IMPORTING THE FIRST AMENDMENT

Importing the First Amendment
Freedom of Expression in American, English and European Law

Edited by

IAN LOVELAND BA, LLM, D Phil.

Professor of Law, Brunel University

·HART·
PUBLISHING
OXFORD
1998

Hart Publishing
Oxford
UK

Distributed in the United States by
Northwestern University Press
625 Colfax, Evanston
Illinois 60208–4210 USA

Distributed in Australia and New Zealand by
Federation Press Pty Ltd
PO Box 45, Annandale
NSW 203, Australia

Distributed in the Netherlands, Belgium and Luxembourg by
Intersentia, Churchillaan 108
B2900 Schoten, Antwerpen
Belgium

Hart Publishing is a specialist legal publisher based in Oxford, England.
To order further copies of this book or to request a list of other
publications please write to:

Hart Publishing, 19 Whitehouse Road, Oxford, OX1 4PA
Telephone: +44 (0)1865 434459 or Fax: +44 (0)1865 794882
e-mail: hartpub@janep.demon.co.uk

British Library Cataloguing in Publication Data
Data Available
ISBN 1–901362–28–0 (cloth)

Typeset in 12pt Sabon
by Hope Services (Abingdon) Ltd.
Printed in Great Britain on acid-free paper
by Bookcraft Ltd., Midsomer Norton, Somerset

To
MADISON

Table of Contents

Preface

This is the second collection of essays I have edited on the application of aspects of American constitutional law to questions and problems currently confronting British lawyers and legislators. The first collection—*A Special Relationship?*—was published in 1995 by Oxford University Press and dealt with a broad range of issues. This volume is more narrowly focused, being concerned solely with questions of freedom of expression.

I have sketched out the intellectual justification for the project in the introductory chapter, and will not rehearse those arguments here. I would however like to take the opportunity to extend my thanks to a number of people who have contributed in various ways to this book. The essays have in the main grown out of papers presented at a conference held at the Institute of Advanced Legal Studies in September 1996. I am much indebted both to the speakers at that conference and to the other academics who took the time and trouble to attend the proceedings and offer their views on the arguments presented. I am also much obliged to Gillian Morris, then Head of Department at Brunel, for making funds available to subsidise the costs of those proceedings.

I am also grateful for the prompt interest that Richard Hart showed in publishing the essays, for his forbearance at my failure to meet our initial deadline, and for his assistance during the publication process.

Lastly, of course, I am indebted to my contributors for the essays that they produced. I should in particular single out Stephen Sedley and John Laws in this regard, whose contributions were produced amidst the many more pressing demands that the High Court imposes upon their time.

Ian Loveland
London, 1998

Table of Cases

Table of Conventions and Treaties

Table of Legislation

Contributors

Professor Eric Barendt, University College London
Professor David Feldman, University of Birmingham
Sir John Laws, The High Court
Professor Leonard Leigh, London School of Economics
Professor Ian Loveland, Brunel University
Professor Gillian Morris, Brunel University
Sir Stephen Sedley, The High Court
Professor Colin Warbrick, Durham University

1

A Free Trade in Ideas—and Outcomes

IAN LOVELAND

I. INTRODUCTION

Recent developments in English public law have brought the language of "fundamental" or "higher" laws appreciably closer to the mainstream of our jurisprudential discourse. It is now almost 400 years since Coke CJ offered his celebrated—and no doubt poorly reported and imaginatively interpreted[1]—dictum in *Dr Bonham's Case*[2] that all English law, whether it emanate from Parliament or the courts, had to conform to the substantive requirements of "common right or reason".

The *Factortame* saga has evidently confirmed that directly effective EC law must now be seen as a "higher" source of legal authority than the provisions of UK statutes. Insofar as domestic courts are indeed willing—as the House of Lords rather delicately puts it—to "disapply" domestic legislative provisions which cannot be reconciled with the requirements of EC law, that law enjoys supra-legislative status within the UK constitution.[3] Whether our courts will retain sufficient fortitude to uphold the *Factortame* rationale in the long term remains to be seen. The answer to the question may turn in part on whether successive cohorts of judges accept the currently dominant explanation that the European Communities Act (ECA) 1972 has in some mystical way altered the "rule of recognition" according to which statutes are interpreted,[4] or whether they are attracted to the more radical critique offered by Murray Hunt which roots the supremacy of EC law within the UK constitution in a dramatic shift in the status of the common law.[5]

Proponents of the argument that EC law now offers the United Kingdom

[1] See S. Thorne, "Dr Bonham's Case" (1938) 54 *LQR* 543: T. Plucknett, "Bonham's Case and Judicial Review" (1926) *Harvard LR* 30.

[2] (1610) 8 Co. Rep. 114.

[3] [1991] 1 AC 603. See P. Craig, "Sovereignty of the United Kingdom Parliament After *Factortame*" [1991] *Yearbook of European Law* 221.

[4] Sir William Wade's essay "Sovereignty—Revolution or Evolution" (1996) 112 *LQR* 568 being the exemplar of this line of argument. The rather limited nature of Wade's arguments is persuasively revealed by T. R. S. Allan, "Parliamentary Sovereignty: Law, Politics and Revolution" (1997) 113 *LQR* 443.

[5] *Using Human Rights Law in English Courts* (Oxford, 1997).

a set of fundamental constitutional values obviously assert an as yet unproven case. Two essential questions remain unanswered. The first is whether Parliament retains the authority to pass legislation which expressly orders our courts to condone specific breaches of EC law. The second, more interestingly, is whether Parliament can expect that an Act purporting to withdraw the United Kingdom from the European Community will be applied by English courts.[6] Yet there seems little likelihood that either political question will be posed by the UK government in the foreseeable future. The present Labour government is markedly less eurosceptic than its Conservative predecessor, and there are surely few psephologists who would predict that Tony Blair's administration will fail to win a second term in office.

This rather suggests that any search for "fundamental law" within the United Kingdom's constitution should move beyond the confines of the EC Treaties and the jurisprudence of the ECJ. Some Scots lawyers (although it seems Lords McKay of Clashfern and Irvine of Lairg would not be numbered among them) would of course deny that British law ever rejected the notion of fundamental rights. From this perspective, the terms of the Treaty of Union are seen as providing the constituent values upon which the creation of the British nation—and thence the British constitution—are based. We have on occasion been offered intriguing dicta by the Scots courts as to the relationship between statute and the Treaty of Union, most notably in *McCormick* v. *Lord Advocate* and *Gibson* v. *Lord Advocate*.[7] Ongoing developments in the devolution of "legislative" power to a new Scots "Parliament" may reawaken academic and popular interest in the *McCormick* thesis, and lend a new, non-EC character to debates about "federalism" within the British constitution.[8]

But curiousity as to the notion of fundamental rights in English law has lately been stimulated—albeit only among the academic audience—by the musings of several senior judges in academic journals.[9] These critiques have lent a somewhat less abstract dimension to the theoretical arguments developed by several academic lawyers in recent years, T. R. S. Allan being foremost among them.[10]

---

[6] The point being whether the UK's departure from the Community can now only be lawfully achieved as matter of EC law (and thus of UK law) by further amendment to the EC treaties. See I. Loveland, "Parliamentary Sovereignty and the EC: the Unfinished Revolution" (1997) 49 *Parliamentary Affairs* 517.

[7] 1953 SC 396 and 1975 SLT 134 respectively. See T. Smith, "The Union of 1907 as Fundamental Law" [1957] *Public Law* 99: C. Munro, *Studies in Constitutional Law* (London, 1987), ch. 4: N. McCormick, "Does the United Kingdom Have a Constitution?" (1978) 29 *Northern Ireland Law Quarterly* 1.

[8] Cf I. Loveland, "Local Authorities", in R. Blackburn and R. Plant (eds.), *Constitutional Reform Now* (London, 1997).

[9] See especially Lord Browne Wilkinson, "The Infiltration of a Bill of Rights" [1992] *Public Law* 397; Sir John Laws, "Is the High Court the Guardian of Fundamental Constitutional Rights" [1994] *Public Law* 59, "Law and Democracy" [1995] *Public Law* 72; Lord Woolf, "Droit Public—English Style" [1995] *Public Law* 57.

[10] Notably in *Law, Liberty and the Constitution* (Oxford, 1995).

Narrowly construed, these judicial writings merely lend a sharper focus to a stream of administrative law decisions which recognise that executive actions which impinge upon certain aspects of individual autonomy should receive what is termed "anxious scrutiny".[11] Within this line of cases, certain moral values have been identified as "fundamental", in the limited sense of being secured against executive infringement which cannot be justified by anything other than the most explicit of statutory commands.

The broader, and academically more exciting, construction of these arguments is that there are some moral values which some judges might be prepared to recognise as beyond parliamentary authority entirely, irrespective of the precision with which the legislature chooses to express its wishes. Such speculation has apparently alarmed politicians of various ideological hues, and prompted Lord Irvine *qua* Lord Chancellor in-waiting to issue a barely coded message warning the judiciary against over-enthusiastic review of government action.[12] Such concerns seem hugely overstated, primarily because they seem to be premised on the assumption that judges cannot differentiate between their academic theorisation and the more prosaic task of actually issuing judgments.

The outcome of the 1997 general election has however moved the argument about fundamental rights on to more practically achievable constitutional grounds. The Blair government's promise to promote legislation which will incorporate the European Convention on Human Rights (ECHR) into UK law will—if carried out—institute a new era in the relationship between the United Kingdom's various organs of government and its citizens, and necessarily between central government and the courts.

Some proponents of constitutional reform might regret the fact that incorporation of the Convention will be carried out through the medium of domestic rather than EC law. The ECJ's recent *Opinion on Community Accession to the European Convention on Human Rights* concluded that incorporation of the ECHR into EC law is not a matter that can be achieved through secondary legislation.[13] Such an initiative would instead require an amendment to the EC Treaties. The outcome of the Amsterdam summit suggests that there is little enthusiasm among the EU's Member States to turn the exhortatory language in the Treaty of Maastricht concerning the Community's respect for human rights into a justiciable element of EC law. The cause for regret on this point is that incorporation of the Convention into EC law would seem to require that the UK's Parliament as well the executive branch of its government would thereafter be constrained by the

[11] For a survey of the cases, see S. de Smith, Lord Woolf and J. Jowell, *Judicial Review of Administrative Action* (London. 1995) pp 325–30.

[12] "Judges and Decisionmakers: The Theory and Practice of *Wednesbury* Review" [1996] *Public Law* 59.

[13] [1996] ECR I–1759. For comment on the opinion and suggestions as to how best to enhance Community protection of human rights see A. Toth, "The European Union and Human Rights: The Way Forward (1997) 34 *CMLRev.* 491.

Convention's requirements. There is little indication that the Blair government regards such an outcome as desirable. While the Blair administration clearly accepts that the courts would be able to enforce the terms of the Convention against all branches of the executive government, its views as to the Convention's impact on legislative autonomy are more opaque.

Following the 1997 election, the debate as to the effects of incorporation on Parliament has been stuctured largely in terms of a choice between the New Zealand and Canadian models of fundamental rights jurisprudence. The New Zealand model is seen as an approach which would would empower our courts only to issue advisory opinions concerning the incompatibility of statute with the Convention. Whether Parliament then chose to accept that advice would be a matter for legislators. It takes little imagination to see such an approach as a quite feeble attempt to restructure constitutional understandings.[14] The Canadian model goes a little further. Its proponents assume that our courts could disapply statutory provisions which conflicted with the Convention unless the provisions in question had been enacted in a form which ordered the courts to apply them "notwithstanding" their inconsistency with the Convention.[15]

Neither technique would secure to the Convention the same status in UK law as is currently enjoyed by the law of the EC, nor—lest it seems the title of this book has been forgotten—as is enjoyed by the constitution of the United States in respect of legislation passed by Congress or the American states. It might thus be thought a matter for regret that Parliament did not incorporate the Convention in terms which mirrored those in the ECA 1972. The nice question which would then have arisen for the courts is whether the Convention's provisions thereby gain supra-legislative status; and if so— reprising the argument over the basis of *Factortame*—whether they do so through a "super-statutory" or "common law" route.

The point which gradually emerges from this ostensibly disparate collection of legal and political developments is that constitutional lawyers are now entering an historical phase in which the legitimacy of traditional understandings of parliamentary sovereignty is being challenged from several directions. English and British public law is in a state, if not of flux, then certainly of unusually rapid development. The purpose of this book is to begin to inform domestic constitutional debate with some of the most sophisticated jurisprudential critiques of the relationship between the citizenry and their governments in a modern democratic State.

The First Amendment to the US Constitution can readily be construed as resting upon an avowedly functionalist moral base, namely to ensure that the process and substance of governance are legitimised by the "informed consent" of those who are governed. The US courts' subsequent interpreta-

---

[14] A. Butler, "The Bill of Rights Debate: Why the New Zealand Bill of Rights Act is a Bad Model for Britain" (1997) 17 *OJLS* 325.

[15] D. Beatty, "The Canadian Charter of Rights: Lessons and Laments" (1997) 60 *MLR* 481.

tion of the First Amendment has provided an extraordinarily rich source of argument as to the specific legal manifestations of this broader moral base. It would be facile to suggest that the American judiciary has been a constant source of liberal enlightenment when faced with freedom of expression issues. As Stephen Sedley observes in the following chapter, the Supreme Court's First Amendment history has clearly been marked by periods of reactionary conservatism, most notably in the 1920s[16] and the early 1950s.[17] Yet even during these eras one can point to individual judgments and to systemic patterns of dissenting opinions—notably those of Holmes and Brandeis in the 1920s—which lend the Court's reasoning a level of complexity and contingency which is less frequently encountered in English civil liberties jurisprudence. One can draw similar conclusions in respect of the way that strands of doctrine have developed over a period of years. The long line of cases refining the notion of symbolic speech[18] is a particular rewarding subject of analysis—whether for pedagogic or political purposes; as is, in a narrower time frame—the much shorter line of recent decisions concerning the constitutional status of laws criminalising racist motivation in crimes of violence.[19] This may be because the legal actors who step upon the Supreme Court's First Amendment stage are playing for such large stakes; not simply in terms of the outcome of the particular case in which they are involved—many of the leading First Amendment decisions have turned on facts of quite remarkable triviality[20]—but because of the broader political principles which all such cases raise. And these are principles concerned not just with freedom of expression *per se*—but also with the nature of the relationship between courts and legislatures and the people that both law-making fora reputedly exist to serve.

II. INFORMED CONSENT AS THE MOST FUNDAMENTAL OF DEMOCRATIC CONSTITUTIONAL PRINCIPLES

One could point to a great many celebrated judicial pronouncements concerning the centrality of First Amendment values to the American constitutional tradition. In the landmark case of *Palko* v. *Connecticut*, Cardozo J characterised it as "the matrix, the indispensable condition of nearly every other form of freedom".[21] Brandeis' judgment in *Whitney* v. *California*

---

[16] See for example *Schenck* v. *US* (1919) 249 US 47; *Abrams* v. *US* (1919) 250 US 616; and *Gitlow* v. *New York* (1925) 268 US 652.

[17] *Dennis* v. *US* (1951) 341 US 494. For an inside and generally dissenting view of the Court's decisions in this era see W. Douglas, *The Court Years* (New York, 1980), ch. 3.

[18] The leading cases being *O'Brien* v. *US* (1968) 391 US 367; *Tinker* v. *Des Moines Independent School District* (1969) 393 US 503; *Cohen* v. *California* (1971) 403 US 15; *Texas* v. *Johnson* (1989) 491 US 397.

[19] See David Feldman, Ch. 8 *infra*.

[20] *People* v. *Cowgill* (1970) 396 US 371 offers an outstanding example.

[21] (1937) 302 US 319 at 327.

enjoys a similarly oft-quoted status. In his view the First Amendment existed to protect the principle that:

> "freedom to think as you will and to speak as you think are indispensable to the discovery and spread of political truth; that without free speech and assembly discussion would be futile; . . . that public discussion is a political duty; and that this should be a fundamental principle of the American government."[22]

Learned Hand J advanced a similarly expansive view in *US* v. *Associated Press* in 1943:

> "The First Amendment presupposes that right conclusions are more likely to gathered out of a multitude of tongues, than through any kind of authoritative selection. To many, this is, and always will be, folly; but we have staked upon it our all."[23]

In more recent years, William Brennan had assumed the mantle of the Court's most trenchant defender of an expansive interpretation of First Amendment freedoms. His judgment in *Sullivan* v. *New York Times*[24] will be addressed in some detail below and in Leonard Leigh's chapter in this volume, but the political base on which his legal argument rested was built in the broadest of terms: "[W]e consider this case against the background of a profound national commitment that debate on public issues should be uninhibited, robust, and wide-open."[25] Brennan's general approach to First Amendment issues—and his judgment in *Sullivan* in particular—had been shaped by the writings of the political philosopher Alexander Meikeljohn.[26] The pertinence of the Meikeljohn thesis to the British context is the specific subject of Sir John Laws' chapter in this volume, but the broad thrust of his approach might usefully be alluded to here. Meikeljohn's views rested on the presumption that:

> "All constitutional authority to govern the people of the United States belongs to the people themselves, acting as members of a corporate body politic. They are, it is true "the governed". But they are also "the governors". Political freedom is not the absence of government. It is self-government. . . .
>
> The revolutionary intent of the First Amendment is, then, to deny to all subordinate agencies authority to abridge the freedom of the electoral power of the people".[27]

---

[22] (1927) 274 US 357. Brandeis' judgment was a curious affair, insofar as it was nominally a concurring opinion, but one couched in language that seemed virtually impossible to reconcile with the result that it supported. On Brandeis' view of the First Amendment in general see L. Paper, *Brandeis* (Secaucus, NJ, 1983), ch. 19.

[23] (1943) 52 F Supp 362 at 372.

[24] (1964) 376 US 254.

[25] (1964) 376 US 254 at 270.

[26] See W. Brennan, "The Supreme Court and the Meiklejohn Interpretation of the First Amendment" (1965) 79 *Harvard LR* 1.

[27] A. Meikeljohn, "The First Amendment is an Absolute" (1961) *Supreme Court Review* 245 at 253–4.

In an influential critique of the Meiklejohn thesis, William Brennan characterised this notion of informed consent as "a fundamental departure from the English and other forms of government . . . [it] was this country's great contribution to the science of government".[28] As David Rabban has more recently observed, that departure was in itself grounded in a radical English opposition to dominant eighteenth century theories of the relationship between the government and the governed.[29] In a sense therefore, contemporary English jurists might plausibly regard the First Amendment as the prodigal daughter whose return home is not only to be warmly welcomed, but to be recognised as long overdue. For it is readily apparent that there are a good many features of our legal system's treatment of the principle of free expression where an outsider's perspective might usefully be brought to bear.

Political and Private Libels

The recent travails of Johnathon Aitken and Neil Hamilton have brought the (in)adequacy of Brtish libel laws into sharp focus. Both men evidently abused their position as members of the government to enrich themselves by clandestinely taking money and favours from sources of dubious repute. Both then issued libel writs against the newspaper and TV stations which exposed their behaviour. And both, no doubt, expected to win their actions, thereby vindicating their (manifestly undeserved) reputations, pocketing substantial awards of damages and perpetrating a sickening deceit on the British people.[30]

Aitken and Hamilton's litigation was facilitated by English libel law, which draws no distinction between "political" and "private" libels, and which in the main loads the dice very heavily in the plaintiff's favour. In both cases, the *Guardian*'s only defence was to prove that its claims were true. It was a matter of great good fortune that such evidence eventually emerged in both cases before the trials were concluded.

Neither case would have come before the American courts had these events occurred in the United States. Since 1964, the Supreme Court's interpretation of the First Amendment in *New York Times* v. *Sullivan*[31] has required state libel laws to place substantial obstacles in the way of

---

[28] *Supra* n. 26, at 11.

[29] D. Rabban, "The Original Meaning of the Free Speech Clause of the First Amendment", in R. Simmons (ed.), *The US Constitution—the First Two Hundred Years* (Manchester, 1989). See also P. Maier, "John Wilkes and American Disillusionment with Britain" (1963) *William and Mary Quarterly* 373.

[30] Not content with attempting to curb press discussion of his behaviour, Hamilton then launched a series of libel writs against his "apolitical" opponent in his constituency during the 1997 general election in an effort to prevent discussion of the issue during the campaign.

[31] (1964) 376 US 254.

defamation suits brought by politicians in respect of stories concerning their political behaviour.

In addition to enabling the press to expose the Hamiltons and Aitkens who infect our body politic, the adoption of the *Sullivan* rule in English law might have the happy effect of deterring putatively corrupt politicians from succumbing to temptation in the first place. Parliament was given the opportunity to take such an initiative in 1996, when new defamation legislation was enacted. That the then Conservative-dominated Commons and Lords chose not to assist press attempts to expose dishonest and corrupt MPs is perhaps unsurprising.[32] Nor might one expect the issue to rank particularly high on the Blair Government's list of priorities. The courts have frequently been invited in recent years—generally by Lord Lester QC—to mould the common law along *Sullivan* lines, but they have as yet declined to do so.[33] Incorporation of the Convention will, it seems, require our courts to take at least some steps in the *Sullivan* direction.[34] But they will look in vain to the ECHR for detailed guidance on this issue. US jurisprudence, in contrast, offers thirty years of intensely litigated experience on which we might draw.[35]

The importation of the Convention into domestic law is also likely to have appreciable implications for the regulation of legislative privilege. As with political libels, this is an issue to which the ECHR thus far has paid scant consideration.[36] This may be because legislators in the Convention's other signatory States are in the main less self-importantly arrogant than their British counterparts. It may, in contrast, suggest that there is a generic predisposition among European judges to tread with undue care when asked to examine the internal proceedings of legislative assemblies.

A familiarity with First Amendment jurisprudence might promptly lead one to question the extent to which the Commons' and Lords' claimed privileges to call for "papers and persons" to assist their inquiries is compatible both with Article 10 of the ECHR's guarentee of freedom of expression (a freedom which undoubtedly includes the right *not* to express certain information) and Article 8 of the ECHR's protection of the right to privacy. One

---

[32] See D. Vick and L. MacPherson, "An Opportunity Lost: The UK's Failed Reform of Defamation Law" (1997) 49 *Federal Communications Law Journal* 621.

[33] Lord Lester will do so again before the Court of Appeal in *Reynolds* v. *Sunday Times*.

[34] The *Sullivan* question has not yet come before the ECHR, but dicta in several criminal libel cases indicate that signatory States' legal systems must ensure that it is more difficult for a politician than a private citizen to win a libel action relating to a political story: see *Lingens* v. *Austria* (1986) 8 EHRR 407; *Castells* v. *Spain* (1992) 14 EHRR 445; and *Oberschlik* v. *Austria* (1991) 19 EHRR 389.

[35] The recent use made of William Brennan's judgment in *Sullivan* in the Australian and Canadian courts is the subject of Leonard Leigh's ch. in this volume, while in ch. 5 Ian Loveland explores the longstanding common law roots of the *Sullivan* doctrine.

[36] *Demicol* v. *Malta* [1992] 14 EHRR 47 is an exception. In *Demicol*, the Court considered that the Maltese legislature's contempt powers were tantamount to the imposition of a criminal penalty. Consequently its proceedings had to comply with the terms of Art. 6 of the ECHR.

might point for example to a series of cases in the 1940 and 1950s in which the Court offered a debased view of First Amendment protections in order to appease the intolerance of a McCarthyite House of Representatives and similarly motivated state legislative assemblies.[37] By the early 1960s, however, a majority on the Court had re-appraised the relationship between the First Amendment and legislative privilege in a fashion which markedly curtailed legislators' powers to force citizens to comply with "requests" to assist legislative investigation.[38] The US Supreme Court has also entertained debate on a question of legislative privilege which has been virtually ignored by UK jurists, namely whether Article 9 of the Bill of Rights (and the corresponding provision in the US Constitution[39]) can any longer be sensibly interpreted as barring libel actions by private citizens against MPs (or Congressman and Senators) who knowingly or recklessly defame such citizens during legislative proceedings.[40] This is a matter which has much exercised constitutional lawyers in recent years, although the bulk of their attention has been directed merely to lamenting the manifest injustice of this state of affairs, rather than to fashioning a common law tool with which to reshape it.[41]

"Public" Executions

Even proponents of more extensive protection for freedom of expression in the United Kingdom have on occasion suggested—as indeed does Stephen Sedley in the next chapter—that the First Amendment simply goes too far in defending the dissemination of information.[42] That sentiment will perhaps be reinforced by the decision of a federal district court in *California First Amemdment Coalition* v. *Calderon*.[43] In *Calderon*, Judge Vaughan Walker held that the general public has a First Amendment right to witness the executions of prisoners convicted of capital crimes.

Calderon might on its face seem an indefensible decision, in effect doing little more than to extend the concept of "entertainment" to the infliction of the death penalty. We might thus think that we in the United Kingdom are fortunate to be spared a constitutional right that seems to pander to the

[37] See especially *Tenney* v. *Brandhove* (1950) 95 L Ed. 1019; *Barr* v. *Matteo* (1959) 3 L Ed. 2d 1434.

[38] *Bond* v. *Floyd* (1966) 17 L. Ed. 2d 624; *Gravel* v. *US* (1972) 33 L Ed. 235.

[39] The "speech and debate clause": Art. 1 s. 6.

[40] Sir John Laws is an exception to the trend. See "Law and Democracy" [1995] *Public Law* 72 at fn. 14. The leading US opinion on the point is *Doe* v. *Macmillan* (1972) 36 L Ed. 2d 912, especially the judgment of Douglas J.

[41] Cf P. Leopold, "Leaks and Squeaks in the Palace of Westminster" [1986] *Public Law* 368; A. Bradley and K. Ewing, *Constitutional and Administrative Law* (London, 1993), 226–7.

[42] See for example A. Bradley, "Free Expression and Acts of Racial Hatred" [1992] *Public Law* 357.

[43] (1997) 956 F Supp. 883.

morbid voyeurism of the public at large and the triumphalist wish for vengeance of the right-wing fringes of the law and order lobby. US opponents of the death penalty might also be appalled by the decision. If execution becomes prime-time entertainment, surely the public will become inured or desensitised to the gravity of what their government is doing in their name. And the logical consequence of this would be that capital punishment will become an increasingly routine part of the criminal justice process.

But paradoxically, *Calderon* might be thought to have just the opposite effect. Thurgood Marshall, the Supreme Court's most inveterate opponent of capital punishment, maintained that much public support for execution would vanish if people really knew what the process entailed. There is some empirical research supporting that contention.[44] Execution is not a clinical, antiseptic activity. Killing someone, even if he does not resist his killers, can be an extraordinarily and overtly violent process. Lethal injection, current the most widely-used killing technique, is not a particularly "difficult" means of executing criminals. The prisoner's head is not ripped off, as sometimes occurs in hanging. He is not fried, with the stench and small explosions of bodily parts that that method entails, as invariably results when electrocution is used. And the injector is unlikely to miss his target, as occcasionally happens when firing squads are deployed.[45]

But the prisoner may go to his death protesting his innocence, so raising doubts about the accuracy of the result reached at trial. He may fight; twisting, turning, seeking desperately to break free, and so convey the enormity and irreversibility of the action the government is about to take. Or he may, as did the man executed in Arkansas in the presence of Governor Clinton during the 1992 Presidential election campaign, plod aimlessly to the electric chair, revealing that his mind has no understanding of what is about to occur, and so reveal the inadequacy of the criminal law's mental impairment defences.[46] Or (like 80 per cent of the prisoners facing the same sentence) he may simply be black, so starkly pointing out that race discrimination is alive and kicking in the contemporary United States' criminal justice system— even if some of its many victims are not.[47]

It may thus be argued that for the public to be exposed to the detailed mechanics of the punishment it inflicts on its most feared criminals is a particularly forceful illustration of the principle of informed consent. It enables them, even perhaps forces them, to face the truth: it places the business of government under a spotlight, rather than cloaking it in an obfuscatory

[44] Especially A. Sarat and N. Widmar, "Public Opinion, the Death Penalty and the Eight Amendment" (1976) *Wisconsin LR* 171.

[45] See F. Grannucci, "Nor Cruel and Unusual Punishments Inflicted" (1969) 57 *California LR* 839; M. Gardner, "Executions and Indignities—An Eight Amendment Assessment of Methods of Inflicting Capital Punishment" (1978) 39 *Ohio State LJ* 96.

[46] C. Olgiati, "The White House via Death Row", *Guardian*, October 12 1993.

[47] See the majority and dissenting arguments in *McCleskey v. Kemp* (1987) 481 US 278.

shroud. As we think of Matrix-Churchill, of the cash-for-questions scandal, and of our governments' pervasive preference for secrecy and covert action, we might perhaps conclude that maybe Judge Walker has got it right after all.

Limits to First Amendment Freedoms

And it is undoubtedly a gross exaggeration to claim that the First Amendment protects *all* speech. The charge frequently raised against *Sullivan* is that it deprives politicians of any defences against deliberately mendacious, partisan press organisations. The charge is quite false; media defendants—or private citizens—who are proven to have wilfully or recklessly published lies about political figures will lose defamation actions, and in all likelihood incur substantial damages liability as a result. Similarly, there has been little dissension amongst even the most ardently liberal judicial and academic views of the First Amendment from the view that government bodies may legitimately impose "time, manner and place" constraints on the dissemination of speech. Although there has—of course—been considerable argument on the question of just how far and in what circumstances such constraints can be imposed.[48]

Some fifty years ago, defenders of the First Amendment against charges of free speech absolutism could have pointed to the judgment of Murphy J in *Chaplinsky* v. *New Hampshire*.[49] *Chaplinsky* restricted First Amemdment protection to speech which served a useful social purpose, a principle which, while not justifying the suppression of minority or unorthodox opinions, nonetheless permitted government regulation of speech which was intended to provoke violence or which was obscene, libellous or profane.

As suggested above, *Chaplinksy's* categorisation of libellous speech as beyond the pale of First Amendment safeguards was subsequently rejected by the Court. In later years, First Amendment protection has also been extended to profanities, on the assumption that the manner in which a political sentiment is expressed can be as important an element of the message the "speaker" wishes to convey as the words she chooses to use.[50]

The matter of obscenity has caused the Court rather greater difficulty. For academic lawyers and their students, the line of cases beginning with *Roth* v. *United States*,[51] and continuing through *Kingsley International Pictures*

---

[48] Contrast, for example, *Chicago Police Department* v. *Mosley* (1972) 408 US 92 with *Grayned* v. *Rockford* (1972) 408 US 104 and *Cox* v. *Louisiana* (1965) 379 US 559.
[49] (1942) 315 US 568. See also Roberts J in *Cantwell* v. *Connecticut* (1940) 310 US 296: "Resorts to epithets or personal abuse is not in any proper sense communication of information or opinion safeguarded by the Constitution."
[50] Cf *Cohen* v. *California* (1971) 403 US 15.
[51] (1957) 354 US 476.

Corp. v. *Regents*[52] to *Memoirs* v. *Massachusetts*[53] and *Miller* v. *California*[54] provides a fascinating study in both the technicalities of legalistic reasoning and the broader issue of judicial attempts to regulate intolerant majoritiarian moralities. Stewart J's celebrated definition of obscenity in *Jacobellis* v. *Ohio*—"I cannot define it, but I know it when I see it"[55]—neatly conveys one lesson that might be drawn from this area of First Amendment jurisprudence: namely that substantive law, even in respect of supposedly "fundamental principles, can be a contingent, unstable phenomenon. It serves as a warning against bland assumptions that civil liberties in this country could necessarily be better protected against governmental interference by the creation of supra-parliamentary legal norms.

In addition, as Colin Warbrick suggests in Chapter 9, the Court's difficulties with obscenity law forcefully reveal the degree of substantive variability inherent in fundamental laws within a federal constitutional structure. As such, it serves as a powerful antidote to suggestions that the supremacy of EC law and the potential supremacy of the Convention law will subject the British people to uniform rules promulgated by the ECJ and the ECHR.

In contrast to the Court's difficulties with obscenity, the First Amendment's treatment of blasphemous speech now offers a rather more coherent body of jurisprudential principle.[56] The First Amendment provides in specific terms that "Congress shall make no law respecting an establishment of religion, nor prohibiting the free exercise thereof". The text flowed directly from Madison and Jefferson's previous experiences in Virginia,[57] and while its subsequent interpretation has proved problematic in respect of such issues as public funding of religious education, its impact on the laws of blasphemy is quite clear.

The Court's forceful comments in *Watson* v. *Jones* in 1872 to the effect that "the law knows no heresy, and is committed to the support of no dogma, the establishment of no sect"[58] were of limited value, since at that time it was assumed that the First Amendment did not control the activities of state governments.[59] By the early 1950s however, the Court had concluded that an offence of blasphemous libel—whether fashioned by an organ of federal or state government—was wholly incompatible with First

---

[52] (1959) 360 US 384.

[53] (1966) 383 US 413.

[54] (1973) 413 US 15.

[55] (1964) 378 US 184. Stewart J did indeed offer a definition of sorts in a subsequent case: *Ginzburg* v. *US* (1966) 383 US 463.

[56] The issue is discussed more fully in Colin Warbrick's ch. *infra*.

[57] See L. Fisher, *Constitutional Rights: Civil Rights and Civil Liberties* (2nd edn; New York, 1995), 722–8.

[58] (1872) 20 L Ed. 66 at 676—quoted in D. Feldman, *Civil Liberties and Human Rights in England and Wales* (Oxford, 1993), 690.

[59] The Court began to apply aspects of the First Amendment to the states in *Gitlow* v. *New York* (1925) 45 S Ct. 625.

Amendment principles. The point was succinctly put in *Joseph Burstyn Inc. v. Wilson*:[60]

> "[F]rom the standpoint of freedom of speech and the press, it is enough to point out that the state has no legitimate interest in protecting any or all religions from views distateful to them. . . . It is not the business of government in our nation to suppress real or imagined attacks upon a particular religious doctrine, whether they appear in publications, speeches or motion pictures."[61]

Wilson concerned an attempt by New York to prevent the screening of Roberto Rosselini's *The Miracle* on the grounds that it was sacriligious in its treatment of the Catholic religion. The assumption seemed somewhat implausible, given that the movie had enjoyed a general release in Italy. But the effect of the Court's judgment was to make questions of sacrilege or blasphemy an irrelevance.[62]

British observers might draw an uncomfortable parallel between the *Wilson* decision and the treatment meted out to allegedly blasphemous films by the English courts and the European Court of Human Rights (ECHR) almost fifty years later.[63] The House of Lords' judgment in *R. v. Lemon*[64] remains an unsightly blot on our civil liberties landscape,[65] and one which it seems incorporation of the Convention will do nothing to remove. The ECHR judgment in *Otto Preminger Institute* v. *Austria*[66] displayed an unfortunate responsiveness to the evidently delicate sensibilities of the more zealous members of Austria's Christian community in upholding the suppression of a caustically anti-religious movie. This pandering to vocal religious minorites was more recently upheld by the ECHR (contrary to the opinion of the Commission) in *Wingrove* v. *The United Kingdom*.[67] Wingrove's movie—*Visions of Ecstacy*—might readily be described as an excursion into the realm of soft pornography. It might equally well be described as a serious attempt to confront the essentially hypocritcal attitude taken by the Catholic Church towards matters of sexuality. The video was however refused a licence by the British Board of Film Classification, not because it was considered obscene, but because it was thought to be blasphemous. In the Board's view, the video was "bound to to give rise to outrage at the unacceptable treatment of a sacred subject".[68]

Although the Commission considered that the Board's decision amounted to a violation of Article 10, the censorship opinion was upheld by the

---

[60] (1952) 343 US 495.
[61] *Ibid.*, at 505.
[62] M. Frankel, *Faith and Freedom* (New York, 1994), 33–5.
[63] Cf D. Pannick, "Religious Feelings and the European Court" [1995] *Public Law* 7.
[64] [1979] 1 QB 10, [1979] AC 617 (HL).
[65] See the succinct argument in favour of abolishing the offence by J. Gray, "Time to Get Rid of the Crime of Blasphemy", *Guardian*, 13 August 1997.
[66] (1995) 19 EHRR 34.
[67] (1996) 24 EHRR 1.
[68] *Ibid.*, at para. 13.

ECHR. The Court's judgment was little more than a reiteration of the *Otto Preminger* rationale. The majority opinion characterised the film as, *inter alia*, "reviling", "scurrilous" and "ludicrous". Prohibiting its circulation could not therefore be regarded as breaching Article 10.

Blasphemy is a common law rather than statutory offence. It owes its existence entirely to the courts. The House of Lords would therefore not be stepping on Parliament's legislative toes in deciding that this particular common law rule had outlived its usefulness. It is perhaps unfortunate that Mr Wingrove accepted counsel's advice not to seek a remedy in the English courts. This may have been an instance when the common law might have proved itself responsive to American influence and produced an outcome which was rather more forceful in defence of free expression than the judgment offered by the European Court of Human Rights.

III.　FROM JUDICIAL TO LEGISLATIVE ACTIVISM

Any sytematic and explicit judicial attempt to reform the common law with reference to First Amendment principles would no doubt be widely regarded as a wholly unconstitutional enterprise. For many observers, such a strategy would amount—as Lord Symonds put it so many years ago—to "a judicial usurpation of the legislative function".[69] Such criticisms were indeed frequently made by the political Right during the final years of the Major Government in respect of wholly orthodox judicial decisions which happened to hold ministerial actions unlawful. *M* v. *The Home Office*,[70] the *Pergau Dam* case,[71] *R.* v. *Criminal Injuries Compensation Board, ex parte Fire Brigades Union*[72] and *R.* v. *Secretary of State for Social Security, ex parte Joint Council for the Welfare of Immigrants*[73] resulted in legal outcomes which could hardly have been unexpected by any observer versed in the basic principles of judicial review. The attack on these decisions revealed an extraordinary degree of constitutional illiteracy (or—less extraordinarily—mendacity) on the part of backbench Conservative MPs and several national newspapers.[74] The rationale for the criticism of the courts appeared to rest largely on the assumption that the preferences of a majority party in

---

[69] *Magor* v. *St Helens Corporation* [1951] 2 All ER 839 at 841. The comment was aimed at Denning LJ's suggestion in the CA in the same case that courts should adopt teleological rather than literalist interpretive techniques when faced with statutes whose text seemed to require bizarre solutions to legal disputes. Denning's heresy has now of course become an orthodoxy in respect of matters pertaining to EC law.

[70] [1993] 3 WLR 433.

[71] [1995] 1 All ER 611.

[72] [1995] 2 AC 513.

[73] [1996] 4 All ER 385.

[74] Including *The Times*: see I. Loveland, "The War Against the Judges" (1997) 68 *Political Quarterly* 162.

the Commons at any given time enjoyed the same constitutional status as the most precisely drafted of statutory provisions.

It nevertheless has to be acknowledged that several of these decisions[75] have interpreted arguably ambiguous laws in ways that inconvenienced the government sufficiently to prompt it to make a legislative response. To that (albeit limited) extent they mark a departure from the judical attitude displayed in such leading cases from the 1970s and 1980s as *Malone* v. *Metropolitan Police Commissioner*[76] and *R.* v. *Inland Revenue Commissioners, ex parte Rossminster*[77] in which (respectively) an ambiguous point of common law and of statutory interpretation were resolved (despite judicial professions of disquiet) in a manner which accommodated rather than obstructed central government's preferences.[78] In both cases, the court had invited the government to promote legislation which would make the law more sensitive to civil liberties issues. Both invitations were of course refused.

If we (cynically) accept—as did the framers of the US Constitution in general and James Madison in particular—that governments are happiest when their actions escape legal control, it makes little sense for a court faced with an uncomfortable dilemma merely to *invite* them to promote legislation which will expose hitherto unregulated powers to closer judicial regulation. One need not be a judicial supremacist to suggest that the courts should resolve ambiguous areas of civil liberties law in a way which inconveniences government bodies.[79] This is not because the court thereby becomes the highest source of legal authority, but because it will force the issue into the legislative arena, where it can be addressed and resolved in the full glare of press and public scrutiny. A judge who follows that course is not attacking the *de jure* sovereignty of Parliament, but is rather questioning the *de facto* usurpation of that sovereignty by the executive.

The Regulation of the Electoral System

It should also be stressed that any extensive investigation of First Amendment principles will present us with initiatives in American political life that appear wholly unpalatable. But this is a reason for being rigorous in our examination of First Amendment principles, and selective in the uses

[75] The *Fire Brigades Union* and *Joint Council* cases being the prime examples.

[76] [1979] Ch. 344.

[77] [1980] AC 952.

[78] Lord Denning's judgment in the CA had adopted the opposite approach.

[79] *Malone* can usefully be seen in the light of two celebrated US cases on telephone tapping. Megarry VC's reasoning in *Malone* echoed that of the US Supreme Court in *Olmstead* v. *US* (1928) 277 US 438. *Olmstead* had been overruled by the Supreme Court 13 years before *Malone* was decided: *Katz* v. *US* (1967) 389 US 347.

we make of them, rather than for concluding that the whole comparative exercise is not worthwhile.

The Supreme Court's continuingly controversial decision in *Buckley* v. *Valeo* has been widely portrayed as in effect equating the power of wealthy individuals to spend copious amounts of money in support of their preferred candidates with a pure exercise of free expression.[80] We might thus be tempted to pat ourselves on our British backs for being spared—at a trivial level—the American-style horrors of political TV ads interrupting the news or coverage of the Ashes Tests and—more soberly—the essentially anti-meritocratic and anti-democratic prospect that a candidate's electoral success is linked more closely to the size of her advertising budget than the cogency and rectitude of her preferred policies.

This is perhaps an unduly celebratory position to adopt. We might at this juncture leave aside the suggestion that *Buckley* v. *Valeo* was a poorly reasoned decision[81] (and regret its apparent adoption by the Australian High Court[82]) and focus instead on the fact that the law surrounding the financing of our electoral system is in many respects in an extremely sorry state. Given the broad consensus that elections to the Commons are fought, won and lost primarily on national rather than local issues, it is little short of an absurdity that the limits on campaign expenditure imposed by British law are focused solely on individual constituency activities and—with the important exception of access to the broadcast media—allow money an entirely free rein in respect of political parties' national campaigning behaviour. In essence, we have *Buckley* v. *Valeo* by default.

The inadequacy of the system is underlined by the absence of any legally enforceable requirement that political parties reveal the sources of their funding. The 1997 controversy concerning allegations that the Chinese government was covertly funding the US Democrat party demonstrates that disclosure provisions will not necessarily ensure that American parties do not receive financial assistance from sources of dubious repute. Yet had such allegations about party funding been aired in Britain, any controversy over the issue would have been over and—for most observers—forgotten in a matter of days. The American system, in contrast, creates a public forum in which a political party's financial integrity is exposed to relentless scrutiny. The American law expresses the simple principle that it is virtually impossible for a voter to give informed consent to her choice of political party if she does not know that the party is receiving substantial amounts of financial aid from undeclared sources.

---

[80] See K. Ewing, "Legal Control of Party Political Finance", in I. Loveland (ed.), *A Special Relationship* (Oxford, 1995).

[81] The Court of Appeals had upheld most of the restrictions which were struck down in the Supreme Court: see S. Wright, "Politics and the Constitution: Is Money Speech?" (1976) 85 *Yale LJ* 1001; "Money and the Pollution of Politics: Is the First Amendment an Obstacle to Political Equality?" (1982) 82 *Columbia LR* 609.

[82] In *Australian Capital Television* v. *Commonwealth of Austrialia* (1992) 66 ALJR 695.

The Blair Government has intimated that it will consider introducing legislation to regulate party political finances more stringently, and in a manner which takes account of the now essentially national nature of the political campaigning process. *Buckley* v. *Valeo* and its progeny will surely provide an important point of reference for that debate, even if only in the negative sense of providing us with a model that we should not follow.

The Control of Sleaze among MPs

As suggested above, importation of *Sullivan* might have a salutory effect on the ethical codes adhered to by MPs and other politicians. There are however rather more direct ways of enhancing the likelihood that politicians' financial dealings are beyond ethical reproach. It is a commonplace feature of American political campaigns that the various candidates make a full disclosure of their income tax returns so that the electorate is aware both of the size and the sources of their wealth. The Whitewater imbroglio indicates that income disclosure is not necesarily a guarantor of a politician's financial probity. But a US politician who lies about her income to the Internal Revenue Service faces political ruin and potential imprisonment. A British politician who does the same in her submission to the Register of Members' Interests runs the risk of little more than a splutter of indignation from her peers, and even that is likely to be muted if she happens to be a member of a governing party with a small Commons majority.

A candidate for office who is secretive about the amount and sources of his/her wealth is more likely to be motivated by the knowledge that she/he has something to hide than by a concern for "privacy" for its own sake. Thus far however it seems that the Nolan Commission on standards in public life has been persuaded by the merits of the privacy argument. The rather feeble recommendations it proposed in respect of entries on the Register of Members Interests remain doubly defective: first because they do not compel the disclosure of the amounts of money earned from extra-parliamentary sources; and secondly because they are mere internal Commons rules and as such have no enforceable legal status. Legislation compelling full and detailed disclosure is the only effective way to ensure that concerned citizens can guarantee that their electoral choices are not made on the basis of mistaken assumptions about a candidate's financial probity.

The Appointment of Senior Judges

Perhaps the most important and most pervasive contextual principle which can be extracted from First Amendment jurisprudence is that so much of what is ostensibly part of the private sphere is on closer examination suffused with an inalienably public character. One need not look too closely to appreciate that the people who make and administer laws have been to a large extent turned into public property.[83]

That government employees are public property—and thence dependant for their legitimacy on the informed consent of the citizenry—is a point no less forceful in respect of judges than in respect of legislators and members of the executive. The—to British eyes—extraordinary process through which Supreme Court judges are now appointed has no basis in the letter of the First Amendment—but offers an exemplary illustration of its spirit. That federal judges are nominated by the President but appointed by the Senate is a nice illustration of the Americans' formal embrace of the principle of the separation of powers. That the Senate's confirmation proceedings are now often brutally adversarial, forcefully investigatory and—just as importantly—the subject of intense press and television coverage conveys the sense that occupation of high judicial office is a trust granted by the people rather than—as in Britain—a gift bestowed by the Prime Minister.

One need have no sympathy whatsoever with Robert Bork—either as a jurist or political ideologue—to wonder if the concerted campaign conducted against his confirmation overstepped the bounds of rational, courteous debate.[84] One might even accept that the deluge of fact and comment about Bork which was aired in the US media may have contained misleading as well as useful information. But through this process, Bork's career and character became a matter of public record. His ideological views on the Constitution were also exposed to public scrutiny—as indeed were those of the members of the Senate Judiciary Committee. And, ultimately, the public was presented with a decision which was manifestly "political" rather than legal in nature: a right-wing judge was rejected by a centrist Senate because he was considered to be an ideological extremist.[85]

The essentially political nature of judicial appointments was similarly laid bare by the more recent nomination of Clarence Thomas. The Senate hearings ensured that his manifest inadequacy for the post he had been nominated to assume was placed squarely before the American public. That the Republican-dominated Senate thereafter chose to ignore the evidence and approve Thomas' nomination might have shocked liberal legal opinion. That Thomas now sits on the Court may be hugely offensive to that same audience. But his inadequacies—like Bork's ideologies—are a matter of common knowledge, and as a consequence whatever contribution he makes to the development of constitutional law will enjoy little legitimacy.[86]

[83] Gill Morris explores a rather different facet of this issue in Ch. 6 below.

[84] Bork makes a convincing argument to this effect: see R. Bork, *The Tempting of America* (New York, 1990) chs. 14–15. For a less partisan view see D. Savage, *Turning Right* (New York, 1992), ch. 4; R. Dworkin, *Freedom's Laws* (Cambridge, Mass., 1996), ch. 12.

[85] Dworkin, *supra* n. 64, ch. 13.

[86] *Ibid.*, ch. 15. For an extended treatment of the nomination see J. Mayer and J. Abramson, *Strange Justice* (New York, 1994).

It may be suggested that there is less need for transparency in the process used to appoint senior judges in the United Kingdom than in the United States, since our courts are less powerful players within the UK constitution than are their (federal) American counterparts in the United States. That presumption must obviously be qualified in the post-*Factortame* era. But references to the (generally) untrammelled sovereignty of Parliament should not lead us to underestimate the enormous legal authority that the common law[87] bestows upon our judiciary.

As a process, the common law is in some respects an extraordinarily secretive source of legal principle. Our courts are open in the senses of being physically accessible to a public audience and having their proceedings reported in the press. They are really rather mysterious, opaque fora however, when one moves to consider the identities and backgrounds of the judges who preside over them. There would be few students in reputable American law schools—and more significantly perhaps few intelligent and well-read laymen -who would not know the names of all nine Supreme Court justices and have at least a hazy idea of their past career and the ideological baggage they bring with them to the bench. Few members of the House of Lords or Court of Appeal enjoy similar prominence in UK law schools, still less in the British public mind. Nor—with a very few exceptions—have those judges left much of a record in their former lives from which an intelligent layman might form some sensible conclusions as to the predilections they bring with them to their office. Few have laid out in academic or mass media writings—as did Bork and Scalia—their personal views on matters of legal doctrine. Even fewer (with the occasional exception of the Lord Chancellor) enter the court with a clearly identifiable party political identity—as did Warren, Black, Douglas, Rehnquist and O'Connor.

To make these points is not to cast doubt on the competence or integrity of High Court judges; nor even to suggest that they might have been found lacking in some necessary judicial quality had their appointment process been conducted by Members of Parliament with the rigour often favoured by the Judiciary Committee of the US Senate. Rather it questions whether judicial independence must necessarily go hand in hand with what is in effect judicial anonymity.

The argument is similarly cogent in respect of the judges who staff the European Court of Justice and the European Court of Human Rights. These lawmakers are not public figures in any meaningful sense. And while their decisions may receive intense and often adverse media scrutiny, their past

---

[87] In which I include principles of statutory interpretation. Obvious recent examples of the courts introducing marked changes to our understanding of public law principles include *Council for the Civil Service Unions* v. *Minister for the Civil Service* [1985] AC 374; *R.* v. *R— (rape: marital exemption)* [1991] 4 All ER 481; *Pepper* v. *Hart* [1993] 1 All ER 42; *R.* v. *Secretary of State for Transport, ex parte Factortame* [1991] 1 AC 603; *R.* v. *Brown* [1992] 3 All ER 75.

lives and present beliefs remain shrouded in anonymity. If we are indeed entering an era in which the judiciary increasingly becomes the guardian of an expanding list of "fundamental" laws, the case for governmental action which enhances public awareness of the personal and professional characteristics of the judges becomes ever stronger.

IV. CONCLUSION—A NON-DEFERENTIAL APPROACH TO COMPARATIVE LAW

The methodological paradigm which I brought to bear in the *Special Relationship* collection three years ago now strikes me as unduly deferential and defensive.[88] Crudely stated, that approach could be characterised as accepting that efforts to import foreign legal principles to address domestic legal problems had to be acutely sensitive to any differences of culture, social history and political tradition between the donee and donor nations. A country's laws, it is suggested, should reflect its people's idiosyncratic political and cultural context; and if that context offered a blunt obstacle to foreign-led reform of the common law or statute, it should be the courts or the legislature rather than the context which should give way. This is, on even limited reflection, a rather unsatisfactory stance to adopt. It has no relevance at all to pedagogic concerns within a law school curriculum, where one might readily argue that the legitimacy of all of a country's political and cultural (and legal) traditions should be open to constant evaluation against both trans-historical and trans-national yardsticks.

Its relevance to our substantive law is also less compelling than might initially be supposed. One can leave aside for the present arguments as to the increasing convergence of American and European cultural traditions, but what one cannot neglect is the argument that it is a facile over-simplification to assume that a society's laws invariably follow, rather than lead, its political culture and social mores.

We might for example—keeping our eyes on the American constitutional landscape—offer up *Plessey* v. *Ferguson*[89] as an illustration of the principle that law should express dominant (if not quite hegemonic) cultural suppositions. We might then offer *Brown* v. *Board of Education*[90] as an exemplar of a jurisprudence which demands that courts should attempt to reconfigure those cultural suppositions on a more enlightened moral base, even when the suppositions concerned have received the ostensibly legitimising stamp of legislative approval. There are surely few observers who could comfortably argue that the methodology and outcome of the *Plessey* judgment were in any sense superior to those of *Brown*.

---

[88] "Introduction—Should We Take Lessons From America?", in I. Loveland (ed.), *A Special Relationship* (Oxford, 1995).
[89] (1896) 163 US 537.
[90] (1954) 347 US 483.

Plessey and *Brown* were cases which turned on the meaning attached to the equal protection clause of the Fourteenth Amendment, and would seem to have no obvious linkage to the values inherent in the First. But both provisions share, along with the rest of the Constitution's terms, the distinction of rejecting the legitimacy of simple majoritarianism as the determinant of society's legal norms. The British constitution has traditionally been assumed to rest on just such a presumption of majoritarian legitimacy. The essays in this book are intended to provoke students, scholars and practising lawyers to consider the extent to which the First Amendment provides a compelling functionalist foundation on we could sensibly build a more assertive rights-based jurisprudential culture. And in so doing, they may add further force to the argument that the time has come for the people of the United Kingdom to fashion a constitutional settlement within which a collection of fundamental political and moral principles are placed far beyond the reach of simple parliamentary majorities.

2

The First Amendment: a Case for Import Controls?

STEPHEN SEDLEY

I. INTRODUCTION

Let me begin with some questions.

Why is this volume about importing the First rather than, say, the Fourteenth Amendment? Why is it not about the need to recognise food and shelter or civil peace as fundamental human rights? Why is it, in other words, that freedom of expression dominates the conversation when the elaboration and enforcement of fundamental rights and freedoms is discussed?

It is perhaps for the same reason as has made the First Amendment both a sacred cow of US constitutional law and the dominant topic of human rights litigation in this country. Constraints on what the press can publish are bad for business, and it is consequently worth the press's while to throw considerable resources into litigation designed to remove or limit constraints. This they have done with resounding success over many years in the United States.[1] The resonance has now been felt in Australia,[2] though Canada has resisted it.[3]

It is worth remembering, first of all, that there is more to First Amendment jurisprudence than the outcome of *Sullivan* v. *The New York Times*.[4] To it Americans also owe the striking down of measures designed

---

[1] The financing of *Near* v. *Minnesota* (1931) 283 US 697 by Colonel Robert McCormick, the owner of the *Chicago Tribune* and a multi-millionaire libertarian, is a paradigmatic example of this. See F. Friendly, *Minnesota Rag* (New York, 1981), ch. 6. In *Near*, the Court held (albeit by a narrow majority) that the First Amendment precluded virtually all prior restraints on newpaper publishing. For further insight into McCormick's motives see Ch. 5 below.

[2] See my comments in "The Sound of Silence: Constitutional Law Without a Constitution" (1994) 110 *LQR* 270, 276, 286 ff. on the Australian High Court's embrace of First Amendment ideas in *Nationwide News Pty. Ltd* v. *Wills* (1992) 108 ALR 681; *Australian Capital Television Pty. Ltd* v. *Commonwealth of Australia* (1992) 66 AJLR 695; and the joined cases of *Theophanous* v. *Herald and Weekly Times* and *Stephens* v. *West Australian Newspapers Ltd*, (1994) 68 ALR 713. The Australian cases are further discussed in Leonard Leigh's chapter in this volume. See also K. Ewing, "New Constitutional Constraints in Australia" [1993] *PL* 256.

[3] See *Libman* v. *Quebec* (1997) 151 DCR 4th 385.

to create a right of reply for individuals traduced in the public media,[5] and the frustration of repeated legislative attempts to create a more level political playing field by limiting the amount of money that candidates can spend on an electoral campaign.[6] Yet the First Amendment, in the hands of the same Supreme Court, for many years afforded no protection at all to soapbox radicals who were repeatedly gaoled for making syndicalist speeches in town squares,[7] nor, even with the new jurisprudence of the later 1930s, to the many victims of the House Un-American Activities Committee.[8]

There are intelligible historical reasons for the shape which the right of free speech has taken in the United States, and it is no part of my task to criticise the jurisprudence of the Supreme Court. The question is whether we should import it into a country which recognises and enforces a variety of constraints upon the bare right of free speech which would certainly be inconsistent with the meanings which the Supreme Court has placed upon the First Amendment.[9]

First, lest I be misunderstood, let me say loud and clear that the Miltonic freedom—the freedom to utter criticism or heresy without fear of suppression or reprisal from those who may be angered or embarrassed by it—is of fundamental importance in any free society. But the right to be wrong is a subtler concept. I am not speaking of the right to be eccentric or misguided or a pain in the neck: these are rights which undoubtedly need constitutional protection. But what canon of civilised living can confer a right to publish factual falsehoods which blight the lives and livelihoods of others? The present English law of fair comment and qualified privilege may be a pretty imperfect way of striking a balance,[10] and a defence of innocent dissemination has been long overdue, but a legal system which cannot protect an indi-

---

[4] (1964) 376 US 354. The preoccupation with *Sullivan* is further evidenced by the fact that two of the chs. in this volume deal (respectively) with its forebears and its progeny.

[5] In *Miami Herald Publishing Co* v. *Tornillo* (1974) 418 US 241 the Burger Court (extending the *Sullivan* principle) unanimously struck down Florida legislation which granted political candidates the right to require newspapers to print a candidate's response to news stories "assailing" his or her character in similarly lengthy and prominent terms to the original story.

[6] *Buckley* v. *Valeo* (1976) 424 US 1. For a powerful warning against borrowing from *Buckley* see K. Ewing, "Legal Control of Party Political Finance", in I. Loveland (ed.), *A Special Relationship* (Oxford, 1995).

[7] See for example *Abrams* v. *US* (1919) 250 US 616; *Debs* v. *US* (1919) 249 US 211; *Gitlow* v. *New York* (1927) 268 US 652; *Whitney* v. *California* (1927) 274 US 357.

[8] Indeed, it seemed to be taken for granted by both the Supreme Court and the lower Federal courts that the First Amendment had no applicability to such issues, which were governed instead by the privileges bestowed on each House of Congress by the Constitution's "speech and debate" clause, a provision modelled on Art. 9 of England's Bill of Rights. See especially *Barsky* v. *US* (1948) 167 F 2d 241; *Tenney* v. *Brandhove* (1950) 95 L Ed. 2d 1019.

[9] For example, the treatment of speech intended to provoke racial hatred; see I. Loveland, "The Criminalisation of Racist Violence", in Loveland, *supra* n. 6. And see also David Feldman', Ch. 8 *infra*.

[10] For example, the latter defence does not yet apply to political libels *per se*, but even here there is a highly debateable terrain.

vidual against the publication of damaging calumny has surrendered one of its most important constitutional functions.

II. THE FINANCIAL DIMENSION OF FIRST AMENDMENT FREEDOMS

Why then is it free speech, of all the rights which are regularly threatened, which is always at the head of the queue for judicial protection? The first reason is very simple. Rights mean nothing if they are incapable of vindication, and litigation to vindicate them generally costs a great deal money. Many, perhaps most, of those whose fundamental rights are violated have no access to legal redress; but the press and broadcast media are not in this class. They have, for the most part, funds which enable a cost-benefit calculation to be made and which make litigation feasible if the possible return is considered worthwhile. Indeed, company law probably allows no other basis of expenditure. With the best of professional representation and advocacy, the media from the *Sunday Times* cases[11] to *Brind*[12] to *Goodwin*[13] have been in a position to make the most of the right of free speech.

The second reason is more complex but, in my view, far more important in the context of human rights. Freedom of speech is not today, in any proper moral appreciation, a freestanding right. I stress the word "today" because the once paradigmatic lone individual with a case to put—though he or she still matters—is not the typical beneficiary of the right. A right to be heard by the world at large is of real significance only to those who have the world's ear—and it is correspondingly the mass media who, as I have said, come to court to claim it. But the mass media have the colossal power not only of communication but of selection, comment and presentation.

The media may and do genuflect to the precept that these awesome powers are to be exercised responsibly, but it is a rule not only entirely devoid of sanctions but one which faces an almost irresistible tide of incentives to disregard it. Every printed or broadcast report has of course to be selected in preference to other stories; it has to be presented in one form or another. Such choices are inevitable and in a free society cannot be justiciable. Journalism as a whole, moreover, is no freer than the rest of society from the vices of sloth and venality. But what then becomes of responsibility?[14]

[11] *Sunday Times* v. *United Kingdom* (1979) 2 EHRR 245 and *Derbyshire County Council* v. *Sunday Times* [1993] 1 All ER 1011. The first case led to legislative changes in the law governing contempt of court; the second held that government bodies could not sue in libel to protect their political reputation. The second of these cases seems to have triggered much of the recent increase in the interest in the applicability of US free speech ideas to British society. See further Ch. 5 below.

[12] [1991] 1 AC 696.

[13] *Goodwin* v. *United Kingdom* (1996) 22 EHRR 123.

[14] *Sullivan* devotees might usefully refer to the close studies of press behaviour in the post-*Sullivan* era offered by R. Smolla in *Suing the Press* (Oxford, 1986) and *Jerry Fallwell* v. *Larry Flint* (Urban, Ill., 1988). See also A. Lewis, *Make No Law* (New York, 1991).

One way of crystallising the problem may be to recognise that free speech has among its moral counterparts the right of others to information. Another is to say that the right to speak freely is circumscribed by a duty to those who depend upon the speaker for information or guidance. But what concept of human rights is it which has nothing to say about the decision of a major news corporation, in return for the power to broadcast throughout China, to exclude the BBC's news reportage because the government of China does not want its citizens to have access to the balanced coverage for which the BBC is valued? Does the Chinese people perhaps have a right of access to information which is at least as valuable as a news corporation's right to broadcast what it finds convenient? And if the Chinese, why not other peoples? What, for example, have the protagonists of the First Amendment to say about the media whiteout in the United States on the work of such a distinguished radical as Noam Chomsky?

A third way of crystallising the issue is to stop thinking of freedom of information as a right which runs only against the State.[15] The mass media too have possession of large funds of information, and their power to manipulate or withhold it is no less than that of government. To postulate it as a right of the individual to be able to be fully and fairly informed by the media of communication, whether in State or in private hands, is to call in question—as I believe the time is long past for doing—the whole fortress model of civil and human rights which conceives them purely as bulwarks of the individual against the power of a hostile State. There are today repositories of corporate power as capable as any State of invading the rights of individuals.

Correspondingly there are contexts in which it is to the State, not merely to its courts, that the individual ought to be able to look for protection from the abuse of corporate power. There is something skewed about a rights paradigm which contemplates a transnational news corporation standing before a constitutional court as a victim of the abuse of State power, while those who depend on the corporation for information have no right to know whether it is telling them the truth about the world and no power to make it do so.

None of these considerations finds any place in the First Amendment. Nor does the more fundamental consideration which these issues throw up. Are rights properly seen as property—which is how the right of free speech generally features in litigation about press freedom—or as a constraint imposed in the public interest on the exercise of power? Although both our history and our jurisprudence have contributed to the unspoken view that it is the former, the flowering of English public law in this generation has brought us

---

[15] As Colin Warbrick notes in Ch. 9 *infra*, the notion of "the state" is one which must be used guardedly when dealing with freedom of expression ideas in federal, quasi-federal or international legal orders.

steadily closer to the concept of public law as a constraint on the misuse of power[16] in the interests not of one but of all citizens. This too is a wholesome shift from which the importation of the First Amendment would draw us back.

III. CONCLUSION

As Ian Loveland has suggested in the previous chapter, I am one of the contributors to this book who holds a rather more sceptical view of the benefits that might accrue to English law from any substantial borrowing of American First Amendment ideas.

The remaining chapters in this book offer a variety of views on the desirability of drawing on First Amendment ideas to order our own understandings of free expression issues. My own argument is that the abandonment (I say nothing about the possible modification) of present constraints on freedom of publication in favour of an uncontrolled market-place, not only of ideas (the high ground of First Amendment jurisprudence), but of everything including suppression and calumny would be not the enhancement but the dilution of human rights, especially in the fuller and more complex forms which they will have to assume in the world of the twenty-first century.

[16] The drift is articulated in Buxton J's judgment in *R v Chief Constable of the North Wales Police, ex parte A13* [1997] 4 All ER 691. The decision concerned North Wales Police disclosing the whereabouts of paedophiles.

TATLER

Charlene and Michel de Carvalho

Heirless

Eccentrics in big houses
- Robin Mirrlees 78 –
  11th Earl of Kingston
  - Stuart Usher
  - Sir John Leslie
  - Lady Maria McCafferty
- Catherine Maxwell Stuart – Socialist lady laird
- Cherry Drummond, Baroness Strange
  Dukes of Atholl – Blair Castle

The Admirable Crichton

Houses – Robert Adam and Quinlan Terry

Psychiatrists

~~Chiefs~~ Socialist Socialites

<u>Gigolos</u>

<u>Sultan of Zanzibar lives in Southsea</u>

<u>Gangsters – Darius Guppy, the Mayfair Men (1939)</u>

<u>Schools</u>

<u>Chiefs</u>

Quentin Kihis Kawananauakoa, Crown Prince of Hawaii

Namedroppers

London Cockneys

Belvoir Castle – Rutland
Broughton – Lord Saye & Sele
Wilton House – the Earl of Pembroke

Princess Theodora (20), Prince Philippos (17)

The Condé Nast Publications Ltd, Vogue House, Hanover Square, London W1S 1JU

T 020 7499 9080 F (Editorial) 020 7499 0451 F (Advertising) 020 7493 1962 F (Promotions) 020 7499 8745 www.condenast.co.uk

Registered office as above. Registered in London 1547376

3

The First Amendment and the Media

ERIC BARENDT*

I. INTRODUCTION

Few areas of First Amendment law are as instructive as that concerning the regulation of the mass media. This is not because there has been a large number of cases. Indeed, until recently only a handful had reached the Supreme Court, while US constitutional law case-books usually devote more space to the general principles of prior restraint and to particular topics such as libel and obscenity than they do to the media. However, with the advent of cable broadcasting and the Internet, more cases have been taken to the Court, so that it has now become possible to speak of a mass media jurisprudence, albeit one which is far from coherent.

That this case law lacks coherence is hardly, as the first two chapters of this book might suggest, a source of surprise. Nor should it be unexpected that this jurisprudence highlights some aspects of the treatment of free speech in the United States which many lawyers and commentators in the United Kingdom and Europe would find troublesome. For example, many court decisions show an unqualified commitment to an unregulated "market place of ideas"[1] and a corresponding suspicion of government attempts to promote public debate by media regulation. Another feature of general First Amendment jurisprudence plays a prominent role in these cases: hostility to "content-based" regulation of speech, broadly defined as regulation which permits the expression of some views or some types of speech, but which prohibits others.[2] For this reason it is virtually impossible to prescribe radio and television programme standards of the type which have traditionally been accepted in Europe, including the United Kingdom.

In assessing the media cases, it must be remembered that the First Amendment guarantee of the freedoms of speech and the press was drafted at a time when the new federal Congress was seen as the only threat to their

* I would like to thank Beth Johnston, Yale University, for her research and for commenting on a draft of this essay.

[1] This idea is associated with the famous dissenting judgment of Holmes J in *Abrams* v. *US* (1919) 250 US 616, 630.

[2] This topic is explored further in section 5 of this essay.

exercise.[3] Moreover, as Stephen Sedley noted in Chapter 2, almost all the early free speech cases in the 1920s and 1930s concerned the prosecution of individual writers, pamphleteers and protestors, many of them members of radical or socialist groups. The First Amendment freedom was asserted only against the *government*. That was so whether the case concerned official censorship, the application of criminal laws relating to the advocacy of insurrection, or restrictions imposed by police officers and local authorities on meetings and processions. In all these circumstances, it is invariably easy to determine the identity of the "speaker", the individual who is entitled to claim the constitutional right. (Indeed, one of the arguments for taking freedom of speech seriously, and giving it constitutional coverage, is that exercise of the freedom is essential to the self-fulfilment of individual speakers.) Furthermore, the evils of censorship and of the use of draconian criminal laws are all too apparent; the government is able, at the least, to control political debate; in some circumstances it may be tempted to use the law to outlaw all dissent or the expression of minority opinion.

This Orwellian perspective has dominated US thinking about the First Amendment.[4] Government is the sole enemy of freedom of speech, as it is of other basic political liberties. Doctrinally this leads to the complex "state action" doctrine, under which the courts must find, sometimes with considerable ingenuity, some element of government or public action before constitutional rights can be asserted. The perspective also explains the general hostility to government regulation, even when, say, it is intended to promote equal opportunities for speech in the course of election campaigns.[5] Further, it justifies the suspicion of content-based rules, under which the government bans some types of speech or opinion, while tolerating the expression of others.[6]

How much of this perspective is relevant to the output of the mass media? The question is crucial, for at the end of the twentieth century virtually all significant speech is mass speech. The soap-box orator, the pamphleteer and individual canvassers now play little part in forming public opinion. The town meeting, where the chairman allows everyone to speak in turn, is no longer a realistic model for the organisation of political debate. All these forms of discussion have been replaced by sound-bites, news clips, and talk-shows where increasingly the boundaries between politics and entertainment are blurred. The evil some fear is not so much Orwell's *Big Brother* as

[3] Madison had initially wished that the provisions of the Bill of Rights should apply to the states as well as to Congress and the President, but was unable to convince a sufficient majority of the Senate of the desirability of this principle.

[4] The term is used in an article challenging the usual assumptions underlying First Amendment thinking: R. Collins and D. Skover, "The First Amendment in an Age of Paratroopers", (1990) 68 *Texas LR* 1087.

[5] *Buckley* v. *Valeo* (1976) 424 US 1.

[6] See G. R. Stone, "Content Regulation and the First Amendment" (1983) 25 *William and Mary LR* 189, 200–33.

the tyranny of pleasure depicted in Aldous Huxley's *Brave New World*.[7] The agenda of political and social debate is not determined exclusively by the government, as the Orwellian perspective holds, but by newspaper barons and media conglomerates. Subversive opinion and the voices of minority groups are not suppressed because they are dangerous to the State. Indeed, they are not suppressed at all. Rather, they find no space on television schedules, the tabloids or even in much of the broadsheet press, because they do not attract large audiences and are unattractive to the advertisers who finance the mass media.[8] Indeed, minority opinion may only get reported, and its merits discussed, when it takes to the streets.[9]

As I will explain in the next section, in most contexts the Supreme Court and other courts have applied, with relatively little modification, their traditional First Amendment principles to the mass media; government regulation of media scheduling or of the press is an unconstitutional abridgement of freedom of speech. That approach is defended by many commentators who argue that the principles developed for print should be applied without modification to the new communications media.[10] Terrestrial broadcasting has so far remained something of an exception to this practice, one which many commentators find an anomaly, explicable only in terms of outmoded or questionable assumptions. Section 2 therefore briefly examines some of the leading US cases, and the principles underlying them. While the courts have usually been hostile to attempts to regulate the content of newspapers and broadcasting schedules, they have often been more sympathetic to *structural* regulation, that is, rules designed to prevent, say, undue concentrations of media ownership or to protect the access of viewers and listeners to a variety of sources of information and ideas. To this extent, at least, the notion that the First Amendment requires a wholly free market-place of ideas is misconceived.

But it is questionable whether special media ownership and other structural rules, now a common feature of media regulation in many countries, can be sharply distinguished from contents-based regulation. This topic is explored in section 3 of this Chapter. The following section examines the coherence of the prevalent attachment to the "market-place of ideas" theory in the mass media context. I argue that whatever its general merits, the theory serves society badly when it is applied to the media, particularly broadcasting and cable. One major weakness of the theory is that only a handful of media magnates seem to enjoy rights to speak in the market-place.

However, it would be misleading to characterise American free speech thinking as uniform. There are lively disagreements on many First

---

[7] Collins and Skover, *supra* n. 4, 1090–106.

[8] An explanation perhaps for Stephen Sedley's unanswered question concerning the US media's "white-out" of Noam Chomskey; see p. 26 above.

[9] Or perhaps to the art galleries; see Warbrick's chapter in this volume.

[10] E.g., see L. Powe, *American Broadcasting and the First Amendment* (California, 1987); T. Krattenmaker and L. Powe, "Converging First Amendment Principles for Converging Communications Media" (1995) 104 *Yale LJ* 1719.

Amendment questions. That is true with regard to the mass media cases. The dissenting tradition in the law schools is represented by such figures as Owen Fiss, Cass Sunstein and Edwin Baker. They argue, for example, for a more discriminating attitude to contents-based regulation of speech, under which, for instance, some programme standards might be allowed, at least insofar as they allow time for the expression of opinion which otherwise would be entirely excluded from television schedules. More fundamentally, this tradition is relatively sympathetic to government regulation which is designed to give time or space for such expression or which is intended to equalise the opportunities for speech by all elements in the community. The tradition rests, it will be argued in section 5, on a richer understanding of the First Amendment than the market-place of ideas approach where only the government is seen as the enemy of freedom of expression. We should, as comparative lawyers, resist the temptation to equate the entirety of First Amendment jurisprudence with its dominant orthodoxies.[11]

II. THE MASS MEDIA CASES

The Press

The First Amendment explicitly covers freedom of the press as well as "the freedom of speech". It is a nice question whether the two terms are simply interchangeable or whether they have separate, distinct meanings. Some writers, notably Potter Stewart in a famous extra-judicial article,[12] have argued that the press is entitled to a special degree of constitutional protection, as the Fourth Estate, the primary independent watch-dog over government and political life. That might entail recognition, say, of press rights of access to institutions, such as prisons, military bases and other places, to which the public are normally denied entry, in order to investigate matters of public interest.[13] A special degree of protection might have repercussions for the scope of incidental press (and general media) rights, such as the journalists' privilege not to reveal their sources of information. But in most contexts, such as the application of the First Amendment to the laws of libel and privacy, it seems to make little difference whether freedom of speech or freedom of the press is invoked; the rule in *New York Times* v. *Sullivan*[14] and the general hostility to hate speech laws cover both the media and individ-

---

[11] Cf Ian Loveland's observation in Ch. 1 regarding *Buckley* v. *Valeo*. For a further demonstration of the merits of discarding the ratio of First Amendment case law while adopting the principles which can be argued to underlie it see the chapter by Morris in this volume.

[12] "Or of the Press" (1975) 26 *Hastings LJ* 631. Also see C. Baker, *Human Liberty and Freedom of Speech* (New York, 1989), ch. 10.

[13] An argument that might be invoked to qualify Stephen Sedley's suggestion in Ch. 2 *supra* that the First Amendment cannot serve as source of positive rights of access to information.

[14] (1964) 367 US 254.

ual writers and speakers, though of course the primary beneficiaries of these principles are the institutional media.

However, in one context the explicit reference of the First Amendment to press freedom may be significant. In *Miami Herald Publishing Co. v. Tornillo*[15] a unanimous Supreme Court held a Florida statute granting political candidates a right to reply to attacks in newspapers violated press freedom, in particular, the discretion of editors to determine the content of their newspapers. The Court's judgment was given by Burger CJ. He noted the decline in the number of newspapers available to the public in most areas of the United States and the concentration of power in the hands of a few press magnates. He also considered the argument that mandatory rights of reply would give readers the benefit of views other than those of editors or press owners. Despite these points, he concluded that the First Amendment outlawed any interference by government, federal or state, with the independent press. Press freedom entails virtually unfettered editorial discretion. Moreover, since the reply right was triggered by the newspaper's attack on a political candidate, the provision amounted to a content-based restriction on press freedom.[16] Burger CJ referred invariably to the Press Clause and freedom of the press rather than freedom of speech, but he did not appear to attach significance to this point. More strangely, he did not refer to the decision five years earlier in *Red Lion*, where the Supreme Court, again unanimously, had upheld a right to reply to personal attacks on the broadcasting media.

Terrestrial Broadcasting

From 1934 broadcasting has been regulated by the Federal Communications Commission (FCC), given broad statutory power to assign frequencies and to allocate licences. The common carrier model, under which licensees would be required like a telephone network to make their stations available for the use of community associations and others was deliberately rejected; it would have unduly burdened broadcasters' freedom. But it was clear from the outset that they did not enjoy the same rights of free speech as newspaper editors and owners. In 1943 the Supreme Court upheld FCC regulations restricting the freedom of local licensees to allow the national networks exclusive access to their broadcasting time;[17] Frankfurter J emphasised that the First Amendment did not confer freedom to broadcast without a licence,

[15] (1974) 418 US 241.

[16] C. Baker, "*Turner Broadcasting*: Content-based Regulation of Persons and Presses" [1994] *Supreme Court Review* 57, 111–14, argues that on this alternative rationale there would be no objection to requiring newspapers, say, to give all candidates some space, as access would not be triggered by anything published in the paper.

[17] *National Broadcasting Company v. US* (1943) 319 US 190.

so the FCC could impose reasonable conditions when it granted an application permission to broadcast.

Most insight into US broadcasting regulation is gained by a brief exploration of the Fairness Doctrine, a set of rules issued by the FCC after the Second World War. It required licensees to devote a reasonable amount of their broadcasting schedule to the presentation of controversial issues and to treat them in a balanced manner. The Doctrine was therefore equivalent to the "due impartiality" provisions in the UK Broadcasting Act 1990, also incorporated in the BBC Broadcasting Agreement.[18] Another aspect of the Doctrine required stations to provide a free right of reply to persons or organisations attacked on a radio or television programme. As it covered all personal attacks, and not just those on election candidates, it was a broader right than that subsequently held incompatible with the First Amendment in *Tornillo*. Both the general Doctrine and the right of reply were held constitutional in the famous *Red Lion* case.[19] The Supreme Court ruled that broadcasters did not enjoy the same rights to free speech as pamphleteers or newspaper editors; the former had been given the privilege to make use of a scarce resource, the airwaves. Channel owners were to be regarded as trustees for the viewing and listening public, whose rights were paramount.

White J's judgment in *Red Lion* adopted the "scarcity" rationale for broadcasting regulation. Whatever its coherence then, it is virtually impossible to defend it now, with the advent of cable and satellite, and with the imminent arrival of digital broadcasting. Moreover, it is hard to see how it could ever have justified restrictions on the transmission of "indecent" or "offensive" programmes, frequently imposed in the broadcasting context. At most, the rationale might have justified some provision for the access to the airwaves of groups who would have liked to acquire a licence, but for whom there was no space on the available frequencies.[20] Though *Red Lion* has never been overruled, its approach is widely regarded as anomalous in relation to general free speech jurisprudence. Moreover, attempts to apply its approach to other media outlets have consistently been rejected; this is true of the press (as already noted), of cable, and most recently of cyberspace. The FCC itself abandoned the Fairness Doctrine (though not the personal attack rule) in 1987, a change upheld by the Circuit Court of Appeals for the District of Columbia.[21] With the greater number of broadcasting channels, it was unnecessary, and probably unconstitutional, to fetter the freedom of broadcasters to choose their own programme schedules.

---

[18] (1996) Cm. 3152, Cl. 5.

[19] *Red Lion Broadcasting Co.* v. *FCC* (1969) 395 US 367.

[20] J. Balkin, "Media Filters, the V-Chip, and the Foundations of Broadcast Regulation" [1996] *Duke LJ* 1131, 1134–5.

[21] *Syracuse Peace Council* v. *FCC* (1989) 867 F 2d. 654.

Unlike the UK statutory rules,[22] the Doctrine never prohibited commercial licensees from stating their own views on contemporary political and social events, or "editorialising" to use the American term. The freedom to editorialise was, however, at first denied the small public broadcasting system established in 1967. The restriction was subsequently held incompatible with the First Amendment.[23] Brennan J said that it amounted to a content-based restriction on the speech of public broadcasters; they had been free to solicit funds and to discuss their own programme schedules (as is the BBC), so it was wrong to stop them expressing views on other matters.

The tenuousness of the "scarcity rationale" does not of course exhaust the arguments for regulation of the broadcasting media. A majority of the Supreme Court in the *Pacifica* case upheld the authority of the FCC to impose sanctions against a Californian radio station for broadcasting "indecent" language in the middle of the afternoon.[24] Stevens J's judgment emphasised that each branch of the media should be treated individually. The broadcasting media are a "uniquely pervasive presence' in modern American society, and are "uniquely accessible" to children, even those unable to read. In contrast, it is unconstitutional to outlaw "indecent" language in newspapers and cyberspace, for such matter, unlike "obscene" material, is covered by the First Amendment. *Pacifica* therefore exceptionally tolerates one type of content-based regulation on the broadcasting media.

Whether the "unique pervasiveness" or accessibility to children rationales for broadcasting regulation are any more acceptable than the "scarcity" argument is another matter.[25] It is very odd to allow greater regulation of a medium, simply because it is the most effective or powerful means of communication. And it can be questioned whether broadcasting is now significantly more accessible to children and young people than the Internet or the telephone,[26] just because it requires fewer active steps to turn it on. But even if they are coherent, it is worth pointing out that the rationales would only justify the regulation of indecent or perhaps excessively violent programmes. Many positive programme standards, routinely imposed in the United Kingdom and most other European countries, for example, the requirement to transmit news and current affairs programmes, could not easily be supported on the *Pacifica* arguments. Such standards would probably be regarded in the United States as unacceptable content-based regulation of the scheduling freedom of broadcasters.

---

[22] Now see Broadcasting Act 1990, s. 6(4).
[23] *FCC v. League of Women Voters of California* (1984) 468 US 364.
[24] *FCC v. Pacifica Foundation* (1978) 438 US 726.
[25] For a criticism of the "pervasiveness" argument, see Balkin, *supra* n. 20, 1134–41.
[26] In *Sable Communications of California* v. *FCC* (1989) 492 US 115, the Court struck down a ban on "dial-a-porn" telephone lines, on the ground that unlike radio and television access it required active steps by the listener.

Cable Broadcasting

The treatment of cable has always been controversial. Should it be assimilated for First Amendment purposes to the position of the unregulated press, or should it be treated in much the same way as terrestrial broadcasting? It has rarely been given the latter position, perhaps because on one view of its scope it would be odd to apply the "scarcity" rationale to systems which could deliver at least 45 to 50 and sometimes more than 100 channels. (Although it should be admitted that in most communities only one system can be accommodated, given the physical constraints in laying cable down and the need to attract an adequate number of subscribers. A cable system is, like BSkyB satellite broadcasting in Britain, almost inevitably a *de facto* monopoly.) On the other hand, there is an obvious objection to treating cable in exactly the same way as newspapers or magazines. Cable is primarily a system for distributing programmes made by specialist programme makers, either the companies who produce largely for the terrestrial channels, or satellite or cable programmers. This makes analysis of the rights to freedom of speech in this context particularly difficult. One question is whether these rights should be ascribed solely to the operators of the cable systems, or whether programme-makers also have First Amendment rights. Secondly, in what circumstances, if any, is it constitutional to enact legislation imposing obligations on cable operators to transmit certain types of programme?

Some answers to these questions have been provided by the Supreme Court in *Turner Broadcasting System, Inc.* v. *FCC.*[27] At issue was the constitutionality of the "must-carry" provisions of the Cable Television Consumer Protection and Competition Act of 1992, requiring cable systems to devote some of their channels to the transmission of local commercial and public television channels. Congress imposed these obligations, because it feared that otherwise cable systems would only transmit the commercial programmes made by cable programmers. That would endanger the survival of local terrestrial channels, and consequently the access of viewers without cable (about 40 per cent of US households) to them. The Court rejected the *Red Lion* approach, since the "scarcity" argument hardly applied. Equally, it did not think it appropriate to treat cable in the same way as the press. Kennedy J for the Court majority recognised that cable operators are able to exercise "bottleneck" or gatekeeper control over the access of viewers to television programming; if they exclude certain programmes, it is impossible for viewers dependent on cable to watch them. This distinguishes cable from the press. Moreover, unlike the right of reply held unconstitutional in *Tornillo*, the must-carry provisions did not require cable operators to alter

---

[27]   (1994) 114 S. Ct 2445.

their own programmes, nor would their implementation give viewers the impression that the operators agreed with any messages or ideas communicated by the terrestrial channels.

The key step in the Court's reasoning was that the must-carry requirement did not amount to content-based regulation. In Kennedy J's view the sections of the 1992 legislation were content-neutral, since they required provision for terrestrial channels, irrespective of their contents. Rather, they encouraged the maintenance of a particular means of transmission, which might be at danger if cable were not compelled to carry its programmes. (In the second *Turner* case decided three years later,[28] the Court found this danger to be a real one, and so approved the must-carry rules.) In these circumstances Kennedy J held it would be wrong to subject the must-carry sections to strict scrutiny to determine whether they were compatible with the First Amendment. A lower level of examination, known as intermediate scrutiny, was more appropriate. On that approach, they should be upheld if they furthered a substantial governmental interest, unrelated to the suppression of free expression.[29] In perhaps the most revealing sentence of his judgment, Kennedy J said that:

> "assuring that the public has access to a multiplicity of information sources is a governmental purpose of the highest order, for it promotes values central to the First Amendment."[30]

The government was also entitled to promote fair competition in the television market between cable and terrestrial broadcasting.

When it denied that the must-carry rules were content-based, the Court in effect characterised them as structural regulation, concerned with the organisation of the broadcasting industry and the promotion of competition between its different sectors. We will see in section 3 that the Supreme Court is more sympathetic to this type of regulation, on the assumption that it poses fewer dangers to free speech principles than direct regulation of the contents of speech. But it may be hard, as we will also see, to distinguish in practice between the two types of media regulation; arguably, however commendable the result in *Turner Broadcasting* may be, the decisions in these cases themselves rested on a questionable characterisation of the provisions in the 1992 legislation.[31]

Whatever its defects, Kennedy J's judgment in *Turner Broadcasting* did attempt doctrinal clarity. In contrast the judgment for the plurality of the Court in the complex *Denver Area* case[32] deliberately avoided it. The case

---

[28] (1997) 117 S Ct. 1174.
[29] For a full statement of the test for intermediate scrutiny, see the draft-card burning case, *US v O'Brien* (1968) 391 US 367, 377.
[30] (1994) 117 S Ct. 2445 at 2470.
[31] This point is discussed further below.
[32] *Denver Area Educational Telecommunications Consortium* v. *FCC* (1996) 116 S Ct. 2374.

concerned the constitutionality of three provisions of the 1992 cable legislation permitting, or in one instance requiring, cable operators to limit access to patently offensive or indecent programming on access channels, that is, channels the operators were statutorily required to make available for use by non-affiliated programmers. Breyer J, giving the plurality judgment, declined to bracket cable with either the press or the terrestrial media. Nor was he willing to characterise the control over indecent programming as a content-based rule which should be subject to strict scrutiny. Breyer J justified his caution by reference to the evolving character of the cable and telecommunications industries. It was enough to judge whether the provisions addressed a complex problem without imposing unnecessarily onerous restrictions on speech.

One difficulty in this area, as already noted, is deciding whose speech is in issue: should the courts be more solicitous of the rights of the independent programmers, or for that matter the viewers of the access channels, or of the editorial freedom of the cable operators? The judgments of Kennedy J and Thomas J were equally critical of Breyer J's pragmatism, but differed on the ascription of First Amendment rights in this context. For the former, the cable operators were to be treated as common carriers or conduits for the access channels, and the indecency rules amounted clearly to a content-based regulation of the programmers' First Amendment rights. Thomas J, with whom Rehnquist CJ and Scalia J concurred, thought that cable operators enjoyed the same editorial rights as newspaper editors, and for that reason would have upheld two of the provisions which the Court plurality, and Kennedy J, regarded as an impermissible violation of the programmers' First Amendment freedom.

The Internet

How should the new media technologies be treated under the First Amendment?[33] On one view, the international network of connected computers known as the Internet differs from the mass media in that it largely provides a system for individual exchanges and the retrieval of information. It is perhaps more akin to an electronic library or intellectual shopping mall than it is to a newspaper or broadcasting channel. On the other hand, newspapers, magazines and video images can be transmitted electronically over the Internet, so to some extent it is an alternative to the traditional media. The general view in the United States has been that it is wrong in principle, as well as impractical, to regulate cyberspace, at least with regard to the con-

---

[33] See the Symposium, "Emerging Media Technology and the First Amendment" (1995) 104 *Yale LJ* 1613.

tent of Internet communications.[34] This has now been confirmed by the Supreme Court. In *Reno (Attorney General of the United States)* v. *American Civil Liberties Union*[35] it held two provisions of the Communications Decency Act 1996, forming Part V. of the Telecommunications Act of 1996, contrary to the First Amendment. They made it an offence to send indecent or patently offensive messages over a telecommunications system to any person under 18 years. The aim was the laudable one of preventing children accessing pornographic material over the Internet, but it failed to pass constitutional muster. In the Court's view the provisions amounted to a content-based restriction on speech. It had the effect of restricting communication to adults, and criminalised the transmission of material which parents might be happy for their children to look at.

Stevens J refused to apply the *Pacifica* radio indecency ruling, in which he had given the Court's judgment. Radio was historically subject, as already explained, to special regulation, on the grounds of scarcity, pervasiveness and the difficulty of precluding access by children. In contrast, some degree of know-how is needed to gain access to pornographic or other material on the Internet. Moreover, broadcasting has been regulated by a specialist agency, the FCC; there is no equivalent body for the Internet. A more appropriate analogy was the telephone, where regulation of indecent messages has been held unconstitutional in the Dial-A-Porn case.[36]

It is hard to disagree with this reasoning. Internet communication does seem to have much in common with the speech and writing of pamphleteers and other individual authors. It is however still unclear whether they will provide a forum for genuine political and social debate similar to that afforded by the broadcasting media, whether they are transmitted terrestrially or by cable or satellite. One difference is that broadcasting is in practice accessible to every member of the community, while the Internet is at the moment used by the better educated and wealthier groups—although take-up is increasing rapidly.

III. STRUCTURAL REGULATION

In the *Turner Broadcasting* case Kennedy J's plurality judgment denied that the must carry obligation amounted to a content-based regulation of the operators' First Amendment freedom; but the principle of viewer access to a multiplicity of information sources should be regarded as a legitimate purpose of government, important enough to justify the obligation imposed on the cable operators. This contrast brings out an important feature of

---

[34] See the general view of the collection of essays in the Symposium, *Emerging Media Technology and the First Amendment*, (1995) 104 *Yale LJ* 1613.

[35] (1997) 65 *Law Week* 4715.

[36] *Sable* v. FCC (1989) 492 US 115.

modern US media jurisprudence. Content-based regulation, in particular the imposition of programme standards, is viewed with great suspicion, while *structural* rules concerning, for instance, the organisation of media industries are treated much more favourably.

Acceptable structural regulation normally takes the form of the application to the media, including the newspaper industry, of the general law of taxation and antitrust law. But the Supreme Court has also approved the application of special structural rules designed to increase or preserve the number of media outlets in a particular community and thereby to protect, it is believed, the diversity of sources of information. (Such rules would also be viewed sympathetically in European jurisdictions as reasonable measures to promote pluralism, a constitutional principle which in France and Italy may justify limits on the rights of channel owners and individual broadcasters.[37]) A leading example of the first category of structural regulation, the application of general rules, is the decision of the Supreme Court in *Associated Press* v. *US*.[38] Members of the Associated Press Service were required to transmit to it every piece of news they collected, and not to divulge it to anyone else. These requirements, in conjunction with other restrictive rules, were held unlawful under the Sherman antitrust legislation. The important point is that Associated Press lost its argument that antitrust regulation could not be applied to the press: as Black J put it: "Freedom of the press from governmental interference under the First Amendment . . . does not sanction repression of that freedom by private interests."[39] Further, the media enjoy no general immunity from tax laws,[40] nor from the principles of contract and promissory estoppel.[41]

In addition to *Turner Broadcasting,* two examples may be given of the Court's treatment of special media regulation. In the *NCCB* case[42] it approved cross-ownership rules, precluding joint newspaper and broadcasting company control of local television or radio stations in areas where the press company published a newspaper. For a unanimous Court Marshall J rejected the argument that the rules amounted to an unconstitutional content-based regulation of the First Amendment rights of newspaper owners. The rules did treat them differently from, say, petrol companies, but they applied irrespective of the contents of the newspapers affected. They were

---

[37] For a recent discussion of the European principle, see R. Craufurd Smith, *Broadcasting Law and Fundamental Rights* (Oxford, 1997), ch. 7.

[38] (1945) 326 US 1.

[39] *Ibid.*, at 20.

[40] *Giragi* v. *Moore* (1937) 301 US 670. But discriminatory tax legislation, which imposes special burdens on the press, is contrary to the First Amendment: *Minneapolis Star & Tribune Co.* v. *Minnesota Commissioner of Revenue* (1983) 460 US 575.

[41] In *Cohen* v. *Cowles Media Co.* (1991) 501 US 663, the Court held that a newspaper was bound by general principles of estoppel to honour a promise not to disclose the identity of an informant.

[42] FCC v. *National Citizens Committee for Broadcasting* (1978) 436 US 775.

structural rules designed to widen the range of information and opinion available to local communities.

Secondly, in *Metro Broadcasting*[43] a bare majority, five to four, of the Court upheld an FCC policy, mandated by Congress, favouring minority group ownership of broadcasting stations. The policy had been adopted in the belief that increased minority group ownership fostered programme diversity, the same argument used in support of the must-carry rules approved in *Turner*. Minority preference was then regarded by the Court majority as a benign classification of racial groups, and hence under a low level of scrutiny held to be compatible with the Fourteenth Amendment's Equal Protection Clause prohibition of racial discrimination. This aspect of the case is no longer good law. The decision in *Metro* has been overruled by a recent Court decision that even benign racial classifications must be subject to strict scrutiny. under the Fourteenth Amendment.[44]

However, *Metro Broadcasting* remains a significant First Amendment decision, insofar as it drew a distinction between policies favouring diversity of ownership and of programming, upheld by the majority, and impermissible content-based regulation. O'Connor J, dissenting in this case as she subsequently did in *Turner*, argued that it was unprecedented for the Court to uphold broadcasting measures intended to promote the dissemination of distinct views or the expression of particular groups, whether of racial minorities or other groups. The FCC policy at issue in the *Metro* case had been formulated as an ownership rule, but it was in her view indistinguishable in substance from a contents or programme rule.

This is a crucial point. Many structural rules are designed to achieve much the same ends as programme standards. Diversity of ownership is one means of achieving programming variety and the expression of a range of different opinions, objects which may also be achieved by such rules as the "due impartiality" principle or requirements to show news, current affairs and other programmes of merit. There is therefore a paradox in the Supreme Court's approach. Under its general attitude to content-based regulation, programme standards are unlikely to survive strict scrutiny in the context of broadcasting, while in the case of cable they would almost certainly be struck down. But if a regulation can be characterised as structural it is more likely to be upheld, even though it is designed indirectly to achieve the same objects as the inadmissible programme standards.

This paradox is also revealed by the *Turner* case. The majority upheld the must-carry regulations as structural rules intended to ensure fair competition between cable and terrestrial broadcasting, and the access of viewers to a wide variety of information sources. But O'Connor J, with whose

---

[43] *Metro Broadcasting Co.* v *FCC* (1990) 495 US 547. For commentary, see M. Rosenfield, "*Metro Broadcasting* v. *FCC*: Affirmative Action at the Crossroads of Constitutional Liberty and Equality" (1991) 38 *UCLA LR* 583.

[44] *Adarand Construction Co.* v *Rena* (1995) 115 S Ct. 2097.

judgment three other members of the Court joined, disagreed with the characterisation of the regulations as content-neutral. Rather, they were designed to give a preference for diversity of views, for educational and public affairs programming, and other material which might not be chosen by the cable operators, their programmers or viewers. This assessment was surely right. Section 5 of the legislation of 1992 specifically required operators to devote a proportion of their channels to public and educational broadcasting. But this requirement is only intelligible if these programmes have distinctive contents or put over views and ideas which otherwise would be absent from the operators' programme schedules.

These difficulties have not escaped the attention of some American commentators.[45] Why, for example, Cass Sunstein has asked, should the Court be so willing to countenance structural regulation when it is so reluctant to tolerate content-based regulation designed to achieve the same end? The characterisation of regulation as either one or the other may be difficult, as the disagreement between the members of the *Turner* Court indicates. Yet everything, certainly too much, seems to depend on how the rule is regarded. Sunstein's answer is that the approach in *Turner* represents a compromise between two perspectives on freedom of speech, both of which present real problems.[46] On the one hand, there is the pure "market-place of ideas" view, hostile to all government regulation. On that perspective, neither content-based nor structural regulation of the media would easily be tolerated. On the other, there is what he terms the Madisonian view or model of freedom of speech, which emphasises the need to encourage vigorous and uninhibited public debate and which is prepared to allow its encouragement, when necessary, by government or other public regulation. Sunstein concludes that the *Turner* compromise can be justified as avoiding the risks which a tolerance of some content-based regulation runs. Some view-point discrimination might creep into media regulation under the guise of broadcasting standards which on their surface merely appear to encourage, say, the expression of minority views or the scheduling of a balanced range of programmes. For Sunstein an insistence on content-neutral regulation may be necessary to save the courts the delicate task of distinguishing between acceptable and unacceptable standards for the media.

Much of this analysis will seem very strange to European readers, accustomed to quite extensive public regulation of the broadcasting media and on the continent, at least, some regulation of the press as well. In the United Kingdom, France, Germany and other countries, government is usually trusted to regulate the media with sensitivity, subject to judicial review. In many continental jurisdictions, regulation to promote pluralism or to provide rights of reply, or even access to the media, is considered perfectly com-

---

[45] See O. Fiss, *The Irony of Free Speech* (Harvard, Conn., 1996), 70–4; C. Sunstein, "The First Amendment in Cyberspace" (1995) 104 *Yale LJ* 1757.
[46] *Ibid.*, at 1777–80.

patible with freedom of expression. But it is not enough to refer to this to show the drawbacks of the US media jurisprudence. It is now time to consider the coherence of the "market-place of ideas" understanding of freedom of speech, particularly in the context of the modern mass media.

IV. A MARKET PLACE OF IDEAS ?

It is almost impossible to exaggerate the central hold of the "market-place of ideas" metaphor on US jurisprudence and general thinking about the First Amendment freedom of speech. From it stems the belief that the best corrective for the expression of pernicious opinion is not regulation, let alone suppression, but more speech. Truth, it is said, will emerge from the competition of ideas in the market-place. Government should therefore abstain from any interference, though it must be pointed out that the intervention of the law is necessary to allocate and to enforce the property rights—for example, to newspaper presses, broadcasting stations and other channels of communication—which underlie the communication of speech. In particular, regulation which discriminates between different views or types of speech is suspect, since it distorts the market and interferes with the free acceptance or rejection of ideas by the public.

This is the central tradition of US free speech jurisprudence. Almost certainly conceived by Holmes J in his famous *Abrams* dissent[47] as a metaphor, it is now taken quite literally as the appropriate framework for First Amendment jurisprudence.[48] There is a free market in speech, as there is for automobiles, oil and soap powders. But the tradition rests on shaky foundations, which appear particularly infirm in the context of mass media communications. The argument makes a number of questionable assumptions. First, it presumes that everyone is free to enter the market-place to communicate their views and to exchange information. Secondly, the market-place theory suggests that speakers and writers present their own views or offer information which they believe to be accurate and likely to contribute to the resolution of some question or other. And thirdly, the market-place theory only makes sense if it is assumed that the audience, in the context of broadcasting listeners and viewers, generally assesses contributions to the market-place of ideas in a rational and intelligent manner.[49]

These assumptions are critical to the coherence of the market-place theory, with its concomitant hostility to any attempt by government, however benignly intended, to regulate its operation. A market-place which few

[47] *Abrams* v. *United States* (1919) 250 US 616, 630.

[48] See F. Schauer, "The Political Incidence of the Free Speech Principle" (1993) 64 *U Colorado LR* 935, 949–52.

[49] See J. Weinberg, "Broadcasting and Speech" (1993) 81 *California LR* 1103, to which the arguments in this section are much indebted.

can enter does nothing for "the principle that debate on public issues should be uninhibited, robust and wide open . . .", a principle to which the Supreme Court showed its commitment in *New York Times* v. *Sullivan*.[50] But the modern mass media are controlled by a handful of groups and networks. Few cities in the United States offer readers a choice of newspapers, while three or four national networks dominate television. The United States, like Europe, has witnessed the growth in multi-media corporations, with interests in films, broadcasting, newspapers and magazines, or some combination of them. The Supreme Court has noted these phenomena, but has declined to lessen their significance by the recognition of rights of reply to the printed press[51] or of an access right to use the broadcasting media for political messages.[52]

It is worth saying a little more about the second weakness of the marketplace argument. One aspect of mass communications is that relatively little of it is the direct expression of the views of the media institution itself, although First Amendment rights are generally ascribed to it, rather than, say, the individual journalist, freelance writer, or independent production company. Many media outlets largely distribute the speech of others, rather than communicate their own ideas or information which they have assembled themselves. This is recognised by requiring some communications systems to act as "common carriers" for all types of message, for the most part irrespective of their contents. Obviously the postal service and telephone systems are treated as "common carriers". Equally the Court's judgment in *Turner Broadcasting* and the approach of Kennedy J in the *Denver Area* case treated cable operators as akin to common carriers with regard to access channels, by denying them full First Amendment editorial discretion to choose exactly which programmes were carried on them. On the other hand, the clear implication of *Tornillo* is that newspaper editors exercise full First Amendment rights; newspapers are not to be treated as public forums, let alone common carriers for the articles and letters of others. Equally, the "common carrier" model, as mentioned in section two, was rejected as appropriate for broadcasting, though perhaps the *Red Lion* decision shows some trace of its approach.

This troublesome aspect of the regulation of media speech has not received the full treatment it deserves.[53] The difficulty is that First Amendment rights may be ascribed to media institutions, or to their controllers such as newspaper editors or broadcasting channel owners, without

[50] (1964) 376 US 254, 270, *per* Brennan J.

[51] In *Miami Herald* v. *Tornillo* (1974) 418 US 241, discussed above.

[52] In *CBS* v. *Democratic National Committee* (1973) 412 US 94, the Court rejected a constitutional right of access to advertise against participation in the Vietnam War; some members of the Court majority took the view that this right would infringe the broadcasters' First Amendment freedoms.

[53] For a notable exception, see M. Meyerson, "Authors, Editors, and Uncommon Carriers: Identifying the 'Speaker' Within the New Media" (1995) 71 *Notre Dame LR* 79.

real consideration whether this is appropriate. When a cable operator or the owner of a radio station declines to allocate time on its channels to the work of an independent producer, is he exercising a real free-speech right, something like the editorial function traditionally given the newspaper editor? Or is it better to conclude that this function is more akin to that of a newsstand, bookshop or a telephone company, acting as a conduit for the views of those claiming access to facilities for the transmission of speech? On one view, distributors are really exercising a property right or commercial freedom when they determine whose speech they are prepared to transmit, rather than claiming an independent free speech right.[54]

These difficulties cannot simply be resolved by reference to the "market-place" theory or to the courts' habitual hostility to government regulation of speech. In the context of the mass media, this approach only works on the assumption that some institution or other enjoys the First Amendment right, so that any regulation to allow individual access to its facilities distorts the market-place of ideas. This point can be illustrated by a brief reference to the *Turner Broadcasting* and the *Denver Area* cases. In both cases the question, put simply, was whether various access provisions of the Cable Television Consumer Protection and Competition Act of 1992 were compatible with the First Amendment. In *Turner* the issue was whether the must-carry provisions limited the freedom of cable operators to determine use of their channels, while in *Denver* it concerned the legitimacy of Congress' grant to the operators of a right to control access programmes on the grounds of indecency or offensiveness. The point is that neither case could be resolved simply by reference to the courts' traditional hostility to regulation of a free market-place. That is largely because it is unclear in this context exactly who can lay claim to the First Amendment freedoms: the cable operators, the programmers granted access by Congress or, for that matter, the viewers, whose rights had been declared "paramount" in the broadcasting context by White J in the *Red Lion* case.[55]

Quite apart from these problems, it can be argued that mass media communication is substantially affected by the pressures of advertisers and their agencies, which influence the contents of newspapers and television schedules.[56] That is the reason commercial broadcasters prefer not to put on documentaries or serious news and arts programmes during peak viewing hours, but will show them, if at all, long after most viewers have switched off and gone to bed. Now scheduling of this sort is inevitable in a private broadcasting system, free at the point of access to the viewers and almost entirely financed by advertising revenue. But the practice makes it difficult to sustain a case that broadcasters are entitled to the same degree of First

---

[54] J. Lichtenberg, "Foundations and Limits of Freedom of the Press", in J. Lichtenberg (ed.), *Democracy and the Mass Media* (Cambridge, 1990), at 102, 120.

[55] *Red Lion Broadcasting Co.* v. *FCC* (1969) 395 US 367, 390.

[56] C. Baker, "Advertising and a Democratic Press" (1992) 140 *U. Pa. LR* 2097, at 2139–68.

Amendment protection as, say, authors and book publishers who have only, or largely, their readership in mind. In the context of the mass media, the free market of ideas is influenced, perhaps distorted, by the other market in which programme schedulers compete for the attention of advertising agents.

The third shaky foundation of the market-place theory of free speech will be discussed more briefly. That is not because there is little to say about it; rather, it is too complex a topic to do it justice within the compass of this essay.[57] For Holmes the best test of truth was the power of the speech to win acceptance in the market-place of ideas.[58] It is difficult to take this proposition very seriously; at best it is a gross over-simplification of John Stuart Mill's rich and complex justification for freedom of speech as a necessary procedure for gaining or defending social and political truths. Holmes himself was an intellectual sceptic who was understandably hostile to any attempt by government to prescribe what is true and false or what is acceptable and unacceptable. But it is equally reasonable to doubt whether any truths will emerge from an unregulated market-place in which a handful of media corporations draw up the agenda of political and social discourse and carefully limit the access of individuals and groups which dissent from their programme.

In the final analysis this part of the Holmes argument rests on the assumption that any regulation of speech will necessarily make it more difficult to discover or win truths than an unregulated free market. That is certainly true of a general censorship system and of vague criminal laws which can be applied selectively to any type of speech the authorities dislike. But it is far from obvious whether we should reach the same conclusion when regulation takes the form of positive requirements on broadcasters to put on current affairs programmes, challenging documentaries and original drama during peak hours, particularly if these standards are devised and enforced by an independent agency. It is also reasonable to be at least agnostic about the impact on free speech of other provisions, such as those mandating rights of reply or access to the media, must-carry rules, or requirements on broadcasters to be impartial or fair in their treatment of political issues. It is one thing to say that regulations of this type interfere with the market-place of ideas, but quite another to conclude that they necessarily restrict freedom of speech. They are intended instead to promote or foster it. They should be approached sympathetically, if critically, because they do not suffer from the vices inherent in a censorship system or in laws criminalising the expression of particular views. The market-place perspective on freedom of speech does not permit this discriminating attitude, but it is allowed by the alternative approach to the First Amendment outlined in the final section of this essay.

[57] For a fuller discussion, see Weinberg, *supra* n. 49, 1157–64.
[58] *Abrams* v. *US* (1919) 250 US 616, 630.

V. THE VALUE OF SPEECH IN A MASS MEDIA SOCIETY

This essay has criticised the media jurisprudence of the US Supreme Court, on the ground that it is unsatisfactory simply to apply to modern mass communications free speech principles developed for individuals and the print media at the beginning of the century. This criticism extends to the market-place perspective which is particularly open to question in this context. It is now time to outline an alternative approach, an aspect of what I termed, in section 1 of this essay, the dissenting tradition in US thinking on freedom of speech.

Cass Sunstein has put forward, as an alternative to the market-place approach, a Madisonian model. This emphasises the importance of the lively discussion of political and social issues.[59] Without informed public debate, democracy becomes a sham, perhaps, as is now widely feared, a branch of the entertainment business. The market-place model treats viewers and listeners as consumers, selecting television programmes or tabloids as if they were choosing goods in a shopping mall. The Madisonian perspective addresses them as citizens, entitled to information and a vigorous exchange of ideas and opinion. As Sunstein argues,[60] it better reflects the values of American constitutionalism.

One important implication of this perspective is that it is legitimate for government to promote the values of free speech, where they are not adequately realised through the operation of the free market. Government already does this through postal subsidies for the distribution of newspapers and election material and by its support of public broadcasting, the arts and research in the humanities. Structural regulation of the media, as noted in section 2 of the essay, is also constitutionally permissible. On the Madisonian approach, the Supreme Court's decision in *Red Lion* might not be the aberration it appears from the market-place perspective. Rather, it is legitimate to question its ruling in *Tornillo* and the Circuit Court's ready acceptance of the repeal of the Fairness Doctrine.[61] Further, the anxiety of the Court in *Turner Broadcasting* to characterise the must-carry provisions as content-neutral, and not content-based, seems unnecessary. For provisions designed to compel the transmission of educational and public affairs programmes should not be subject to strict scrutiny. The Court's hostility to content-based regulation should not extend to standards imposed to raise programme quality and the range of views expressed on broadcasting schedules—the requirements often now known as pluralism.

As has often been pointed out in this essay, a prominent feature of recent US free speech jurisprudence is a marked hostility to content-based

[59] *Supra* n. 45, 1759–65.
[60] *Ibid.*, 1763.
[61] See p. 34 above.

regulation. This is closely linked to the market-place theory, under which any regulation of speech, however benignly intended, is regarded as distorting free exchange between players in the market. It is fundamentally wrong for the law to skew the course of public debate or favour the expression of particular views. But both the underlying justifications for, and the scope of, the distinction between content-based and content-neutral restrictions are far from clear.[62] There is no doubt that view-point discrimination should always be subject to very strict scrutiny. It is hard to see how any regulation permitting, say, the statement of Republican views but forbidding the expression of Democratic sympathies could be justified under the First Amendment. It is less clear whether the courts should be so suspicious of rules which discriminate between, say, political and commercial speech, or which single out sexually explicit or indecent material for greater regulation. After all the Court has held that there are distinctions in the degree of protection afforded by the First Amendment to various categories of speech. However, in a number of cases in the last twenty-five years the Court has held that these subject-matter restrictions are as undesirable as view-point discrimination, and so should be subject to the same strict scrutiny.[63] This perspective, for instance, influenced the Court's treatment of the rule precluding editorialising by public broadcasters,[64] its approach in *Turner Broadcasting* and *Denver* to cable regulation and its recent Internet decision. It also influenced the FCC decision to repeal the Fairness Doctrine. There are now indeed very few programme standards in US broadcasting, apart from the indecency rules.[65]

This suspicion of programme standards is surely wrong. The evil of viewpoint discrimination is that government distorts debate by suppressing messages it dislikes or by favouring the expression of ideas to which it is sympathetic. This does not generally apply to subject-matter discrimination. For instance, a rule forbidding broadcasters editorialising restricts their freedom to use their privileged position to influence public debate—a purpose quite different from the evil of view-point discrimination. It is clearly right to subject public broadcasters to an editorialising ban, and it is probably sensible to apply it to private channels as well. There is admittedly room for argument here. But surely there is no basis for suspicion of positive standards, requiring channels to devote some time to educational, cultural and

[62] Among the many articles on this topic are P. B. Stephan, "The First Amendment and Content Discrimination", (1982) 68 *Va. LR 203*; G. R. Stone, "Restrictions of Speech Because of its Content: The Peculiar Case of Subject-Matter Restrictions", (1978) 46 *U. Chicago LR* 81. The topic is also examined by David Feldman in Ch. 8 of this volume.

[63] The leading case is *Police Department* v *Mosley* (1972) 406 US 92.

[64] The rule was held unconstitutional in *FCC* v. *League of Women Voters of California* (1984) 468 US 384.

[65] A ban on broadcasting indecent material from 6.00 a.m. to 10.00 p.m. has been held constitutional by the DC Circuit Court of Appeals as sufficiently narrow to serve compelling interest in protecting children: *Action for Children's Television* v. *FCC* (1995) 58 F 3d. 654.

current affairs programmes. They do not suppress speech, but are rather intended to encourage that lively debate which in other contexts, such as libel cases involving public figures, the Supreme Court is anxious to promote. So a second advantageous implication of the Madisonian approach to free speech is that we can apply the distinction between content-based and content-neutral restrictions more sensitively. Regulations designed to suppress speech should be viewed with great suspicion, but rules designed to enhance diversity of view and to foster public discussion should be regarded more benevolently, even if as a matter of form they might be characterised as content-based.

A third advantage of the Madisonian perspective may be that it is easier to resolve the intractable problem mentioned in the previous section: who enjoys rights to free speech in the context of broadcasting and cable or, for that matter, the press? Is it the owner, editor, programmer, station controller, licensee or cable operator? Do viewers and listeners have any rights in this context? If we apply the market-place of ideas model to the mass media, we must ascribe the free speech right to one of these individuals or groups, for their interests conflict. Either, for instance, the cable operator is free to choose which programmes it carries or the programme companies have a First Amendment right that it carries their programmes under contract without censorship. However, the market-place model offers no guidance on how this should be done, though it may be noted that it seems to grant the First Amendment freedom to those with the property rights in, say, the newspaper, the licence or cable system.

The Madisonian perspective is more helpful. It asserts that the legislature and regulatory agencies must be involved in resolving these conflicts between participators in the free speech market. It is therefore for the law or regulation to determine which institution exercises control over, say, broadcasting schedules or whether an individual enjoys a right of reply in the press or on the broadcasting media. Such regulation must of course promote the values of freedom of speech—lively debate and a diversity of view—within the particular branch of the media, and the courts may invalidate it if it fails to do this. The question which individuals or institutions enjoy First Amendment rights then becomes peripheral. Indeed, it is impossible to conclude that any particular individual or institution—editor, broadcasting licensee or cable operator—necessarily enjoys a First Amendment right irrespective of the context. What is important is that laws are framed to foster the values of freedom of speech, to the service of which the freedoms of the press and broadcasting media and the rights of editors and licensees are instrumental or subordinate.[66]

Much American thinking on freedom of speech in general, and the media freedom in particular, seems dominated, almost distorted, by a fear of

---

[66] I have made these arguments in *Broadcasting Law* (Oxford, 1995), ch. 2.

government, or at least a distrust of its capacity to do any good. That explains its enthusiasm for the uninhibited operation of the free market in the context of the media, as in other areas of economic activity. But the dangers now are surely sensationalism, the trivialisation of political debate, and the balkanisation of the media which occurs when citizens no longer communicate with each other on a handful of television channels and in a small number of newspaper columns. Indeed, if the Internet were eventually to replace the broadcasting media, and newspaper reading further declines, what media would provide the platform for political and electoral debate? It would be misleading and unfair to conclude that US media jurisprudence has entirely ignored these problems. But its preoccupation with the evils of big government has meant that it has not yet begun to do them justice.

4

Of Free Speech and Individual Reputation: New York Times v. Sullivan in Canada and Australia

LEONARD LEIGH*

I. INTRODUCTION

Democracies value inquiry: democracies value dissent. Democratic systems are committed not only to inquiry into governmental policies but also into the integrity of those whom they entrust with the management of public affairs, for to a marked extent these are issues which cannot be separated. The priapic tendencies of a David Lloyd George may not, it is true, impede the due and energetic conduct of matters of state, but they may well have an influence on the tenor and tone of public affairs. It is well that the public be informed of matters of state, and of personal matters concerning politicians and public officials to the extent that they cast light on the former. Both high-mindedness and a desire to sell copies contribute to the way in which the media bring political information before the public, and democratic government may well be the incidental beneficiary of muckraking carried on for purposes which those engaged in the exercise would rather dissemble.

There is, however, as courts and commentators are prepared to admit, a countervailing private interest in the integrity of individual reputation. This interest is, however, not private alone, partly because as citizens we have an obvious collective as well as individual interest in preventing or, where necessary, compensating for traduction, and partly because if public lives become the object of unredressed calumny, good people may be discouraged from participating in public affairs or driven from public life.[1] The question is, then, not one of balancing public and private interests, balance being a dubious metaphor in any event, but of reaching a conciliation

---

* I should like to thank the London School of Economics and Political Science for providing me with a research assistant and to Miss Lisa Clarke BA, barrister, for the exemplary way in which she performed her duties as such.

[1] This is fully recognised by the Supreme Court of Canada in *Hill* v. *Church of Scientology of Toronto* (1995) 126 DLR (4th) 129 at 160 and 167 (Cory J, *per curiam*). Ian Loveland also broaches the issue in Ch. 5 of this volume.

between interests which cannot be clearly separated and which, in any event, interact.

The inquiry is not simple. It is sometimes said that one must protect the essential functions of the media. This is the point from which Brennan J started in *New York Times* v. *Sullivan*, the case which set the prevailing pattern for American approaches to the subject.[2] But that begs the question: what do we conceive the essential functions of the media to be? And in relation to what?

American doctrine deals with a constitutional freedom, the justification for which is put in broad functional terms. Australian doctrine sees matters more narrowly, arguably as a limitation on the enacting power of the Commonwealth Parliament and state legislatures in the interest of securing the essential conditions without which representative democracy would become impossible of achievement. This is, of course, narrower, both in its scope and in its ethos, for such an analysis renders the individual a mere incidental beneficiary of a limitation, not the bearer of a right.[3]

Any inquiry into these matters must also consider both whether individuals have, apart from an action for defamation, other adequate and less intrusive means of vindicating reputation. This, in turn, involves an inquiry into the position of the individual (should he as a public figure be obliged to accept a greater measure of ill than a private person) and his possibilities of securing redress, but also the incidental price that may be paid for such hardy perennial suggestions as a right to reply in the same coin as the original defamation itself. In *New York Times* v. *Sullivan* the US Supreme Court constitutionalised the law of defamation. In so doing, the Court created a body of doctrine which serves as an obvious reference point for courts and commentators elsewhere. Yet it could not be assumed that that doctrine would serve, even in a modified form, as an acceptable export model to other systems whose only, or at any rate most striking, similarities to the United States are their status as functioning democracies. Federalism does not necessarily offer much of a nexus, nor does it follow that the fact that Canada has a Charter of Rights and Freedoms will dictate the development of doctrine cast in the American mould. Constitutional structure, traditions, pre-existing bodies of law and the presence of particular social problems in any given jurisdiction all have a part to play in the formulation of a satisfactory response to the interplay of public interest and private right.[4]

---

[2] *New York Times Co.* v. *Sullivan* (1964) 376 US 254, 11 L Ed. 2d 686.

[3] See in general *Theophanous* v. *The Herald and Weekly Times Limited* (1994) 68 ALJ 713 and cases cited below.

[4] An illustration of this would seem to be *Derbyshire County Council* v. *Times Newspapers Ltd.* [1993] 2 WLR 449, where the HL refers to American doctrine to hold that a local authority may not sue for defamation in respect of criticisms of its conduct, but where also the right of individual councillors to sue is preserved unaffected. See also *Hector* v. *Attorney-General of Antigua* [1990] 2 WLR 606 (PC), where press freedom was held not to be secured adequately by a defence of truth alone.

II. *NEW YORK TIMES* V. *SULLIVAN* AND THEREAFTER

A sketch of *Sullivan* and its progeny is a necessary prelude to evaluating the response of Canadian and Australian courts to American doctrine. I use the word "sketch" advisedly. I shall do no more than outline the doctrine in and developed from *Sullivan* and the principal criticisms of it.

Sullivan was, as is well known, a response to particular problems thrown up by the Civil Rights movement.[5] The case involved allegedly defamatory statements or advertisements published in the *New York Times* which related to the conduct of Sullivan, as a police chief, in relation to civil rights demonstrations in Alabama. The newspaper lost in the Alabama courts (defamation being then seen as peculiarly a subject for state laws) and was threatened with a succession of crushing money judgments the effect of which would have been either to force the newspaper out of business or force it to abandon coverage of civil rights demonstrations.[6]

In a compromise judgment, Brennan J for the court enunciated two propositions of the greatest importance. These were; first, that a privilege was needed for certain official conduct and that therefore an official criticised in respect of it could not recover unless he could prove actual malice; and, secondly, that the Supreme Court could review the entire record of the trial court, thus ensuring the possibility of a wide-ranging factual review of the proceedings. From this it followed that erroneous statements honestly, and even negligently, made would be protected.[7] Wide though this principle was, it was narrower than the absolute privilege for which Black and Douglas JJ contended.

Goldberg and Douglas JJ signalled a reservation to the Court's judgment: the "actual malice" doctrine would not apply to defamatory statements directed against the *private* conduct of a public official or private citizen. From this it followed that First Amendment guarantees indeed dictated the shape, in part at least, of state defamation laws.

It is not, however, the purpose of this essay to discuss American federalism as such.[8] We may, instead, turn to certain of the doctrinal developments which followed *Sullivan*. The *Sullivan* judgment was somewhat loosely

---

[5] The "problems" are described and analysed in M. Tushnett, *Making Civil Rights Law* (Oxford, 1995). Tushnett's study, which ascribes much First Amendment innovation to the NAACP's struggle for racial equality, stands as a forceful counterpoint to Stephen Sedley's critique in Ch. 2 of this volume.

[6] See further P. Leval, "Strangers On A Train" (1993) 91 *Michigan Law Review* 1138, a review of A. Lewis, *Make No Law: The Sullivan Case and the First Amendment* (New York, 1991).

[7] It must, of course, be remembered that the defence of "fair comment" in Alabama depended on the defendant proving that his allegations were true in all their particulars: (1964) 376 US 254 at 267.

[8] That task has been broached directly in this volume by Coiln Warbrick's chapter, and is performed indirectly by the chapters by David Feldman and Ian Loveland.

delineated. To begin with, it spoke of a "public official". This left open the questions of "who is a public official?" and "when does defamatory comment concern his status and functions as a public offical?". Should the basic question be the public significance of the conduct criticised rather than any particular governmental status of the person criticized?[9]

In *Rosenblatt* v. *Baer*,[10] the Court held that the "public official" designation applied at the very least to those among the hierarchy of government employees who have, or appear to the public to have, substantial responsibility or control over the conduct of governmental affairs. That formula at least corresponds to the rationale of preserving public debate over matters of political and constitutional importance.

The dynamic of *Sullivan* soon produced a considerable further step. The Supreme Court in *Rosenbloom* v. *Metromedia Inc.*[11] identified the value as one of preserving debate on public issues. From that premiss it drew the conclusion that in terms of the First Amendment it made no sense to distinguish between "public" and "private" figures.

In *Gertz* v. *Welch* the *Sullivan* rule was extended to inhibit recovery by a "public person".[12] To the difficulties encountered in relation to public officials were soon added difficulties in relation to this new and nebulous concept. In the words of Powell J, "public persons" are: "[t]hose who by reason of the notoriety of their achievements or the vigor and success with which they seek the public's attention, are properly classed as public figures".[13]

Not much is said about the matter in respect of which the public's attention is sought. The Court made clear, however (under the heading of "public officials"), that individuals who seek government office must accept the risk of close scrutiny, and that such scrutiny extends to such matters as fitness for office. Those classified as "public figures" can also achieve notoriety by thrusting themselves into controversy. Such persons have, it is said, greater access themselves to the media and are better able to protect themselves than purely private individuals who do not face the same constitutional hurdles to recovery.[14] To the obvious dangers to individual reputation which all this poses the court replied that it would not lightly assume that a citizen's participation in community and professional affairs rendered him a public figure for all purposes.

The extension so created appears logical in the light of the court's premiss. It has, however, been said that in extending *Sullivan* the Court increasingly lost contact with the principles which underlay that case.[15]

---

[9] E. Barrett, P. Bruton and J. Honnold, *Constitutional Law: Cases and Materials* (3rd edn., Mineola, NY., 1968), 1416.

[10] (1966) 383 US 75.

[11] (1971) 403 US 29, 29 L Ed. 2d 296.

[12] (1974) 418 US 323, 41 L Ed. 2d 789.

[13] *Ibid.*, at 806.

[14] Brennan J dissented on this point.

[15] E. Kagan, "A Libel Story: *Sullivan* Then and Now" (1993) 18 *Law and Social Inquiry* 197.

Unfortunately also, the concept of public figure has been said to be so nebulous as to pose real problems for lower courts.[16] Tests for determining these issues have certainly evolved, but they have been said to leave problems concerning how broad a public controversy may be, what is needed by way of the individual's relationship to the controversy, and whether the defamation should relate to the plaintiff's role in the controversy.[17]

In the result, a plaintiff, whether he be a public official or a private individual speaking out on a matter of public concern, must bear the burden of showing falsity as well as fault in order to recover.[18] Even a private person who seeks to prove that he was defamed in relation to a matter of public interest bears an enhanced burden because the Supreme Court had held that in such cases the states cannot impose liability without some showing of fault on the part of the defamer and cannot permit the award of punitive damages without a showing of actual malice.[19]

To these difficulties may be added problems in defining the fault element. Truth is a defence where the person defamed is a public official or a public figure.[20] A defamation action will thus succeed only where what was said was false. Even within this limitation the plaintiff must prove a high degree of fault. Actual malice need not involve spite or ill-will, but a plaintiff must, in order to succeed, show that the defendant had a high awareness of the probable falsity of the statement or acted with reckless disregard whether the statement was true or false.[21] Evidence of motive or want of care may in some circumstances be relevant to prove actual malice, but they are no more than evidential considerations. It seems clear that the test is to a degree attitudinal, with the dangers which that presents, namely, that "reckless disregard" (to take a phrase used in the judgments) will be a product of the manner in which the court in any given case regards the facts.[22]

Furthermore, the Court does not distinguish for these purposes between false statements of fact and questionable opinions, reasoning that even though false statements of fact have little intrinsic value to public debate they are nonetheless inevitable in a free debate.[23] From this, given the

---

[16] See for example E. Walker, "Defamation Law: Public Figures—Who Are They?" (1993) 45 *Baylor Law Review* 955.

[17] D. Dalton, "Defining the Limited Purpose Public Figure" (1992) 70 *University of Detroit Mercy Law Review* 47.

[18] *Philadelphia Newspapers Inc.* v. *Hepps* (1986) 475 US 767, 89 L Ed. 2d 383.

[19] *Milkovich* v. *Lorain Journal Co.* (1986) 497 US 1, 111 L Ed. 2d 1.

[20] *Cox Broadcasting Corp.* v. *Cohn* (1975) 420 US 469, 43 L Ed. 2d 328. The Court left open the question whether truth is always a defence where a private individual is defamed, but the logic of the judgments would suggest that it is where the matter complained of is one of public concern. This would seem also to follow logically from *Milkovich* v. *Lorain Journal Co.* (1986) 497 US 1, 111 L Ed. 2d 1.

[21] *Harte-Hanks Inc.* v. *Connaughton* (1990) 491 US 657, 105 L Ed. 2d 562; *Hustler Magazine and Flynt* v. *Falwell* (1988) 485 US 46, 99 L Ed. 2d 41.

[22] *Harte-Hanks Inc.* v. *Connaughton* (1990) 105 L Ed. 2d 562 at 589.

[23] Of course, in the case of opinions, malice cannot relate to truth or falsity but there seems little if any authority concerning to what it might relate.

Court's basic premisses, to place publishers under strict liability for publishing untruths would chill debate.[24]

In the result, where speech concerns a matter of public interest (as distinguished from a mere private matter such as a publication concerning a firm's credit rating),[25] recovery becomes impossibly difficult. A survey of Texas cases following *Sullivan* discloses that in no case since that decision was announced has a public official or figure overcome the hurdles set by the Court's First Amendment jurisprudence.[26]

It is not surprising that this has led to disquiet, nor is it surprising that the Court's willingness to review the factual record should cause unease in a system wedded to jury trial.[27] To a foreign observer the balance struck by the Supreme Court seems at times gravely flawed. For example, a retired army officer who received widespread media attention when he accused his superior officers of concealing war crimes made himself a public figure with the consequences in litigation for defamation which that entailed.[28] It is easy to see what the fate of the whistleblower will be, particularly if he acts in an unpopular cause.

It is important to note that these misgivings are also shared by American scholars and judges. *Sullivan*, it has been noted, has a dark side: it allows grievous injury to reputation to flourish unredressed.[29] This is a product of the rule that judgment cannot be had against the media even where the offending organ has acted grossly negligently.[30] As Ian Loveland suggests in Chapter 5 of this volume, there is much to be said in favour of the argument that such a price is worth paying. However, this should not blind us to the similarly forceful arguments suggesting that *Sullivan* pays too little attention to both the private and public interest in the protection of politicans' reputations from untruthful slurs. Even Justices of the Supreme Court have been seen to speculate whether a better, more just way of promoting free speech values could not be found.

In *Dun and Bradstreet* v. *Greenmoss Builders Inc.*,[31] Burger CJ suggested that *Gertz* should be overruled. White J (who joined in the judgment in *Sullivan*) went further, noting the difficulties in the way of a public official or public figure, and concluding that the balance struck by the court in that case was improvident. It might have been better to limit or forbid punitive damages. As White J observed:

---

[24] *Hustler Magazine and Flynt* v. *Falwell* (1988) 485 US 46, 99 L Ed. 2d 41 (1988).

[25] *Dun and Bradstreet* v. *Greenmoss Builders Inc.* (1985) 472 US 749, 86 L Ed. 2d 93.

[26] R. Schoen, "Defamation and Privileges In The Texas Supreme Court Since *New York Times*" (1996) 37 *South Texas Law Review* 81.

[27] See M. Sorini, "Factual Malice: Rediscovering the Seventh Amendment in Public Person Libel Cases" (1994) 82 *Georgetown Law Journal* 529.

[28] *Herbert* v. *Lando* (1979) 441 US 153, 60 L Ed. 2d 115.

[29] Kagan, *supra* n. 15.

[30] Leval, *supra* n. 6.

[31] (1985) 472 US 749, 86 L Ed. 2d 593.

"these First Amendment values are not at all served by circulating false statements of fact about public officials. On the contrary, erroneous information frustrates these values. They are even more disserved when the statements falsely impugn the honesty of those men and women and hence lessen confidence in government."[32]

In any event, the proposition that the actual malice standard promotes public debate is, surely, questionable.[33] Indeed, it may in contrast conduce to media irresponsibility and result in a flood of untrue (and thus corruptive) political information entering the arena of debate.

Notwithstanding general adherence by members of the Court to *Sullivan* and its progeny, disquieting questions concerning it arise in the United States, and these have had an influence on the varying receptions it has recently been afforded in Canada and Australia.

III. CANADA

The desirability of importing *Sullivan* into Canadian law was extensively dealt with by the Supreme Court of Canada in *Hill* v. *Church of Scientology of Toronto*.[34] A brief account of the constitutional structure of Canada would seem desirable before entering upon the details of that case.

The Constitution Act 1982 allocates legislative power according to two exclusive lists to the Parliament of Canada and the Legislatures of the Provinces respectively. The Constitution contains few concurrent powers and few constitutional limitations, and until the advent of the Canadian Charter of Rights and Freedoms was silent as to individual rights.

The Supreme Court of Canada had, it is true, twice enunciated constitutional limitations pertaining to free speech. In *Reference re Alberta Statutes*, the Supreme Court of Canada ruled on a batch of social credit statutes, one of which, the Accurate News and Information Act, would have imposed onerous duties upon newspapers to "correct" inaccurate news stories.[35] While a majority of the Court held the legislation invalid on narrow grounds, Duff CJC (Davis J concurring) enunciated what for Canada was a substantial limitation upon provincial legislative power. The British North America Act 1867 (now the Canada Act 1867) presupposes, His Lordship remarked, a parliament working under the influence of public opinion and public discussion. The examination of policy from all viewpoints is the breath of life of parliamentary institutions. From that premiss, the Chief Justice concluded:

---

32 *Ibid.*, at 608.
33 Kagan, *supra* n. 15.
34 (1995) 126 DLR (4th) 129 (SCC).
35 [1938] SCR 100.

"Any attempt to abrogate this right of public debate or to suppress the traditional forms of the exercise of this right (in public meeting and through the press) would in our opinion be incompetent to the legislatures of the provinces. . . ."[36]

The conclusion was based essentially on the ground that any such attempt would contradict the parliamentary basis of Canadian constitutionalism. It would, furthermore, transcend provincial concerns and could not be considered a matter of property and civil rights within the province so as to fall within the provincial legislative list.[37]

In a later decision, *Switzman* v. *Elbling*, one Justice of the Supreme Court, Abbott J, took this as the premiss for a true constitutional limitation. In a dictum in a case relating to provincial legislation, His Lordship, after referring with approval to Duff CJC's statement in the earlier decision, said this:

"I am also of opinion that as our constitutional Act now stands Parliament itself could not abrogate this right of discussion and debate. The power of Parliament to limit it is, in my view, restricted to such powers as may be exercisable under its exclusive legislative jurisdiction with respect to criminal law and to make laws for the peace, order and good government of Canada."[38]

This dictum was not built upon by Canadian courts, which were instead able to strike down certain illiberal legislation by reference to normal doctrines of constitutional interpretation. This is perhaps readily understandable, given that Canadian courts, notwithstanding their geographical proximity to the United States, were unaccustomed to thinking in terms of constitutional limitations. As Carol Harlow has observed, Canada's constitutional law has long been informed more by British than by American principle.[39]

An attempt to import *Sullivan* into Canadian law had to await the Canadian Charter of Rights and Freedoms, 1982. The Charter contains two relevant provisions. The first is section 2(b), which provides:

"2. Everyone has the following fundamental freedoms:
    . . .
    (b) freedom of thought, belief, opinion and expression, including freedom of
        the press and other media of communication."

The second is section 32, which applies the Charter to the Parliament and government of Canada and the legislatures and government of each province. The focus of the Charter is, therefore, on state action.

The potential applicability of *Sullivan* under the Charter was raised in *Hill* v. *Church of Scientology of Toronto (Manning et al. v. Hill)*.[40] In a

---

[36] At 109.
[37] See Canada Act 1867, s. 92(13). It is worth noting that the point was fully argued, it having been raised in argument by J Ralston KC. The appeal books in the library of the Supreme Court of Canada make this clear.
[38] [1957] SCR 285 at 328.
[39] C. Harlow, "A Special Relationship? American Influences on Judicial Review in England", in I. Loveland (ed.), *A Special Relationship?* (Oxford, 1995).
[40] (1995) 126 DLR (4th) 129 (SCC).

statement read on the steps of Osgoode Hall, the appellant Manning (a lawyer) commented upon allegations contained in a notice of motion by which Scientology intended to commence criminal contempt proceedings against Hill, a Crown Attorney. The allegations, found to be quite untrue, were that Hill misled a judge of the Ontario Supreme Court and had breached certain orders relating to documents belonging to Scientology. The defamatory allegations thus made had never been properly investigated by the appellants.

Two issues arose on appeal: first, whether the common law of defamation breached section 2(b) of the Charter; and secondly, what damages could properly be assessed in the action. The first question represented an attempt to import into Canada the restrictive *Sullivan* rule where defamation concerned a public official.

This attempt fell at the first hurdle. The Court reiterated its established view that section 2(b), by virtue of section 32, only applies to legislative or governmental action. The common law of defamation is affected by the Charter only to the extent that it serves as the basis for some governmental action which infringes a guaranteed right or freedom.[41] The exclusion of private activity from the Charter was a matter of considered policy, not of chance.[42]

Hill, as a Crown Attorney, was a servant of the Crown. The Court was not prepared to deduce from that that his constitutional status should be determined by the nature of the allegation against him, namely, that he acted for the Crown. The determination of whether state involvement existed should rather be dependent upon the circumstances surrounding the institution of the libel proceedings. Actions taken by Crown Attorneys which are outside the scope of their statutory duties (for example, in excess of power) are independent of and distinct from their actions as agents of government. In *Hill*, the appellants impugned the respondent's character, competence and integrity and not that of government. Hill responded by instituting proceedings in his own capacity.

The court's unwillingness to distinguish between classes of individuals for the purpose of determining who is a public official represents a recognition of the problems which drawing such a distinction has produced in the United States. It would also seem to amount to a conscious rejection of that body of doctrine. Instead, the Court focused on the damage to Hill's reputation as a lawyer. It held that the respondents failed to satisfy the governmental action criteria of section 32 of the Charter.

Their Lordships then turned to a further question: whether changes or modifications to the common law of defamation were necessary in order to

---

[41] (1995) 126 DLR (4th) 129 at 148, *per* Cory J (Gonthier, McLachlin, Iacobucci and Major JJ concurring), relying on *Retail, Wholesale, and Departmental Store Union Local 580* v. *Dolphin Delivery Ltd.* [1986] 2 SCR 573, *per* McIntyre J L'Heureux-Dubé J essentially concurred on this point, concluding that the Charter only applies indirectly to the common law.

[42] Here the Court relied on *McKinney* v. *University of Guelph* [1990] 3 SCR 229.

bring it into conformity with the Charter? Here, the court proceeded with some subtlety. The Charter applies, indeed, to the common law and the courts ought so to develop principles of common law as to accord with Charter values.[43] But, as Charter rights do not exist in the absence of state action, the most that the private litigant can do is to argue that the common law is inconsistent with Charter values.

It would seem to follow that the Court's duty is one of development (or interpretation) of common law in such a way as to favour the values set out in the Charter. This in turn presupposes an interaction between public and private law, since the private law standard may well depend upon statements concerning the content and breadth of Charter guarantees derived from pro-nouncements in constitutional and administrative law cases, whereas in public law matters, the Court's interpretation of the value may derive from the approach which it took or takes in a private action.

But Charter values themselves are multi-faceted. The Charter reflects the innate dignity of the individual which underlies all Charter rights. Applied to defamation, the Charter would seem to require that the individual's inter-est in his own integrity be protected by rules which are compatible with the furtherance of this value, and that the value implicit in section 2(b) of free-dom of speech generally must be read in collocation with it.[44]

The Court then addressed the *Sullivan* rule explicitly. Operating that rule, which requires the public official to prove that the defamer acted with actual malice, obliges the Court to make subjective judgments concerning who is a public figure and what is a matter of legitimate public concern. The burden on a public official who wishes to sue for defamation is heavy. Two evils result from this: first, the stream of information about public officials is often polluted by false information; and secondly, the reputation and polit-ical life of the defeated plaintiff may be destroyed by falsehoods that might have been avoided had reasonable care been taken to investigate the facts. These, as the court remarked, are perverse results in terms of First Amendment values. Consequently, the *Sullivan* rule does not sufficiently protect reputation.

Hill was, in any event, not an apt vehicle for a full consideration of *Sullivan*. It did not involve the media, nor any political controversy, nor any political commentary concerning government policy. There was no evidence in Canada of any tendency to large jury awards which would chill media coverage of political issues. In Canada there is no broad privilege accorded to public statements by government officials which needs to be counterbal-anced by a similar right for private individuals.

In respect, then, of actions for defamation between private litigants, a majority of the court led by Cory J saw no reason to incorporate *Sullivan*

---

[43] See also *per* L'Heureux-Dubé J at 190.

[44] The Court also notes that reputation is intimately related to another right, that of privacy: *Reg.* v. *Dyment* [1988] 2 SCR 417.

into Canadian law. The law of defamation provides defences of fair comment and of qualified privilege, and those who publish statements should assume a reasonable level of responsibility. The common law of defamation thus complies with Charter standards. The common law defence of qualified privilege will be defeated, in cases where it would otherwise apply, by showing that the statement was actuated by "malice". In Canadian law this means spite, ill-will or any indirect motive or ulterior purpose that conflicts with the sense of duty or mutual interest which the occasion created. It may also be established by showing that the defendant spoke dishonestly or in knowing or reckless disregard for the truth.[45] Qualified privilege may also be defeated when the limits of the duty or interest have been exceeded. In *Hill*, the Court held that the principle required that "the information communicated must be reasonably appropriate in the context of the circumstances existing on the occasion when that information was given".[46]

It follows that the substantive law of defamation accords with Charter values. The Court indicated that the only real effect the Charter would have in such circumstances, save that already noted of acting as a point of reference when change to the common law is contemplated, may be to liberalise procedure by indicating a wider measure of discovery and access to documents and other information. Even so, the guarantee embodied in section 2(b) of the Charter is subject to reasonable limits that may be demonstrably justified in a free and democratic society. This suggests that, for example, restrictions on reporting the name of a complainant in a sexual assault case may well be sustained.

Finally, in relation to damages, the Supreme Court was unwilling to interfere with jury awards in the absence of apt legislation and held that it is right that the jury should estimate what figure is required in order to vindicate the plaintiff's reputation. This, in turn, provokes the reflection that even were legislation capping awards to be introduced into Canada, it could not apply differentially as between classes of persons without falling foul of section 15 of the Charter, the provision which guarantees equality before the law. Thus, it would seem that neither a more nor a less liberal rule relating to recovery could apply in the case of a defamed public official.

In sum, the *Sullivan* rule has been rejected in Canada in respect of public officials. The Court in *Hill* did not even reach the more dubious category of "public figure" which has so frequently been the subject of First Amendment litigation and scholarship in the USA. Of course this partially reflects the different wording of the constitutional guarantee in Canada. But, as the judgment in *Hill* makes manifest, it also rejects the balance which the US Supreme Court established in *Sullivan* as improvident and unnecessary in Canada. The abuses which gave rise to *Sullivan* in the United States were

---

[45] Ian Loveland explores in Ch. 5 the many meanings which have been attached to this notion.

[46] (1995) 126 DLR (4th) 129 at 171, *per* Cory J

greater in their duration and intensity than those, intimately associated with the Cold War, which made an appearance in Canada, particularly at provincial level, in the immediate post-war period. Thus neither the historical basis for *Sullivan* nor any present necessity indicated the need to adopt any such preclusive doctrine.

IV. AUSTRALIA

In Australia, however, in a clutch of cases which have been described as an astonishing development in the light of its past case law, the High Court has sought to carve out more extensive protections for political comment.[47]

The Constitution Act 1900, apart from a few powers which are expressed to be within the exclusive power of the Commonwealth Parliament[48] bestows a wide measure of concurrent power on the Commonwealth Parliament and the state legislatures, with paramountcy in the Commonwealth Parliament.[49] Two principal limitations to power appear in the Constitution, the former of which has been a source of considerable incidental benefit to individuals challenging regulatory action. These are, first, section 92, which requires that trade, commerce and intercourse among the states is to be free; and, secondly, section 116 which forbids the establishment of religion. The High Court is well accustomed to dealing with constitutional limitations imposed by these provisions.[50]

The immediate catalyst for the Australian development was not the law of defamation. It was, instead, a challenge to legislation which prohibited political advertising during election periods and to legislation prohibiting criticism of the Australian Industrial Relations Commission which might bring it into disrepute.

In *Australian Capital Television Pty. v. Commonwealth of Australia*[51] (a case dealing with political advertising), Mason CJ, referred to Canadian authority in enunciating an implied limitation within the Australian Constitution which restrained both Commonwealth and state power in the interests of freedom of political expression.[52] This limitation reflects the central importance of free discussion in a representative parliamentary system of government. In Mason CJ's judgment the talk is of a freedom to communicate, the justification for which is put in much the same way as it was put

---

[47] See T. Jones, "Freedom of Political Communication in Australia" (1996) 45 *ICLQ* 392. See further F. Trindade, "Political Discussion And The Law Of Defamation" (1995) 111 *LQR* 199.

[48] Constitution Act 1900, s. 52.

[49] *Ibid.*, s. 51, 1l.(i)–(xxxix).

[50] S. 117 of the Constitution does provide against any one state discriminating against a subject of the Queen resident in any other state. No account is taken of it here.

[51] (1992–93) 177 CLR 106.

[52] *Reference re Alberta Statutes* [1938] SCR 100; *Switzman v. Elbling, supra* n. 38.

by Duff CJC in *Reference re Alberta Statutes*. To both men, public participation in political discussions is a central element of the political process.

The freedom (or limitation, if one prefers the characterisation adopted by another member of the Court, Brennan J) is wide because it extends to all aspects of political affairs. But it is restricted nonetheless to matters of political expression and admits of such limitations as can be shown to be compellingly justified in order to protect a competing public interest. Brennan J in particular sounded a cautionary note: the value stated is not so transcendent as to override all other interests which the law might protect.

This development was then applied to the law of defamation in *Theophanous* v. *The Herald and Weekly Times Limited*.[53] Action was brought by the plaintiff, a member of the House of Representatives, against the defendant newspaper in respect of the plaintiff's alleged views concerning immigration, and in particular his alleged bias in favour of Greek immigrants. The defence was privilege with a denial of malice in making the statement.

Mason CJ (Toohey and Gaudron JJ concurring) restated the proposition advanced in the earlier case concerning the implied freedom of expression under the Commonwealth Constitution.[54] In their Honours' view, this implication is linked to political discussion and political discourse, but does not extend to freedom of expression generally. It is not, however, limited to matters relating to the government of the Commonwealth, but relates to political discussion in the context of that communication and discussion which is necessary to ensure the efficacious working of representative democracy. Their Honours' focus is thus narrower than that of *Sullivan* and its American *sequelae*. It also states a value but leaves to be worked out what instances will fall within it, and one may expect standards to vary over time and in relation to context. Entertainment and politics are, as their Honours remark, different, but may in any given case merge.

If the focus is narrower than that adopted by the American Supreme Court, it is nonetheless wide and its limits are not easily foreseeable. Their Honours, for example, cite Barendt for the wide proposition that;

> "political speech refers to all speech relevant to the development of public opinion in the whole range of issues which an intelligent citizen should think about."[55]

They nonetheless do not abandon the focus on the working of representative parliamentary institutions. Even granting the narrowness of the Court's focus, one commentator at least considers that the decision is likely to have a considerable impact on the law of defamation in Australia.[56]

---

[53] (1994–5) 182 CLR 104.

[54] It should be noted that Dawson J (dissenting) rejected any such implication.

[55] E. Barendt, *Freedom of Speech* (Oxford, 1985), 152.

[56] S. Walker, "The Impact of the High Court's Free Speech Cases on Defamation Law" (1995) 17 *Sydney LR* 43.

Their Honours then addressed the question whether the law of defamation raised a constitutional issue. They agreed with the House of Lords in *Derbyshire*[57] that institutions of central and local government should not be able to sue for defamation lest political discussion be unduly abridged.[58] They further concluded, however, having examined *Sullivan en route*, that political discussion must be protected against onerous criminal and civil liability if the constitutional implication of a freedom to communicate is to be effective in securing its purpose.

Where, then, was the balance between the competing interests of freedom of speech and individual reputation to be drawn? The common law was not developed in the light of the constitutional limitation, and it could not, therefore, be said (contrary to the view of Brennan J dissenting) that there was no inconsistency between the common law principles and the freedom. The common law defence of fair comment applies only to opinion. Qualified privilege depends on an absence of malice and on the person making the communication having an interest or duty in its making and on the recipient having a corresponding interest or duty in receiving it. The requirement for reciprocity of interest at common law means that qualified privilege is usually not available when the information has been disseminated to the public generally. The defendant may, if he is to succeed, have to prove truth, which is often difficult to do.

It may, parenthetically, be noted that their Honours did not seek to develop, in connection with qualified privilege, any proposition about reciprocity flowing from concepts of individuals' civic duty. It is central to the dissenting judgments, particularly of Brennan and McHugh JJ, that qualified privilege does apply in relation to political comment and that the common law defences do strike a fair balance between the need for free expression and the individual's interest in reputation.[59]

Where, then, is the balance to be struck? Their Honours dismissed summarily the position taken up by Black J in the US Supreme Court in the *Sullivan* case that political statements ought to carry an absolute privilege. They also refuse to accept the whole of *Sullivan*. First, the extension of that case to "public figures" would go too far. Such an extension would reach far beyond the representative government rationale advanced above. Secondly, *Sullivan* tilts the balance too far away from the protection of individual reputation and would do so even if it were restricted to individuals who are public officials. To this extent the High Court shares the same reservations as the Supreme Court of Canada.

Their Honours, however, also conclude (again contrary to Brennan J, who found no evidence for the proposition) that existing law unduly limits

---

[57] See Ian Loveland's comments on the *Derbyshire* case in ch. 5 below.

[58] *Derbyshire County Council* v. *Times Newspapers Ltd.* [1993] AC 534.

[59] That one can also find such reasoning in many US state jurisdictions in the years prior to *Sullivan* is the point made by Ian Loveland in Ch. 5.

freedom of communication in political matters. The reconciliation suggested is that the defendant should be required to establish that the circumstances were such as to make it reasonable to publish the impugned material without establishing whether it was true or false. But the publisher should nonetheless be required to show that he acted reasonably in so doing, either by taking steps to check the accuracy of the account or by establishing that it was otherwise justified in publishing without taking adequate steps to check. A more severe rule would unduly inhibit discussion. It is thus felt to be appropriate that the plaintiff be deprived of a trial on truth or falsity, but to formulate a test in those terms would be to run counter to the implied freedom. "Actual malice" need not be included because the issues are subsumed under reasonable publication. It is for the defendant to show that the publication falls within the constitutional protection. Common law qualified privilege must for the future be viewed in the light of the constitutional limitation.

It does not follow from the foregoing discussion that other, concurring Justices necessarily accept in full the propositions attributed to the Chief Justice. Deane J suggested a somewhat narrower context, construed by reference to heads of enacting power. He would also confine the doctrine to statements about official conduct or consequent suitability for office in the case of a holder of high public office (a somewhat indeterminate formula) since this most closely responds to the representative government rationale, lying at the heart of political communication.

The basic premiss of *Theophanous* was restated in *Stephens* v. *West Australian Newspapers Ltd.*[60] and must be taken to have established a new constitutional doctrine in Australia, notwithstanding the continued dissent by three members of the court, Brennan, McHugh and Dawson JJ. In particular, the later case holds that in pleading qualified privilege it is unnecessary to allege a duty on the part of the newspaper to publish the matter complained of to its readers. The balance thus reached certainly has an appeal and, whatever else may be said of it, appears better suited to reconcile the competing interests of private reputation and democratic government than does *Sullivan*.[61]

V. CONCLUSIONS

What, then, may be said of the reception of *Sullivan* v. *New York Times* in Canada and Australia respectively? The first, and obvious, point is that while the values which it enunciates are generally agreed, the doctrine which it created in response to them is not. This, in the light of the criticism advanced of that doctrine by American writers (and reprised in this volume by Stephen Sedley in Chapter 2), is hardly surprising. In any event, constitutional

---

[60] (1994) 68 ALJR 765.
[61] See further S. Walker, *supra* n. 56.

structures differ (a feature most marked in Canada where the Charter of Rights and Freedoms was designedly cast in narrower terms than its American counterpart). That we should not blandly accept that such structural differences preclude the effective importation of specific rules was a point forcefully made in the opening chapter—but such arguments offer us only a question rather than an answer. Relatedly, the political and social history of endemic, violent and nominally "legal" racial abuse of blacks by whites in the United States to which *Sullivan* v. *The New York Times* arguably lends the case a considerable degree of historial and geographical specificity.

It is, however, interesting that *Sullivan* either served or may serve as a catalyst for change in both Australia and Canada. The Canadian Supreme Court, in accepting the statement of values embodied in that case, at least envisages a possible gradual adaptation of defamation law to bring it into conformity with Charter values. A majority on the High Court of Australia identifies a need to correct the balance between freedom of expression and individual reputation in a relatively narrow and somewhat indeterminate context, and suggests a formula (attested to in some American writings) which should permit an ample measure of practical immunity to suit in respect of political expression whilst leaving the grosser forms of personal abuse within and without that context to the common law.

In neither jurisdiction do courts welcome the American extension from matters of a political nature in respect of government to matters of public interest, or the extension from "public official" to "public figure". In Canada, certainly, and among some Australian judges, there is an obvious reluctance to make assumptions about the "chilling effect" of possible libel actions, even though the propensity of some politicians to issue writs in order to force financially advantageous settlements is not unknown.[62] There seems to be a greater readiness in Canada and Australia to admit the multifaceted aspects which these interests represent and a consequent unwillingness to adopt what seems almost to be a "flat earth" approach to the problem, though that uncivil reflection may simply reflect ignorance of American conditions which justify the full rigour of *Sullivan* and the doctrine deduced from it.

Finally, a British reflection. It seems unlikely that *Sullivan* would be followed by the courts here, even in the limited sense of being adopted as a common law rule. Nor did either the government or the opposition expressed any enthusiasm for the principle during the parliamentary passage of the Defamation Act 1996.[63] But perhaps the time has come to do what the Australian High Court has begun to do and what the Supreme Court of

---

[62] In England it has been said that the late Reginald Maudling used this tactic to stifle inquiry arising out of the Poulsen affair which involved corrupt dealings with government.

[63] See A. Sharland and I. Loveland, "The Defamation Act 1996 and Political Libels" [1997] *Public Law* 113.

Canada envisages. That is to review common law defences to defamation in the interests of free expression generally. That is perhaps a responsibility which falls squarely on the shoulders of the courts in all democracies which retain a common law legal system. And in the British context, the need for review is lent added impetus by the possibility that our present law on political libels might be found wanting if examined by the European Court of Human Rights.[64]

In recent months, two further developments have lent further force to this contention. The election of the Labour Government in May 1997 brought with it a commitment to promote legislation to incorporate the Convention into English law. Following the passage of the Human Rights Act 1998 we will surely not have to wait too long before a media defendant in a political libel action invokes Article 10 in an attempt to persuade the courts to reform our defamation laws.

Equally, the notion that our common law now demands that courts distinguish between political and private libels has been lent further credibility by the Australian High Court's decision in *Lange* v. *Australian Broadcasting Corporation*.[65] The action was brought by David Lange, the former Prime Minister of New Zealand, in respect of an allegedly defamatory ABC story. Lange had invited the court to overrule both *Theophanous* and *Stephens* and to hold that Australian common law did not extend the qualified privilege defence to political libels. The High Court, in which Brennan now sits as Chief Justice following Anthony Mason's retirement, appeared *de facto* if not *de jure* to reject the "constitutional" basis of the freedom of communication principle endorsed by the majority in *Theophanous* and *Stephens*. It nevertheless accepted that the qualified privilege defence was available in such circumstances: Australian common law, if not Australian constitutional law, had now evolved to the point where it demanded that plaintiffs in political libel actions be faced with substantial obstacles to success.

It would of course be open to the Australian legislature to reverse *Lange*, a feat it could not have achieved in respect of *Theophanous*. It would similarly seem to be the case should English law recognise either a common law or European Convention on Human Rights base for applying a qualified privilege defence to political libels in this country, that the UK Parliament might also seek to reverse such a conclusion. Whether our courts would permit it to do so remains an unanswered question. As Sir John Laws will suggest in Chapter 7 below, the consequences of the intended Human Rights Act for the relationship between Parliament and the courts may not be fully developed by the mere text of the intended legislation. He also indicates that

---

[64] Ian Loveland has discussed this issue in "Reform of Libel Law: the Public Law Dimension" (1997) 46 *ICLQ* 561.

[65] *Lange v Australian Broadcasting Corporation* (1997) 145 ACR 96. For early comment on the case's British implications see P. Milmo, "When Privilege is a Valid Defence", *The Times*, 12 August 1997.

future parliamentary incursions into fundamental common law principles—of which freedom of speech is undoubtedly one—may be afforded a less deferential treatment by the courts than has hitherto been the case.

In the more immediate term, the common law's approach to political libels will shortly be put to the test in the Court of Appeal in the litigation between Albert Reynolds, the former Taieisoch of Ireland, and the *Sunday Times*. Anthony Lester QC will be urging the court to adopt a qualified privilege rule, invoking *Sullivan, Chicago, Lange* and the ECHR as compelling arguments for so doing. If the Court of Appeal accepts that invitation, it might plausibly be argued that English law is not adopting First Amendment case law in a narrow, judicial sense. But it would seem difficult to sustain the argument that its broader principles have not found their way back—albeit by a long and circuitous route—to these shores.

5

City of Chicago *v.* Tribune Co.—*in Contexts?*

IAN LOVELAND

I. INTRODUCTION

As noted in the introductory chapter, the initial impetus both for this volume of essays and the previously published *A Special Relationship* collection was the House of Lords' decision in *Derbyshire County Council* v. *Times Newspapers*.[1] In delivering that judgment for a unanimous House, Lord Keith appeared to be strongly influenced by the decision of the Illinois Supreme Court in a 1923 case called *City of Chicago* v. *Tribune Co.*[2] Both cases reached the same conclusion—that an elected government body was simply not competent to bring an action in libel to defend its political reputation. The decisions derived from different legal roots: *Chicago* in Article 2 section 4 of the Illinois Constitution[3]—"Every person may freely speak, write and publish on all subjects, being responsible for the abuse of that liberty"—and *Derbyshire* in the English common law. Nevertheless, the rationale underpinning the judgments was the same—that permitting such actions would chill potentially well-founded criticism of government policy and so unacceptably impinge upon freedom of political expression.

The press stories which provoked the *Chicago* litigation had accused the Mayor and the city council of being so corrupt and incompetent that the city itself was bankrupt. There could be no doubt that such stories might undermine the city's reputation, both as an institution of government and as a commercial actor. Yet the Illinois Supreme Court, its unanimous opinion delivered by Thompson CJ, was equally convinced that there was no doubt that the city could do nothing to suppress the dissemination of such stories. The judgment rested on two foundations, extracted in large

---

[1] [1993] 1 All ER 1011.

[2] (1923) 139 NE 87. For contemporary comment see Note, "Torts—Power of a Municipal Corporation to Sue for Libel"(1923) 21 *Michigan LR* 915; Note, "Libel and Slander—Suit by Municipal Corporation" (1923) 23 *Columbia LR* 685: Note, "Libel and Slander—Municipal Corporations" (1929) 28 *Michigan LR* 460.

[3] The judgment made no reference at all to the First Amendment. At that time, the First Amendment was not assumed to apply to the states. However, as will become clear in the course of this essay, the Illinois jurisprudence of the early 20th century accurately foreshadowed protections for political speech later to be recognised by the US Supreme Court.

part from Madison's views on freedom of speech and Cooley's celebrated textbook, *Constitutional Limitations*. The first lay in drawing a distinction between the British and American systems of government. The second lay in the rejection of a distinction between criminal and civil libel laws.

Thompson CJ observed that while the British Parliament and Crown exercised legislative and executive authority over the British people, the organs of the federal government of the United States and of the State of Illinois were "founded upon the fundamental principle that the citizen is the fountain of all authority".[4] There was thus no scope for the English doctrine of seditious libel to flourish in American soil except in respect of speech which threatened to provoke imminent violence. The ill-advised and short-lived efforts of the Adams administration to promote a more expensive criminal libel law in the Sedition Act 1798 confirmed that such restraints on political speech were a quintessentially un-American phenomenon.[5] Such powers as government bodies possessed were granted on trust by the relevant electorate. Informed electoral choices demanded that citizens be afforded *absolute* protection against prosecution for criticising government bodies, except in the narrow instance of criticism likely to promote violent disorder.[6]

Having thus limited the legitimate scope of criminal libel, Thompson CJ saw no difficulty in drawing an analogy between criminal and civil actions. Indeed, civil actions could be substantially more effective prohibitors of speech than criminal prosecutions. Among the considerations that led Thompson CJ to this conclusion were the facts that civil libel actions, unlike criminal prosecutions, did not require a grand jury investigation; that they did not grant the defendant the presumption of innocence; that they imposed a lesser standard of proof on the plaintiff; that there was no ceiling to the damages that might be awarded; and that there was no double jeopardy rule.

Thompson CJ stressed that the protection against civil liability for defaming a government body was *absolute*; no action of any sort would be permissible. There was no question of the Court trying to strike a "balance" between freedom of political speech and the government's reputation; the government body had no corporate or public interest in its reputation to weigh in the scales. Thompson CJ thought it likely that such a rule would on occasion lead to unfounded and malevolent criticism being aired. This however was a lesser evil than running the risk that political debate would be discouraged by the threat of defamation actions:

> "[I]t is better that an occasional individual or newspaper that is so perverted in its judgment and so misguided in in his or its civic duty should go free than that all

---

[4] (1923) 139 NE 87 at 90.

[5] On the Sedition Act see L. Levy, *Emergence of a Free Press* (New York, 1985), ch. 8; A. Lewis, *Make No Law* (New York, 1991), ch. 7.

[6] The test thus seems broadly comparable to the "clear and present danger" concept used by the US Supreme Court after World War I in the 1920s; see *Schenk* v. *US* (1919) 249 US 47 and *Abrams* v. *US* (1919) 250 US 616.

of the citizens should be put in jeopardy of imprisonment or economic subjugation if they venture to criticise an inefficient or corrupt government."[7]

In my initial critique of *Derbyshire* (and thus implicitly of *Chicago*),[8] I expressed several reservations about the conclusion that Lord Keith had reached and about the indications his judgment offered for future developments in the law regulating political libels. I suggested that the *Derbyshire* rule's absolutist nature was far too blunt a tool with which to regulate the flow of political (dis)information, since it allowed individuals, political parties or newspapers to disseminate what they *knew* to be lies. As such, it might corrupt rather than enhance the capacity of voters to make informed decisions about political issues.[9] It is difficult to see any legitimate scope for affording protection to the "perverted" *and* "misguided" political commentators that Thompson CJ was prepared to tolerate.

I also suggested that a modifed version of *Sullivan* v. *New York Times*[10] offered a more satisfactory means of enhancing the supply of political information to the electorate. This argument operated at two levels.

The first was that if one's concern was to prevent libel laws blocking the flow of speech which enabled voters to make informed decisions about how they wished to allocate political power, it made little sense to draw distinctions between government bodies and the elected politicians who formulated the policies those bodies put into practice. William Brennan's judgment in *Sullivan* had classed such a distinction as "legal alchemy", an artificial construct which was wilfully blind to the fact that government bodies are essentially a means through which individuals with particular ideological preferences seek to effect their favoured political ends.

The second was that *Sullivan's* requirement that the plaintiff prove that the defendant knew his story was false, or was recklessly indifferent to its truth, did not grant the press (or anyone else) absolute freedom to defame politicians. It protected defendants who had taken reasonable care to ascertain the truth of their claims, those who had been careless in checking their facts, and even those who chose to publish information whose accuracy was at that time impossible to establish: but it provided no shield for deliberate mendacity or wanton disregard of truth.

---

[7] At 91. The passage echoes Madison's celebrated observation, which Thompson CJ had earlier quoted (at 89), that: "Some degree of abuse is inseperable from the proper use of everything, and in no instance is this more true than in that of the press. It has accordingly been decided by the practice of the states that it is better to leave a few of the noxious branches to their luxuriant growth than by pruning them away to injure the vigour of those yielding the proper fruits."

[8] "Defamation of Government: Taking Lessons from America?" (1994) 14 *Legal Studies* 206.

[9] A good example is offered by a Conservative party political broadcast on television which told such outrageous and readily discoverable lies about a Labour-controlled local authority that one cannot possibly conceive that their disseminators thought them true: see P. Routledge, "Birmingham Ire at Tory Travesty", *Independent on Sunday*, 4 April 1994.

[10] (1964) 376 US 254.

However, while Lord Keith had made reference to *Sullivan* in *Derbyshire*, he displayed little enthusiasm for importing its ratio into the English common law. Elected politicians, be they MPs or local councillors, were not to be subject to any special legal disability when initiating libel actions: they were to all intents and purposes private individuals for the purposes of defamation law. Thus damage to a politician's reputation is presumed to follow automatically from the publication of defamatory material. The burden then falls on the publisher to prove the truth of her story, or to try to invoke the limited defences of fair comment or qualified privilege.

In the years since *Derbyshire* was decided, British MPs have made regular resort to the courts to commence libel proceedings against unfavourable newspaper reporting.[11] And while the Australian High Court has recently embraced the *Sullivan* principle,[12] William Brennan's arguments have made little headway in this country, either in the courts or—during the passage of the Defamation Act 1996—in the legislature.

This chapter has two broad objectives. The first is to ask whether the *Chicago* decision can simply be dismissed as an unprincipled judicial reaction to the idiosyncracies of Illinois politics in the early twentieth century, and as such must be viewed as an authority which should carry little weight in the modern English common law. As will be seen below, factors unique to Chicago itself offer an ambiguous answer to that inquiry. However a rather wider contextualisation of the decision, in this instance into the prevailing political defamation jurisprudence of other North-Eastern, Atlantic and Mid-Western states, suggests that *Chicago* enjoyed a well-established *legal* pedigree, sired by a substantial array of judicial decisions which placed substantial obstacles in the path of *elected politicians* who tried to bring libel actions in respect of false political information. That conclusion then leads us to the second objective of this chapter. Simply put, this is to suggest that English lawyers would be well advised to accept the invitation made by Leonard Leigh in Chapter 4 to explore whether an extension to the doctrine of qualified privilege would enable English law to achieve *Sullivan* v. *New York* constitutional law ends through distinctly less controversial common law means.

II. *CHICAGO*—THE POLITICAL CONTEXT

Analysts who begin a study of defamation law jurisprudence by invoking the name of Al Capone might readily be accused by English observers of sacri-

---

[11] For a sample see I. Loveland, "Privacy and Political Speech: An Agenda for the Constitutionalisation of the Law of Libel", in P. Birks (ed.), *Extending Obligations* (Oxford, 1997).

[12] *Theophanous* v. *Herald and Weekly Times* (1994) 68 ALR 713; *Stephens* v. *West Australia Newspapers Ltd* (1994) 68 ALR 765.

ficing plausibility to sensationalism. Yet on even the most cursory inspection of the political context surrounding the *Chicago* litigation, it rapidly becomes evident that Capone's influence on Chicago's politics in the 1920s was a major factor in the case. The key players, however, were two major figures in Republican party politics: William "Big Bill" Thompson and Colonel Robert McCormick.

The City

By the end of World War I, Chicago could plausibly claim to be the United States' "second city". Its geographical location had enabled it to become a vital hub for the transport of manufactured goods, raw materials and agricultural produce. The commercial traffic was rapidly followed by an extensive network of financial markets; the Chicago stock and futures exchanges trailed only London and New York in importance.

The city's population, fuelled by successive waves of immigrants from Europe and latterly the southern states, had rocketed to some three million, much of it contained in rigidly segregated and frequently mutually antipathetic ethnic neighbourhoods.[13] The residential segregation provided the basis for political organisation. Prior to 1930, Chicago was very much a two-party city, just as Illinois was a two-party state. Democrats and Republicans fought keenly for all elected offices. Neither gained a secure long-term hold on power, and the fractionated structure and staggered electoral cycles of the city and state's many governmental offices ensured that each party was in constant possession of important *loci* of government authority. For each party, and more importantly for individuals within them, the key to power lay in their ability to mobilise and maintain support in the city's various ethnic neighbourhoods. Machine politics were well-established in Chicago by 1900. The networks of official patronage on which machine politics relied, in the form of all manner of jobs, access to government contracts and "helpful" exercises of official authority on such matters as land zoning or commercial licensing, were both extensive and complex, and necessarily demanded that the city be an exponent of "big government". They also produced extremely elaborate hierarchies within political parties. Progress to the top of Chicago's particular greasy pole demanded long years of devoted service and the sequential occupancy of a great many party and/or governmental offices.[14]

---

[13] See especially H. Zorbaugh, *The Gold Coast and the Slum* (Chicago, Ill., 1929).

[14] B. Gleason, *Daley of Chicago* (New York, 1974), especially ch. 10: M. Royko, *Boss* (London, 1971), 119–21. The point is nicely ilustrated in M. Holly and P. Jones, *Biographical Dictionary of American Mayors* (Conn., 1981), 60–1. Charting the rise through the political hierarchy of Anton Cermak, Mayor of Chicago 1931–3, the authors note he moved *upwards* from state legislator to Chicago councillor to Chicago municipal judge.

Chicago dominated Illinois politics. The Mayor of Chicago was a more powerful political figure than the Governor of Illinois: an elected member of the City Council wielded greater influence than a member of the state legislature. One perhaps overstates the case a little to say that organised crime dominated Chicago's politics, but it was certainly a major player on the political stage. This arose in part from the essentially corrupt and violent nature of the electoral process. Politicians in many of the longer-established ethnic neighbourhoods were keen supporters of "Athletic Clubs" for local young men, these being organisations which combined sporting pursuits with a little headbreaking and intimidation at election times. Illegality of this kind was a perfectly normal characteristic of the electoral process, and existed happily alongside such less physical but equally unlawful practices as paying electors to vote (ideally early and often) for particular candidates and ballot stuffing.[15] More traditional "non-political" forms of criminal activity were also widespread. The tide of political progressivism which swept much of the United States in the early 1900s had established itself quite firmly in Illinois law and Chicago's own municipal ordinances; gambling and prostitution were illegal and the sale of alcohol was strictly licensed. These laws existed primarily at the formal level however. In practice, Chicago played host to a huge and thriving vice economy—much of it run as a business empire by competing criminal gangs, among which Capone's enterprise had achieved pre-eminent status by the mid-1920s. That such laws be honoured more in the breach than the observance was seemingly a widely accepted feature of Chicago's political *mores*.

William Thompson, The Chicago Tribune and Colonel Robert H. McCormick

Mayor William "Big Bill" Thompson (1867–1944) was the driving force behind the *Chicago* litigation. The son of a prominent businessman—and descendant of a hero of the revolutionary war—Thompson had defied his family's plans for him to enter Yale and instead spent his early adulthood as a ranch-hand in the west. In his mid-20s, Thompson returned to Chicago to take control of the family firm, become an eminent member of elite social circles through his control of the Chicago Athletic Club, and enter Republican party politics. After some twenty years of steady progress through the party ranks—during which his steady advancement owed much to his assiduous courting of the black, Swedish and German communities and the patronage of William Lorimer, a Congressman and subsequently US Senator—Thompson stood close to the pinnacle of Illinois politics. In 1915

---

[15] Zorbaugh, *supra* n. 13, 153–6: Royko, *supra* n. 14, ch. 2; M. Haller, "Organised Crime in Urban Society: Chicago in the Twentieth Century" (1971) 5 *J of Social History* 210.

he was Republican candidate for Mayor of Chicago, and achieved a crushing victory over his Democrat rival, aided in part by the support of the Democrat defeated in his party's primary.[16]

The *Chicago Tribune* was founded in 1847 by Joseph Medill and bequeathed as part of a substantial financial trust to his daughter's children—the Pattersons and McCormicks.[17] The paper had made its mark as an enemy of political corruption in 1909, when it ran a story claiming that an Illinois state legislator had accepted a bribe to cast his vote for William Lorimer as candidate for the US Senate.[18] Despite being deluged with libel actions by the various politicians caught up in the episode, the *Tribune* stood by its story. Three years later, a Senate investigation vindicated the *Tribune's* claims, and unseated Lorimer. Lorimer's political career never recovered from this episode, but by this time Thompson's career had assumed sufficient momentum to withstand his patron's fall.[19] Lorimer's role as Thompson's mentor was subsequently assumed by one Fred Lundin. Lundin was a one-term US Congressman, of Swedish extraction, who had made a fortune selling quack medicines and chose to build a political power base in the shadows rather than the limelight of Illinois politics.[20]

By 1920, the *Tribune* was edited by Colonel Robert McCormick, partner in a major Chicago law firm, and World War I veteran. McCormick was later to achieve a legendary place in First Amendment history by financing the defendants' case in the *Near* v. *Minnesota*[21] litigation, the first Supreme Court decision to extend First Amendment protection to newspapers closed down by state legislation.[22] McCormick had himself appeared as one of the counsel for the *Tribune* in the *Chicago* litigation, and was later to author a book on the freedom of the press. McCormick was a libertarian rather than a liberal. In building up his paper, he had taken both advice and financial aid from Lord Northcliffe,[23] who then owned the *Times* and used it as a constant vehicle to attack Asquith's Liberal governments.[24] As one might expect of the keeper of such bedfellows, McCormick adhered to a somewhat selective version of the rule of law. The *Tribune* was not averse to adopting strong-arm tactics to further its commercial ends. In 1910, the *Tribune* became involved in a price war with Randolph Hearst's *Chicago Examiner*.

[16] G. Schottenhamel, "How Big Bill Thompson Won Control of Chicago" [1952] *Journal of the Illinois State Historical Society* 30.

[17] H. Emery and E. Emery, *The Press and America* (6th edn., 1988), 359–61.

[18] Members of the national Senate were elected by state legislatures until the passage of the Seventeenth Amendment in 1913.

[19] L. Wendt, *Chicago Tribune* (New York, 1979), 368–70: L. Wendt and H. Kogan, *Big Bill of Chicago* (New York, 1953), 74–7.

[20] See H. Zink, *City Bosses in the US* (Durham, NC, 1930), ch. 15.

[21] (1931) 283 US 697.

[22] See F. Friendly, *Minnesota Rag* (New York, 1982), ch. 6.

[23] F. Waldrop, *McCormick of Chicago* (NJ, 1966), ch. 12.

[24] For a flavour of Northcliffe's politics see R. Jenkins, *Asquith* (3rd edn., London, 1977), 355–6, 444–5.

The war was as much a physical as fiscal campaign: both sides employed squads of "sluggers" to threaten and assault news vendors who showed evidence of favouritism to the other.[25]

McCormick and his paper were also thoroughly and vitriolically racist. The tone and substance of its coverage of race relations issues is neatly illustrated by a headline offering the paper's views on the northern migration of American blacks:

> "HALF A MILLION DARKIES FROM DIXIE SWARM
> TO THE NORTH TO BETTER THEMSELVES"[26]

McCormick allied his distate for racial equality with a similar hostility to even modest initiatives in support of economic egalitarianism: his declining years were devoted to a splenetic and mandacious campaign against Franklin Roosevelt and the New Deal. In 1916, he ran a story accusing Henry Ford of being unpatriotic and (incredibly) an anarchist. Ford sued for libel and won—albeit a token sum of six cents![27]

McCormick and Thompson had been friends in the early years of the century, and McCormick had achieved some social glory as a crew member on one of Thompson's many racing yachts. Their paths had however parted over the Lorimer bribery case, and the *Tribune's* racism and antipathy towards big government suggested that Mayor Thompson's first adminstration would not enjoy favourable coverage in McCormick's pages. Thompson had been consistently forthright in offering rhetorical and practical support for black civil rights. In addition to nurturing the careers of black politicians, Thompson appointed blacks to important positions in city government, and was almost the only leading white politician in the country to condemn as racist propaganda D. W. Griffith's notorious movie, *Birth of A Nation*, when it was released in 1915.[28]

However, the immediate cause of the antagonism between McCormick and Thompson arose in 1917. Thompson's assiduous courting of Chicago's ethnic German vote (and hopes of attracting greater Irish support) had led him to adopt a distinctively anti-British public persona in the early stages of World War I,[29] and he remained an advocate of isolationism and neutrality even after the US entry into the war in 1917. Such views were bitterly opposed both by the *Tribune* and, equally significantly, by the then Governor of Illinois, Frank Lowden, a man whose blossoming Presidential ambitions demanded that his state swing wholeheartedly behind the US war effort. Thompson had campaigned for Lowden in 1916, but thereafter his antipathy towards Britian led him to pursue policies which seem to be doing

---

[25] S. Longstreet, *Chicago 1860–1919* (New York, 1973), 453–6.

[26] Quoted in W. Tuttle, *Race Riot* (New York, 1972), 105.

[27] Friendly, *supra* n. 22, 69–73.

[28] Tuttle , *supra* n. 26, ch. x: Wendt and Kogan, *supra* n. 19, 167–8.

[29] Wendt and Kogan, *supra* n. 19, ch. 13.

much to undermine Lowden's Presidential aspirations. Immediately after US entry, Thompson invited a pacifist group, The People's Council of America for Democracy and Terms of Peace, to hold meetings in Chicago. Lowden (acting, it seems, quite beyond his jurisdiction) attempted to order the Chicago police to prohibit any such meeting, an order which Thompson rapidly countermanded.

Neither the Mayor nor the Governor was prepared to back down on this issue. Chicagoans were then treated to the extraordinary sight of city police under express orders from the (Republican) Mayor preparing physically to resist the efforts of the state militia acting under express orders from the (Republican) Governor of Illinois to eject The People's Council from the state. Thompson was subsequently condemned by his own (then predominantly Democrat) council, and hanged in effigy by some of his citizens.[30]

The following year, Lowden avidly backed Robert McCormick's brother Medell against Thompson in the Illinois Republican's US Senate primary. McCormick's success in this race set the scene for a bitterly contested mayoral campaign in Chicago in 1919. Thompson premised his campaign substantially on a run against the Chicago press in general, much of which he tarred with the brush of being a duplicitous supporter of big business interests.[31] Thompson's iron grip on the black and German vote helped him to victory in the Republican primaries, and the presence of a Democrat, an Independent Democrat and a Labor candidate in the general election so split the anti-Thompson forces that the Mayor was returned to power having garnered only 38 per cent of the vote. On this occasion, the *Chicago Daily Journal* assumed the *Tribune's* anti-black role, its election day headline read that "NEGROES ELECT BIG BILL".[32] From this point onwards, the *Tribune* and Thompson were constantly at daggers drawn.

This personal animosity was lent a sharper focus by the Republican primaries in the 1920 Presidential and gubernatorial elections. Thompson had managed to persuade Republican party leaders to hold the party Convention in Chicago, a factor which might be thought (in the days when the convention had a significant role in choosing the nominee) to enhance Lowden's prospects. However Thompson spectacularly refused to endorse Lowden at the conference, on the ground that the Governor had breached electoral laws in previous state campaigns. Thompson's move effectively ended Lowden's candidacy.[33] In the subsequent gubernatorial primaries, the *Tribune* had thrown its weight wholeheartedly behind Lowden's chosen successor, John Ogelsby. Thompson and his particular faction of the Republican machine fell in behind Len Small, who ultimately won both the primary and general election campaigns. Many of the stories of which the city complained in

---

[30] Tuttle, *supra* n. 26, 204–6: Wendt and Kogan, *supra* n. 19, 158–9.
[31] Schottenhamel, *supra* n. 16, 37–8.
[32] Quoted in Tuttle, *supra* n. 26, 202.
[33] Wendt and Kogan, *supra* n. 19, 176–85.

Chicago were verbatim reports and approving comments of Oglesby's campaign speeches.[34]

Furthermore, from 1923 onwards, the flames of McCormick and Thompson's essentially local feud were fanned by an alteration in the USA's fundamental laws. The first Thompson administration had proved remarkably tolerant of illegal vice activities, be they prostitution, gambling or unlicenced liquor sales. There is little doubt that Thompson and many of his appointees were intimately involved with organised crime, and thence with Capone, even prior to the passage of the Eighteenth Amendment.[35] The Eighteenth Amendment, introduced in 1919 as Thompson began his second mayoral term, introduced Prohibition, providing that "[t]he manufacture, sale, or transportation of intoxicating liquors within . . . the United States . . . is hereby prohibited". Prohibition provided extraordinary opportunities for organised crime to exploit a mass market, in which many of the customers were nominally law-abiding and respectable citizens for whom the Eighteenth Amendment had little legitimacy.[36]

An effective and widespread black market in booze obviously demanded a local police force that was at least incompetent and ideally thoroughly corrupt. The city police force was to a large extent one of the Mayor's personal fiefdoms, and Mayor Thompson showed little enthusiasm for using his political power to give the Eighteenth Amendment practical effect.[37] McCormick's libertarianism did not extend to championing Thompson-led subversion of the Eighteenth Amendment, and his constant anti-Thompson campaigning appeared to strike a powerful chord with large sections of the Chicago electorate. Thompson suffered a serious illness in 1922 and 1923, and managed also to antagonise two of his most powerful Republican allies.[38] The first of these was Robert Crowe, the State Attorney for Cook County. Crowe publicly split from Thompson on the ground that the Mayor was frustraiting his efforts to prosecute infraction of the vice laws. He subsequently launched corruption proceedings against several of Thompson's appointees to the School Board. The appointees -defended by Clarence Darrow—were eventually acquitted, but the publicity surrounding the case did much to undermine Thompson's electoral credibility.[39] More significantly, Thompson broke with his second patron, Fred Lundin, thus depriving himself of a significant strand of effective organisational power.[40]

[34] *City of Chicago* v. *Tribune Co* (1923) 139 NE 86 at 87.
[35] In 1917 Thompson's Chief of Police, Stephen Healey, turned state's evidence during an investigation of vice gangs' bribery of city authoritities: Tuttle, *supra* n. 26, 194–5. Thompson himself decided to disband an evidently non-corrupt and thus successful special police vice-squad in 1917: *ibid.* See also Zorbaugh, *supra* n. 13, 116–20.
[36] W. Stuart, *The Twenty Incredible Years* (New York, 1935), 190–7.
[37] Zorbaugh, *supra* n. 13, 116–20: Gleason, *supra* n. 14, 279–81.
[38] Schottenhamel, *supra* n. 16, 39–41; J. Schmidt, *The Mayor Who Cleaned Up Chicago* (De Kalb, Ill., 1989), 65–7.
[39] Wendt and Kogan, *supra* n. 19, ch. 18.
[40] *Ibid.*, 191–5.

The combined effect of these three factors led Thompson to withdraw from the 1923 primary campaign. Although out of office, he contrived to remain in the public eye by buying a large yacht and setting sail, via the Chicago Draininage Canal and the Mississippi river, for Borneo, where he evidently planned to capture tree-climbing fish!

The 1923 race was eventually won by William Dever, a moderate Democrat who was by contemporary standards a model of fiscal and moral rectitude.[41] That Chicagoans retained doubts about the desirablity of such qualities was demonstrated in 1927, when they dumped Dever and re-elected Thompson. Thompson had abandoned his tree fish escapade, made his peace with other factions of the party and launched his 1927 campaign with a vitriolic campaign of Anglophobia, castigating the alleged British influence on history teaching in American schools and most famously threatening to "bust King George VI on the snoot" should he ever venture to Chicago.[42] The propaganda was aimed squarely at garnering the German and Irish votes, and manifestly hit its target.

The Thompson campaign's financial axles were liberally greased by Capone, by then the dominant figure in Chicago's underworld.[43] Thompson was to serve one more term, before losing the 1931 election to Democrat Anton Cermak, whose victory signalled the emerging dominance of the Democratic party machine in Chicago politics. Cermak was to be assassinated in 1933, in what is regarded in some quarters as a Capone-financed hit in retaliation against Cermak's less accommodating approach to Capone's activities.[44] The *Tribune* rejoiced in Thompson's defeat:

> "Thompson has meant filth, corruption, obscenity, idiocy and bankruptcy. He has given the city an international reputation for moronic buffoonery, barbaric crime, triumphant hoodlumism, unchecked graft and a dejected citizenship. He made Chicago a byword for the collapse of American civilisation. In his attempt to continue this he excelled himself as a liar and defamer of character."[45]

Thompson and McCormick would seem on even a cursory inspection to be a pair of unsavoury political demagogues,[46] squabbling for position in a city

---

[41] Thompson had, in a fit of pique, quietly worked on Dever's behalf, by urging black voters to vote against his Republican successor; Schmidt, *supra* n. 38, 73–4.

[42] Two quite extraordinary anti-British campaign speeches are reproduced in full in Wendt and Kogan, *supra* n. 19, 228–30 and 269. Thompson was also the motive force behind a 1923 Illinois staute which proclaimed "American" as the state's official language: Stuart, *supra* n. 36, 197–8.

[43] Wendt and Kogan, *supra* n. 19, ch. 29.

[44] Gleason, *supra* n. 14, 169–71.

[45] Quoted in Wendt and Kogan, *supra* n. 19, at 333.

[46] In contrast, there is no obvious evidence to suggest that the Illinois Supreme Court's judgment in *Chicago* was motivated by partisan political considerations. As suggested in part II of this essay, the decision reached had well-established jurispruential roots. The (7) members of the Court were at that time elected on a district basis for 9-year terms. The then Thompson CJ (no relation to Mayor Thompson) was a Democrat. He had served for 7 years as the State Attorney for Rock Island County, before being elected to the Court in 1919 at the young age

ravaged by ethnic and religious bigotry, containing an electoral system riven with violence and dishonesty, and riddled with a quasi-legitimate criminal economy in booze, drugs and prostitution. And the harder one looks, the more evidence one uncovers to reinforce that preliminary conclusion. The "sovereign people" of whom Thompson CJ spoke in *Chicago* exercised a rather compromised form of political authority over their elected representatives. Such a context would not seem a propitious source for a constituent legal principle which can be invoked across oceans and across decades as a guide to regulating political discourse in a society which presumably regards itself as a mature and uncorrupt democracy.

III.   *CHICAGO*—THE JURISPRUDENTIAL CONTEXT

In addition to pushing the City into launching a libel action against the *Tribune*, Mayor Thompson had commenced his own action over the same allegations. This was discontinued after just one day, when it became clear that his arguments had little realistic prospect of surmounting the legal obstacles that Illinois law placed in the path of "political" libel plaintiffs. Like the English common law in the aftermath of *Derbyshire*, Illinois defamation law in 1923 drew a clear distinction between actions initiated by government bodies and those commenced by the politicians and public officials who staffed them. Under English libel law (then and now), the politican/public servant is treated as if she is an ordinary private citizen; her political identity is irrelevant to the law regulating her claim.[47] But the Illinois distinction was not framed in so starkly dichotomous terms. Mayor Thompson's action was subject to the rule promulgated by the Illinois Court of Appeals' 1905 judgment in *Ambrosious* v. *O'Farrell*.[48] That rule held that the publication of political information about candidates for elected public office attracted the protection of qualified privilege. The qualified privilege defence to a defamation action provides that on certain occasions—those in which the disseminator and the audience of a libel are under a reciprocal set of legal, moral or social rights and duties to divulge and consume the information concerned—the plainitiff can only recover in respect of false stories if she can demonstrate that the disseminator was motivated

of 34. During his time on the Court, he produced a substantial body of academic work. He resigned from the Court in 1928 to run for Governor: although successful in securing the Democratic nomination, he was defeated in the general election. He thereafter entered private practice, and built a considerable reputation as a trial lawyer and pillar of the Illinois and national legal establishments.

[47] In slander, in contrast, there seems to be an obscure defence known as "the public officer" doctrine, which in some circumstances requires elected officials to demonstrate pecuniary loss if they are to recover damages; see *Alexander* v. *Jenkins* [1892] 1 QB 797, discussed further below.

[48] (1905) 199 Ill. App. 265.

by "malice". The defence places formidable obstacles in the path of a libel plaintiff, and may (depending on the precise meaning attached to "malice"[49]) offer an escape route from laibility to all but the malevolent and wilfully dishonest publisher. As such, it is broadly comparable to the *Sullivan* defence.[50]

The broad test for deciding if an occasion of qualified privilege arises derives from the 1834 decision in *Toogood* v. *Spryng*[51]—would extending protection to the information concerned contribute to the "common convenience and welfare of society"? The test would seem to be a dynamic one, inviting courts to determine the prevailing state of societal *mores* before determining whether a qualified privilege arose. English common law had not by 1920 (and still has not today) accepted that the dissemination of political information about politicians to the electorate creates an occasion of qualified privilege. The Illinois Court of Appeals took a different view.

The *Ambrosious* litigation was initiated by a municipal judge in the city of Colinsville. A group of citizens circulated and presented to the city council a petition which accused O'Farrell of being in the pocket of organised crime; he "has been guilty of the most brazen malfeasance, allowing thugs, criminals and desperadoes of all character to escape without punishment". At first instance, the trial judge had instructed the jury that malice was to be implied from the mere fact of publication of libellous material (which the petition undoubtedly was); i.e. the ordinary (English) common law rules applied.

The Court of Appeals overturned this instruction. It concluded as a matter of Illinois *common law* that citizens who publicised libellous political material in this way:

"may not be held to liability in damages even though the charge is that of a crime and may not be proved . . . if they act in good faith without malice or ill-will toward the person of the official complained of".[52]

The Court of Appeals derived this rule from the long-established political principle that citizens should be able to petition their rulers for a redress of grievances. That base might suggest that the rule would have a limited scope—reaching only to commuications to other government bodies (and ancillary publication, such as in city council minutes or reports of proceedings where the matter was discussed).

However, the Court then offered a "reason" for the rule which was rooted in contemporary political realities:

---

[49] Which, as we shall see below, is a term bearing various meanings.

[50] The obvious difference being that *Sullivan* is a supra-legislative construct, whereas qualified privilege, being a common law rule, is a sub-legislative construct.

[51] (1834) 1 C M & R 181.

[52] (1905) 199 Ill. App. 265 at 269.

"Often it is a matter of common knowledge that there is failure to execute the laws and enforce the ordinances, especially those relating to the sale of intoxicating liquor, gambling and prostitution, and yet without the aid of the very officials whose conduct is questioned, the truth of the charge of maladministration could not be proved."[53]

This "reason" would suggest the rule must have a wide scope, embracing publication in or by the press whenever the allegations maintained that large swathes of the government machinery were incompetent or corrupt. The wider view evidently seemed the more persuasive to the players in the *Chicago* litigation; given the Court of Appeals' explicit reference in *Ambrosious* to "liquor, gambling and prostitution" it is little wonder that Big Bill Thompson felt he had little chance of winning his own libel action against the *Tribune*.

The expansive interpretation of the *Ambrosious* principle was re-affirmed in the immediate aftermath of *Chicago,* but given a constitutional law rather than common law root. The plaintiff in *Ogren* v. *Rockford Star*[54] was a socialist candidate for Mayor in Rockford. The trigger for his suit (echoing *Sullivan*) was a series of adverts placed in the *Star* by one of his opponents, which, *inter alia*, suggested he was an anarchist and a terrorist. The Court of Appeals concluded that the adverts could plausibly be construed as expressions of opinion rather than claims of fact. However, even if they were to be regarded as facts, their publication attracted qualified privilege. If libellous, they triggered liability only if the plaintiff demonstrated they were both false and published with malice.

Like the Supreme Court in *Chicago*, the Court of Appeals derived its decision from Article 2, section 4 of the Illinois Constitution. The Court reasoned that a candidate for public office "put his character at issue, so far as it may respect his fitness and qualification for office".[55] He was no longer a purely "private" person, and so forfeited some of the protection bestowed on private citizens by the ordinary law of libel. His private interest was surrendered to the public's interest in being able to make informed choices about their governors—and the press was an entirely proper vehicle for facilitating that choice:

"It was certainly the legal right and duty of any newspaper to make such publication. It is through the medium of the public press that the people . . . become informed of the record of candidates for office, and of the principles for which they stand and advocate. If this right is abridged then those candidates will be deprived of a means to become fully informed of the candidates and what they represent."[56]

---

[53]   At 270.
[54]   (1925) 237 Ill. App. 349.
[55]   At 357.
[56]   At 358.

The victims of maliciously[57] motivated untruths would still be able to recover damages, but the victims of honest or even careless error could not do so.

This then was the Illinois *legal context* in which *Chicago* was based. The judgment grew out of existing legal rules, fashioned to serve the political purpose of enhancing politicians' accountability to their electorate. The decision was not an isolated aberration in Illinois jurisprudence. More significantly, neither were the Illinois decisions in *Ambrosious* and *Ogren* isolated aberrations in the state libel jurisprudence in the early twentieth century. Rather they typified a pervasive strand of legal thought which had been developed (with varying degreees of sophistication) by many other state Supreme Courts. The following sections briefly review those decisions, analysing both the conclusions that were reached and the reasoning that underpinned them.

Pennsylvania

The leading authority on this issue in Pennslyvania was the 1886 judgment of the state Supreme Court in *Briggs* v. *Garrett*.[58] The plaintiff in *Briggs* was a minor political figure—a state judge seeking re-election to his seat on the bench. Garrett was the president of a Philadelphia pressure group, the "Committee of One Hundred", which existed to foster discussion of the merits of candidates for public office. Garret had publicised a letter to the Committee which had accused Briggs of corruption in the discharge of his public duties. The accusation was readily discovered to be false—Briggs had not been the presiding judge in the case to which the letter referred. The Pennsylvania Supreme Court faced two questions. First, did the dissemination of such information in this fashion create an occasion of qualified privilege? And secondly, if qualified privilege did apply to this information, was the defendant's failure to take the simple step needed to establish the falsity of the charge tantamount to malice?

Paxson J gave the majority opinion. The terms of the Pennsylvania Constitution offered little clear guidance on the answers to these questions. As in Illinois, the state constitution provided that "[t]he free communication of thoughts and opinions is one of the invaluable rights of man, and every citizen may freely speak, write and print on any subject, being responsible for the abuse of that liberty".[59] The issue before the Court was whether Garret had abused that liberty—a question to which the text of the Constitution offered no obvious answer.

---

[57] The Court did not define malice—the tone of its judgment suggests it was thinking of this test in terms of knowing falsehood.
[58] (1886) 11 Pa. 406, 2 ATL 513.
[59] Art 1. s.7.

Paxson J began his search for the answer by returning to the English common law's concept of "qualified privilege". He took the *Toogood* v. *Sprying* test as his starting point and found it led him onto a path which English courts had yet to tread. He saw no scope for doubting that the "common convenience and welfare" of late nineteenth-century Pennsylvania demanded that candidates for so important an elected office necessarily cast aside substantial portions of their "private" identity:

> "When Judge Briggs accepted the nomination as a candidate . . . he threw out a challenge to the entire body of voters of the county of Philadelphia to canvass his qualifications and fitness for that position. That involved . . . not only his official conduct...but, generally, his fitness for the position of judge. In this may be included many things beyond mere legal knowledge. . . . There may be faults of temper, mental idiosyncracies, and such manner and walk of conversation in private life as a people jealous of the reputation of their judiciary would never tolerate."[60]

Exposure to criticism on such matters was an unseverable concomitant of the pursuit of important public office. Electors were both entitled and obliged to disseminate and consume information pertaining to a candidate's fitness to serve: merely to be a citizen and a voter was sufficient to embroil an individual in a network of reciprocal rights and duties to circulate political knowledge and opinions with all her/his fellow voters.

In Paxson J's opnion, it was quite specious to argue that citizens could enjoy effective freedom of speech on political matters if their comments and assertions were subject to the ordinary laws of libel:

> "If the voters may not speak, write or print anything but such facts as they can establish with judicial certainty, the right does not exist, unless in such form as a prudent man would hesitate to exercise it."[61]

This presumption led Paxson J both to hold that political libels of this sort attracted qualified privilege *and* to offer a narrow definition of the "malice" needed to defeat the defence. Initially, he suggested that malice could be established only if the plaintiff demonstrated that the defendant *knew* that the information was false. Such knowledge could be inferred from the surrounding circumstances. However simply making a mistake did not make the defendant malicious. Paxson J then shifted his ground somewhat, and concluded that malice could arise if the defendant had no "probable cause" to believe that the information was true. But this did not seem to cast a positive duty of inquiry on the disseminator: since Garrett had no reason to believe the charge made in the letter to be false, he had not acted maliciously in publicising it. In reaching this conclusion, Paxson J seems in effect to have reworked qualified privilege into a form which is to all intents and purposes identical to the *Sullivan* principle.

---

[60] (1886) 2 ATL 513 at 518–19.
[61] At 523.

Nor (again pre-empting William Brennan in *Sullivan*) was Paxson J swayed by the argument that affording qualified privilege of this sort to such communications would expose political figures to constant and unfounded criticism:

> "It is mistakes not lies that are protected under the doctrine of privilege. . . . A man may not charge a public officer with being a thief, knowing it to be false, and in the absence of reasonable probable cause the *scienter* will be presumed. . . . Public officials are not outlaws, to be hounded and maligned at the will of every person who may have incurred their emnity. . . . There is no room for the application of the doctrine of privilege to such instances."[62]

The Court did not deliver a unanimous opinion. Mercer CJ, joined by two other Justices, issued dissenting judgments. However, their dissent did not challenge the propriety of according qualified privilege to libellous political information. Their disagreement centred rather on whether Garrett did indeed display malice in publicising the defamatory letter. In Mercer CJs view, this test owed much more to the concept of negligence than to that of intent. Purveyors of political libels were fixed with constructive notice of readily discoverable falsehoods. Since the palpable falsity of this charge could so easily have been established, Garrett's failure to investigate the story before publicising it was tantamount to malice.

The unanimity which eluded the Court in *Briggs* emerged two years later in *Press Co. Ltd.* v. *Stewart.*[63] The judgment afford a quite extraordinarily wide latitude to the concept of "political" information. Stewart was the owner of a journalism and secretarial school, which had recently opened for business in Philadelphia in a blaze of publicity. A Press Co. newspaper had run a story casting doubt on Stewart's competence and *bona fides*. The Court unanimously concluded that such a story attracted qualified privilege:

> "If we are asked why this article is so privileged, I answer because it was proper for public information. The plaintiff was holding himself out to the world as a teacher and guide of youth. He was seeking to attract them to his place by signs, placards and advertisments. . . . This gave him a *quasi* public character. Whether he was a proper person to instruct the young, and whether his school was a proper place for them to receive instruction, were matters of importance to the public, and the Press was in the strict line of its duty when it sought such information, and gave it to the public."[64]

Given the breadth of this definition of "political knowledge", the Court's unamimous 1893 decision in *Jackson* v. *Pittsburgh Times*[65] to grant qualified privilege status to stories concerning occupants of *unelected* public office is not surprising. The plaintiff in *Jackson* was an officer in the state

[62] At 521 and 523.
[63] (1888) 119 Pa. 584, 14 ATL 51.
[64] At 53: original emphasis.
[65] (1893) 152 Pa. 406, 25 ATL 613.

militia who was accused in a *Times* story of being drunk on duty. The Court was content to allow a claim of qualified privilege here, even though it was satisifed that the *Times* had run an exaggerated and sensationalistic story.

Thus by 1900 the Pennsylvania Supreme Court had pushed the boundaries of qualified privilege not simply into the sphere of *electoral* politics, but also into the much more expansive and amorphous area of the "public interest" generally. In the mid-West, the Iowan Supreme Court had proceeded rather more cautiously.

Iowa

The Iowa courts had reached the conclusion arrived at in *Briggs* v. *Garrett* some years before their Pennslyvanian counterpart. The plaintiff in the 1882 case *Bays* v. *Hunt*[66] was a candidate for (an unspecified) public office accused by the plaintiff of religious and financial dishonesty. At trial, the plaintiff had apparently accepted that his public status removed him from the ordinary libel laws, and exempted the defendant from liability as long as the defendant could show "probable cause" for believing the false statements to be true: i.e. negligence test. However the trial court instructed the jury that malice in respect of information disseminated for the sole purpose of assisting electors in evaluating the qualifications and character of candidates for public office demanded that the plaintiff show the defendant lacked an honest belief in the truth of the story: i.e. a knowing falsity test. The Iowa Supreme Court unanimously approved this instruction, seemingly believing the point was so clearly established that it did not need to be justified by argument from first principles.

The Court's 1899 decision in *State* v. *Hoskins*[67] reiterated this conclusion, but confined the doctrine to a limited geographical area. Publication of false political information about a candidate for a judgeship was privileged only if the circulation of the libel was substantially limited to the relevant electorate. Statewide publication in relation to candidates for municipal office, or out-of-state publication in respect of state office, would not attract qualified privilege.

The Iowa Court also took a narrower view than its Pennsylvania counterpart of what amounted to "public" office. In *Klos* v. *Zahorik*,[68] the Court accepted that a clergyman was a public officer for these purposes. However in *Morse* v. *Times-Republican Printing Co.* in 1904[69] it refused to adopt the Pennsylvania notion that certain types of commercial enterprise had a "public character". The plaintiff in *Morse* was a life insurance salesman, accused

---

66 (1882) 60 Iowa 251, 14 NW 785.
67 (1899) 109 Iowa 656, 80 NW 1063.
68 (1900) 84 NW 1046.
69 (1904) 124 Iowa 707, 100 NW 867.

by the defendant of illegal and unethical practices that had imposed substantial losses on many Iowa citizens. Such a person, the Court concluded, "is not a public officer, nor is his character a matter of general public interest".[70]

In *Salinger* v. *Cowles*,[71] decided just a year before *Chicago*, Iowa's Supreme Court firmly and unanimously confirmed the relevance of the doctrine to public officers, in this case to one of its own members. Salinger had been falsely accused of using his judicial office to "persuade" a railway company to employ one of his friend's children. The rationale behind the conclusion was but briefly argued. Candidates for public office relinquish that part of their private identity which is protected by the ordinary law of libel: the "public trust" which they seek necessarily exposes their behaviour and character to rigorous and potentially inaccurate crtiticism.

The application of qualified privilege to political libels seemed to be embraced almost without the need for argument by the Iowa Court. The doctrine had also been accepted as unproblematic in Minnesota,[72] South Dakota,[73] Maine,[74] New Hampshire,[75] Vermont[76] and Texas.[77] However, the most carefully and convincingly argued application of the qualified privilege doctrine to political information was provided by the Kansas Supreme Court, in its 1908 judgment in *Coleman* v. *McClennan*,[78] a decision which, given its predominantly *English* doctrinal roots, might be thought of as of especial relevance to the argument developed in this essay.

Kansas

Both *Sullivan* and *Derbyshire* had premised their innovations in respect of civil defamation laws in part by analogy with previous decisions restricting the scope of *criminal* libel laws. A similar process is evident in Kansan defamation law. The legal seed from which *Coleman* bloomed in 1908 had been sown over twenty years earlier in *State* v. *Balch*.[79]

Balch had been convicted of criminal libel for circulating a pamphlet during an election for County Attorney which (falsely) accused one of the candidates of vote-rigging at an earlier election. The trial judge had instructed the jury that if they considered the allegations defamatory and

[70] At 873.
[71] (1922) 191 NW 167.
[72] *Marks* v. *Baker* (1881) 9 NW 678; *Friedell* v. *Blakely Printing Co.* (1925) 203 NW 974.
[73] *Myers* v. *Longstaff* (1900) 84 NW 233.
[74] *O'Rourke* v. *Publishing Co.*, 36 Atl. 398.
[75] *State* v. *Burnham*, 9 NH 34; *Palmer* v. *Concord*, 48 NH 211.
[76] *Shurtleff* v. *Stevens*, 31 Am. Rep. 698; *Posnett* v. *Marble*, 20 Atl. 813.
[77] *Express Printing Co.* v. *Copeland*, 64 Tex. 354.
[78] (1908) 98 Pac. 281.
[79] (1884) 31 Kan. 465, 2 Pac. 609.

untrue, malice had to be presumed, irrespective of the defendant's motives and behaviour. The Supreme Court quashed the conviction. Citing several cases from other states—including *Briggs* v. *Garrett*—the Court held that instructions to the jury should have recognised a "good faith" defence in respect of false and defamatory information:

> "If the supposed article was circulated only among the voters of Chase County, and only for the purpose of giving what the defendant believed to be truthful information, and only for the purpose of enabling such voters to cast their ballots more intelligently . . . the article was privileged and the defendants should have been acquitted."[80]

The test of "good faith" was cast very generously in the defendant's favour. An honest belief, even if negligently or recklessly held, would be sufficient.

Valentine J's opinion made no reference to the Kansas constitution. This may mean either that the rule was so manifestly a constituent legal value that it did not to be identified as such,[81] or that it was simply a matter of common law. Classifying the rule as one of common law (and hence sub-legislative) rather than constitutional law (and so supra-legislative) has obvious attractions if one is concerned with its transferability to English soil. That it was indeed the former rather than the latter was one of the points confirmed by the Kansas Supreme Court's 1908 decision in *Coleman* v. *McClennan*.[82]

Coleman v. McClennan

In 1904, Coleman held office as Kansas' Attorney-General. McClennan was the owner of a Topeka newspaper, which ran a story accusing Coleman of unethical and possibly illegal financial practices. The trial judge at the ensuing libel action had issued instructions to the jury which echoed the ratio of *State* v. *Balch*: a false story about a candidate for public office would attract qualified privilege if it had been published for the purpose of enabling voters to vote more intelligently and (and here the trial judge narrowed the *Balch* holding) the defendant had taken reasonable care to establish the truth of any factual allegations. The judge imposed what was in effect a "good faith plus due diligence" test on reporters of political information. Coleman's appeal, which contended that no qualified privilege arose in such circumstances, was firmly and lengthily rebutted by the Kansas Supreme Court in a unanimous opinion authored by Burch J.

Burch J began by referring to Article 11 of the Kansas constitution's Bill of Rights: "[t]he liberty of the press shall be inviolate; all all persons may

---

[80]   (1884) 2 Pac. 609 at 614.

[81]   Analogous to the pre-constitutional or natural law rights alluded to in the Ninth Amendment to the US Constitution. See particularly the judgment of Golberg J and Warren CJ, in *Griswold* v. *Connecticut* (1964) 381 US 479.

[82]   (1908) 98 Pac. 281.

freely speak, write or publish their sentiments on all subjects, being responsible for the abuse of that liberty." He considered the plain text of s. 11 of
little assistance in answering the question before him, since it offered no definition of either "liberty" or "abuse". The provisions of Article 11 also had
to be construed in the light of Article 18 of the Bill of Rights: "[a]ll persons
for injuries suffered in person, reputation, or property, shall have remedy by
due course of law, and justice administered without delay." The meanings
of all such terms, he felt, were to be found in "the common law".

But he did not regard the "common law" as a simple source of formal
rules. He appeared to construe it primarily as a methodological tool rather
than a repository of substantive principles. In so doing, he closely the followed the technique used by Cockburn CJ in *Wason v. Walter*:[83] the common law was an elastic phenomenon, which:

> "enables those who administer it to adapt it to the varying conditions of society,
> and to the requirements and habits of the age in which we live, so as to avoid the
> inconsistencies and injustice which arise when the law is no longer in harmony
> with the wants and usages and interests of the generations to which it is immedi-
> ately applied."[84]

Wason was of course an *English* case. Cockburn CJ's decision had provided
absolute protection from libel actions to verbatim reports of parliamentary
proceedings which contained defamatory material. MPs who made defamatory statements in the course of parliamentary proceedings and the official
publishers of such information enjoyed absolute privilege under statute;[85]
Wason extended similar protection at common law to secondhand reports
of such proceedings.

Cockburn CJ's reasoning offers a powerful, if partial, rebuttal to the
rationale that guided Thompson CJ's opinion in *Chicago,* for it is clearly
rooted in twin presumptions that the political legitimacy of Britain's system
of government had by 1868 come to rest on the informed consent of the citizenry and that such informed consent was greatly aided by the rapidly
growing circulation of the press:

> "Where would our confidence be in the government of the country or in the legis-
> lature by which our laws are framed . . .—where would be our attachment to
> the constitution under which we live -if the proceedings of the great council of the
> realm were shrouded in secrecy and concealed from the knowledge of the
> nation."[86]

In Cockburn CJ's opinion, the English *common law* had now to articulate the political principle which Thompson CJ was sixty years later to claim

---

[83] (1868) LR 4 QB 73.

[84] (1908) 98 Pac. 281 at 284, quoting *Wason* v. *Walter* (1868) LR 4 QB 73 at 93.

[85] From Art. 9 of the Bill of Rights 1689 and the Parliamentary Papers Act 1840 respectively.

[86] (1868) LR 4 QB 73 at 89.

as a distinctive *constitutional law* consequence of the United States' decision to reject a British system of governance. Clearly, Cockburn's judgment was subject to legislative reversal: it thus possessed a potential ephemerality which did not attach to the *Chicago* decision or to the later judgment of the Pennsylvania Supreme Court in *Briggs*. Parliament did not choose to reverse the decision however, which indicates that Cockburn CJ's innovation accurately estimated the weight of legislative and popular opinon on this particular question.

The question facing Burch J in *Coleman* was manifestly rather different from the one before Cockburn CJ in *Wason*. The "occasion" to which he was asked to attach privilege was not the verbatim recitation of legislative proceedings—but *all* political information which bore on the voters' capacity to make informed electoral choices. In that respect, he was being invited to go much further than *Wason*. On the other hand, he was being asked to extend only qualified and not absolute privilege to the information concerned. Had Burch J favoured a rigid, substantive conception of *stare decisis*, *Wason* would have been of little assistance in legitimising a decision in MacClennan's favour. However his judgment suggested that the key element of *Wason* was not its substantive holding, but its methodological exhortation that the common law should serve "the wants and usages and interests of the generations to which it is immediately applied".

Burch J argued that the "wants, usages and interests" of Kansan society in 1908 had moved on considerably from those of Britain in 1868. Yet his reasoning on this issue was *not* informed by distinctively American principles. Rather it rested on foundations which would seem of equal applicability to any representative democracy. The first of these lay in the changing nature and role of the mass media in (then) contemporary society: the second in the empirical basis for the public policy considerations generally invoked to refute the argument that political information should attract qualified privilege.

On the first point, Burch J indicated that technological advances in communicative technology now presented the Court with the opportunity to develop the notion of the "liberty of the press" in a manner which gave meaningful effect to the principle that government officals be accountable to their electorate:

> "The press as we know it today is almost as modern as the telephone and the phonograph. The functions which it performs at the present stage of our social development, if not substantially different in kind from what they have been, are magnified many fold, and the opportunities for its influence are multiplied many times. Judicial interpretation must take cognisance of these facts."[87]

Burch J inferred that the principles of representative democracy on which American forms of government had always been based in theory were only

[87] (1908) 98 Pac. 281 at 283–4.

now, as a result of the increased reach and scope of media reporting, capable of being realised in fact.

Adopting a similar rationale to that employed in *Briggs, Stewart, Ogren* and *Salinger* the Kansan Supreme Court observed that a private citizen forfeited part of her constitutional entitlement to the protection of her reputation when she asked the electorate to entrust her with temporary control of even a small part of its political authority:

> "by becoming a candidate . . . a man tenders as an issue to be tried out publicly before the people or the appointing power his honesty, integrity and fitness for the office to be fulfilled."[88]

At this point, Burch J took an analytical step which had been omitted in the previously discussed decisions. He suggested that it was a facile oversimplification to view the question before the Court—as the English and some other Americn state courts had done—as simply one of balancing the electorate's public interest in the dissemination of political information against an individual politician's private interest in having the law deter unwarranted attacks on her reputation. By seeking to become *qua* politician a *public* persona, an individual lost that element of his entitlement to the protection of reputation which was rooted in the notion of reputation as *private* property. Such protection as the common law afforded politicians against political libels therefore had to be rooted in a purely public interest, which had to stand in the balance with the public interest in maximal dissemination of political information.

In reviewing the decisions of those state and Federal courts which had rejected the qualified privilege defence for political libels,[89] Burch J suggested that the "public interest" which had led courts to reject a qualified privilege defence for political libels had been assumed rather than argued. The assumption was that diluting the purely private identity of politicians for libel law purposes would offer the press legal *carte blanche* to run the most scurrilous and unsubsantiated stories: this would in turn lead many highly qualified citizens to choose not to run for public office: and the consequence of this would be that the public would suffer the misfortune of having a less able field from which to choose their governors.

Burch J felt such criticisms were strongly reminiscent of English predictions about the likely effect of Fox's Libel Act; predictions which he thought had been proven entirely misplaced. The American authorities against granting qualified privilege were, he thought, equally lacking in any secure empirical foundation. Such empirical data as Kansan society could provide suggested the fears were groundless:

---

[88] (1908) 98 Pac. 281 at 285.
[89] Especially *Post Publishing Co* v. *Hallam* (1893) 59 Fed 530: *King* v. *Root* (1829) 4 Wend (NY) 114.

"Without speaking for other states in which the liberal rule applied in Balch's Case prevails, it may be said that here at least men of unimpeachable character from all political parties continually present themselves as candidates in sufficient numbers to fill the public offices and and manage the public institutions."[90]

The Court appeared to be arguing that theoretical issues of political principle—namely to maximise politicians' accountability to their electorates—pointed firmly in favour of expansive defences to political libel suits. Such theoretical presumptions could be rebutted only by compelling empirical evidence as to the pernicious effects of such a legal doctrine. In the absence of such evidence, the Court's responsibility was to enhance rather than restrict the likelihood that electoral decisions were made on the basis of fully informed consent.

Having concluded that qualified privilege must attach to political information, the Court then offered extremely expansive definitions both of what it considered "political" and of what was meant by "malice". On the first point, the Court held that the privilege would apply not just to occupants of and candidates for elected public office, but also to:

"all officers and agents of government, municipal, state and national; to the managment of all public institutions, educational, charitable and penal; to the conduct of all public enterprises affected with a public interest, transporation, banking, insurance; and to innumerable other subjects involving the public welfare."[91]

This formula went rather further than those adopted by any other of the states at this time, and accurately foreshadows the long reach that the US Supreme Court was to attach to the *Sullivan* principle sixty years later.[92]

The Court displayed a similar preference for the protection of speech over reputation in concluding that malice demanded the plaintiff prove "actual evilmindedness" (i.e. knowing falsity) on the defendant's part. Such intent could in principle be inferred from the circumstances surrounding publication: and while it could conceivably be equated with reckless indifference to the truth, it would seem to leave no scope for attaching liability to even grossly negligent failures to recognise the falsity of a story.

Burch J dismissed suggestions that granting qualified privilege to political libels would leave politicians entirely at the mercy of a dishonest and vindictive press. The Court's holding:

"offers no protection to the unscrupulous defamer and traducer of private character. The fulminations in many of the decisions about a Telemonian shield of privilege from beneath which scurrilous newspapers may hurl the javelins of false and malicious slander against private character with impunity are beside the

---

[90] (1908) 98 Pac. 281 at 289.
[91] (1908) 98 Pac. 281 at 289.
[92] See especially *Time Inc.* v. *Hill* (1967) 385 US 374; *Rosenbloom* v. *Metromedia* (1971) 403 US 29.

point. Good faith and bad faith are as easily proved in a libel case as in other branches of the law."[93]

An alternative way of expressing this is that permitting the dissemination of known political lies does not increase the amount of information available to the electorate. Rather such dissemination necessarily places *dis*information in the political domain: it has no other purpose and no other function than to muddle, complicate and corrupt the exercise of informed electoral consent.

The various elements of the Court's conclusion were arrived at not as a matter of Kansan *constitutional law*, but of Kansan *common law*. The Constitution did not require so extensive a protection of press freedom on political issues.[94] Thus, if the Kansas legislature found the rule unacceptable, it was legally competent to alter it. Burch J thought this was unlikely to happen, given that he was in effect applying to the civil law the rule that the Court had applied to the criminal law twenty years earlier in *Balch*—a decision which the legislature had not thought it appropriate to amend or overrule.

IV. CONCLUSION

The application of the qualified privilege defence to political libels was by no means a universal characteristic of American state defamation laws in the pre-*Sullivan* era. Prior to World War II, a narrow majority of states retained a distinctively English approach to this question -a public/private libel law divide simply did not exist in much of the United States. That state opinion should divide so starkly on this question is an unremarkable consequence of the United States' constitutional structure—permitting a geographically segmented pluralism on matters of appreciable political signficance is the predominant purpose of a federal polity. The objective of the US Supreme Court in *Sullivan* in 1964 was to lend the Kansas/Illinois/ Pennslyvnia *et al.* approach to political libels a *national* dimension: those (predominantly southern) states which permitted their libel laws to be used to suppress

---

[93] (1908) 98 Pac. 281 at 292.

[94] This is perhaps the most contentious and potentially fascinating jurisprudential point in *Coleman*. The extension of liberty to defame necessarily curtails individuals' right to enjoyment of their property, insofar as the Kansan constitution construed reputation as a form of property. The issue which Burch J raised—but really did not answer—is how a common law liberty can override a constitutional liberty. Had *Coleman* been decided as a matter of constitutional law, the jurisprudential rationale would simply have been that the Court had struck a particular balance between competing but hierarchically equivalent legal norms. While many observers might consider the balance struck to be erroneous, the methodological legitimacy of the Court's approach would be readily defensible. Yet to allow the *common law* to nibble away at the edges of constitutional entitlement seems to turn orthodox understandings of the constitutional–legislative–common law relationship upside down.

well-founded criticism of elected officials were to be compelled to recognise the "sovereignty" of their respective peoples (and of the national people) by having their political libel laws pulled into line with those of their less intrusive (generally northern) neighbours. *Sullivan* thus lent a federal constitutional identity to a principle that had previously been a creation merely of state constitutional or common law.

In England and Wales, the common law obviously has a "national" scope. We have thus been denied the opportunity to reach informed conclusions about the public policy implications of deploying different degrees of legal protection to false political speech. This entire argument takes place in an empirical vaccuum. We simply do not know if extending a qualified privilege defence to political information would lead newspapers or political activists to publish more outrageous falsehoods about politicians. We cannot tell if the defence would in contrast offer voters more (and more accurate) information to weigh in the balance when deciding their political affiliations. We can only guess whether a more expansive defence would lead dozens or hundreds of our most talented and principled citizens to forswear pursuit of public office. We can but speculate about the correctness of claims that the prospect of more exacting media coverage would deter corrupt and incompetent citizens from seeking positions of political power. The "chilling effect" popularised in *Sullivan* and long embraced by *Sullivan's* state law predecessors is as empirically elusive a phenomenon as the Yeti or the Loch Ness monster—and one, morever, which very few people have ever tried to track down. But for defenders of the English *status quo* to reject a *Colemanesque* reform of our common law on the basis of that principle's shaky empirical foundations is a feeble argument, since the empirical basis of the current law is equally untested.

It is perhaps overly glib to suggest that the only way that the issue could be put to the test would be to change the law, and then wait to see if the press becomes irresponsible and the calibre of our MPs declines. The legislature, it appears, is unwilling to conduct such an experiment. During the passage of the Defamation Act 1996, Lord Williams raised the possibility of Parliament introducing a *Sullivan* defence in respect of political libels. Lord Mackay, on behalf of the government, replied that any such reform would be a matter for the courts. One has to look rather hard to find innovations of that sort in the English common law. One such intitiative arises in the so-called "public officer" defence in actions for slander. The defendant in the 1892 case of *Alexander* v. *Jenkins*[95] had accused the plaintiff, a local councillor, of being an habitual drunkard who was unfit to hold public office. The Court of Appeal concluded that such a plaintiff could recover only if he could demonstrate that the slander caused special damage. The holding was confined to occupants of non-salaried office (which would then have

---

[95] [1892] 1 QB 797.

included all councillors and MPs) in respect of allegations which, if true, would not have legally disqualified the plaintiff from holding the position concerned.

Had the *Alexander* rule been updated to reflect changing political conditions, it might have afforded a straightforward route to granting political libels rather more extensive legal protection than their "private" counterparts. It seems however to have drifted into obscurity. The depths of that obscurity are illustrated by the Court of Appeal's 1941 judgment in *De Buse* v. *McCarthy*.[96] The defendant was the Town Clerk of Stepney Council, who had placed a council committee report containing allegations of financial malpractice against the plaintiff (a council employee) in the borough's libraries, where it was available for public inspection. At first instance, Wrottesly J had instructed the jury that the publication attracted qualified privilege. This instruction was overturned by the Court of Appeal, which saw no basis for assuming that ratepayers and their council had any reciprocal interest or duty in communicating such information. Even the most narrow interpretation of *Ambrosious* would have found a qualified privilege on these facts.

The closest English parallel to *Briggs* and *Coleman* is arguably offered by Pearson J's judgment in *Webb* v. *Times Publishing*.[97] The ratio of that decision extended qualified privilege to contemporaneous reports of those foreign court proceedings which contained information of legitimate public interest to a British readership. However Pearson J indicated obiter that he believed English libel law now (1960) contained a defence of "fair information on a matter of public interest". The defence had a potentially expansive reach. It would embrace any information which "a reasonable man . . . wishing to be well informed, will be glad to read . . . and would think he ought to read . . . if he has the time available".[98]

In Pearson J's view of a modern democracy, the citizen has a duty as well as interest in being informed about public issues, a duty and interest which obviously could not be meaningfully indulged unless one recognised a reciprocal duty and interest on the part of the press to disseminate such information. Pearson J's principle would certainly stretch as far as the *Coleman* test, but even if restrictively construed would surely reach as far as stories addressing an MP's fitness for office.

The Court of Appeal in *Blackshaw* v. *Lord*[99] approved a narrow construction of *Webb*; the reports of some foreign court hearings could indeed attract qualified privilege. However it firmly dismissed Pearson J's wider principle. Defamation law did not and should not recognise a defence of "fair information on a matter of public interest". The Court of Appeal based

[96] [1942] 1 KB 156.
[97] [1960] 2 QB 535.
[98] [1960] 2 QB 535 at 569.
[99] [1984] 1 QB 9.

its decision primarily on an uncritical affirmation of a case from the 1870s—
Purcell v. *Sowler*.[100] *Purcell* had concerned a newspaper report of a meeting
of Poor Law Guardians which repeated accustions of malpractice made
against the plaintiff at the meeting. The Court in *Purcell* denied that the electorate, still less the public at large, had any legitimate interest in hearing allegations of coruption and malpractice on the part of public officials. The only
audience to which the possessor of such information could disseminate it
with the benefit of qualified privilege would be other government officials
whose legal responsibilities empowered them to investigate such allegations.
In Dunn LJ's view, "*Purcell*, which has stood for over 100 years, remains
good law". Political information *per se* was not, then and now, a matter
which bound citizens and the media together in a reciprocal relationship of
dissemination and consumption.

That *Purcell* had stood for over 100 years might sensibly be thought a
very good reason for considering it thoroughly *bad* law, entirely out of tune
with the "wants, usages and interests" of contemporary society.
Blackshaw's dismissal of a wide reading of *Webb* demands that we either
reject Cockburn CJ's view in *Wason* that the common law must respond to
changing perceptions of the correct political basis of the relationship
between citizens and members of the legislature, or that we accept that that
relationship has not changed substantially in the past 120 years.

Neither contention is sustainable. In recent years, the common law's
dynamicism has, if anything, accelerated, especially in the fields of constitu-
tional law and defamation law.[101] Decisions such as *Pepper* v. *Hart*, *M* v.
The Home Office and *Factortame*[102] have ushered in a quiet revolution in
judicial control of both executive and legisaltive decision-making, while
Prebble v. *New Zealand TV*, *Rantzen* v. *MGN Ltd* and *Elton John* v. *MGN
Ltd*.[103] have wrought significant changes (the first now overturned by the
Defamation Act 1996) in the law of libel.

It is also beyond argument that the formal, institutional basis of the political relationship between the citizenry and the government has changed
markedly in the past century. *Purcell* was decided at a time when barely 30
per cent of adults were entitled to vote in parliamentary elections; when the
Queen thought she was still entitled to engage in party politicking to veto
government policies and Prime Ministers of whom she disapproved; when
the House of Lords possessed co-equal status with the Commons in the legislative process; when—to put the matter crudely—Britain could not plausibly be described as a universally representative democracy.

---

[100]   (1877) LR 2 CP 215.
[101]   The term "common law" is used here in an expansive sense, to include principles of
statutory interpretation.
[102]   [1993] 1 All ER 42, [1994] 1 AC 377, [1991] 1 AC 603 respectively.
[103]   [1994] 3 NZLR 1, [1993] 4 All ER 975, [1996] 2 All ER 35 respectively.

That we would now regard our constitution as resting on that political basis is an incontrovertible theoretical proposition. From an empirical perspective, it is similarly incontrovertible that the reporting of parliamentary proceedings does not offer a quantitatively and qualititively adequate source of political information on the basis of which voters can make informed electoral choices. In an electoral system dominated by two political parties, much of the most significant political decision-making necessarily takes place outside Parliament. Similarly, the executive's *de facto* control of the legislature thoroughly undermines the principle that the Commons and Lords are effective vehicles for calling central gvernment to account. We are increasingly told by political commentators and MPs themselves that the Commons is unable properly to scrutinise the executive, that legislation is often hurriedly conceived and poorly thought out.[104]

In these circumstances, the onus falls on individual citizens and the press to compile and disseminate critical information about politicians' fitness for public office. I have argued elsewhere that there are strong reasons deriving from the jurisprudence of the European Court of Human Rights (ECHR) for believing that the English courts must increase the obstacles which face MPs who initiate libel actions over stories dealing with their political beliefs and behaviour.[105] Should the courts not jump in that direction, it seems quite possible that the European Court will accept an invitation from a defendant newspaper to push them off their present perch in the forseeable future. Extending the qualified privilege defence to political libels would be an adequate pre-emptive strike for an English court to launch. It would also undercut the accusations of "judicial supremacism" which would no doubt be bandied about by MPs of both parties if the courts were explicitly to embrace the *Sullivan* defence as a necessary feature of UK adherence to the European Convention on Human Rights.

The present system is politically and logically unsatisfactory; it makes little sense for the common law to have embraced *Chicago* while rejecting *Sullivan*. *Chicago* itself was not a geographically and jurisprudentially anachronistic starting point from which *Sullivan* was to be developed forty years later; rather it was a logical extension of a principle that had already been firmly established in many American states in respect of actions brought by politicians and public officials. *Derbyshire*, as well as being intrinsically simplistic, is a castle built on air. It represents poor policy and shoddy scholarship. There is much to be said in favour of careful comparative legal analysis, if only

---

[104] See for example J. McEldowney, *Public Law* (London, 1994) ch. 9: C. Turpin, *British Government and the Constitution* (3rd edn., London, 1995), ch. 7: Lord Hailsham, *The Dilemma of Democracy* (London, 1978), ch. 20: P. Bennet and S. Pullinger, *Making the Commons Work* (London, 1991): House of Commons Public Service Committee, *Ministerial Responsibility and Accountability* (London, 1996).

[105] The Court has produced dicta to this effect in several criminal libel cases; see *Lingens* v. *Austria* (1986) 8 EHRR 407; *Castells* v. *Spain* (1992) 14 EHRR 445; Oberschlik v. Austria (1991) 13 EHRR 389.

because it may ultimately reinforce our belief in the rectitude of our own legal solutions to particular political and social problems. There is nothing to be said in favour of plucking attractive principles from the foreign jurisprudential air without having first made a serious effort to understand the legal tradition from which they emerge and the political purpose they are intended to serve.

6

Political Activities of Public Servants and Freedom of Expression

GILLIAN S. MORRIS

I. INTRODUCTION

"[I]t cannot be gainsaid that the State has interests as an employer in regulating the speech of its employees that differ significantly from those it possesses in connection with regulation of the speech of the citizenry in general. The problem in any case is to arrive at a balance between the interests of the teacher, as a citizen, in commenting upon matters of public concern and the interest of the State, as an employer, in promoting the efficiency of the public services it performs through its employees."[1]

In many legal systems public servants are prevented from engaging in political activities of a kind which, for other groups, would be viewed as fundamental attributes of citizenship. These restrictions may take a variety of forms, including banning the articulation of political views, even in a personal capacity; forbidding participation in the organisation of political parties or political campaigns; and requiring resignation as the price of standing for political office. The significant interference with freedom of expression which restrictions of this nature constitute is commonly justified by reference to the concept of a "politically neutral" public service whose effective operation would be compromised if the political preferences of its staff were apparent. Three major arguments are usually marshalled (with varying degrees of emphasis) in support of this position: that elected representatives could not otherwise depend upon policy being impartially formulated and executed; those subject to administrative discretions could not be confident that their exercise will be free from political bias; and preferment in the public service may otherwise become governed by political nepotism. Some systems go further in penalising even the private expression of political preferences by denying access to, or advancement within, the public service to individuals who are (or have been) associated with organisations deemed subversive to the State, even though these organisations are not unlawful in domestic law.

[1] *Pickering* v. *Board of Education of Township High School District 205, Will County, Illinois* (1968) 391 US 563 at 568.

In the United States and Canada the legitimacy of constraints on public servants' freedom of political expression has been the subject of challenges in their respective Supreme Courts. It has also been an important issue for the organs which supervise the application of the European Convention of Human Rights (ECHR). In Britain, the scope for challenging restrictions of this nature in domestic law has, to date, been very limited although incorporation of the ECHR may change this.[2] However, it has become an important political issue over the past decade, due in part to dramatic new restrictions imposed on local government workers in 1989, which the European Commission on Human Rights considers to violate Article 10 ECHR.

This chapter considers the extent to which constraints on the freedom of political expression of public servants can be justified in the contemporary democratic State. It begins by outlining the current position in Britain where, although public servants as a group are not constrained, individual categories of workers are subject to distinctive restrictions. It then examines how the issue has been dealt with under the ECHR, compares this with the jurisprudence of the Canadian and US courts respectively, and assesses how far existing British provisions could be open to challenge in the light of the principles developed in those jurisdictions. The conclusion proposes some criteria against which the propriety of restrictions should be judged, particularly in a context where public services may be delivered by staff employed by private, as well as public, sector bodies.

II. RESTRICTIONS ON PUBLIC SERVANTS IN BRITAIN

There are four major groups of British public servants whose freedom of political expression is constrained: civil servants, the police, judges and local government workers. All members of the first three groups, and holders of "politically restricted" local government posts[3] (together with members of the armed forces and holders of specified public offices), are barred by statute from membership of the House of Commons and the European Parliament.[4] Beyond that, each is subject to additional restrictions which differ widely in their scope and operation. Those on civil servants are set out in the Civil Service Management Code, promulgated under the Civil Service Order in Council 1995, as amended;[5] for local government workers and the

---

[2] At the time of writing the Human Rights Bill, which is intended to incorporate much of the Convention into domestic law, is before Parliament.

[3] Local Government and Housing Act 1989, ss. 2, 3. See *infra* for discussion of this concept.

[4] House of Commons Disqualification Act 1975, s. 1 and Sched. 1, Part III; European Parliament Elections Act 1978, s. 5.

[5] Civil Service Management Code, April 1996. Although the Code does not of itself prescribe terms and conditions of service, it sets out regulations and instructions to departments and agencies and, where they are given discretion to determine terms and conditions, the rules and principles to which they must adhere: see introduction to the Code, para. 2.

police they are specified in legislation. The constraint on judges, who are expected not to become involved in party political activities (the Lord Chancellor, who heads the English judiciary, apart[6]), rests purely on constitutional convention, although an individual who continuously flouted this principle might, ultimately, face dismissal.[7] A common difficulty in the case of all these groups, however, is distinguishing between the "political" and the non-political (particularly the "professional" or "trade union") sphere. In the context of charity law, trusts for "political purposes" have been said to include those whose "direct and principal purpose" is to further the interests of a particular political party; to procure changes in the laws of this or a foreign country; or to procure a reversal of government policy or particular decisions of governmental authorities in this or a foreign country,[8] a definition which was also recently adopted in relation to the statutory ban on political advertising.[9] By this standard, comments by judges upon proposed changes to the criminal justice system, by chief constables on the resources available to the police, and by local authority chief executives on government housing policies could cross this line. More significantly in this context, none of the provisions imposing restrictions offers any assistance in defining the crucial concept of a "political party", beyond an unhelpful reference in the local government regulations to the exclusion of organisations whose objects relate solely to matters arising in States outside the EU.[10] The Sex Discrimination Act 1975 makes special provision for participation in a political party if "it has as its main object, or one of its main objects, the promotion of Parliamentary candidatures for the Parliament of the United Kingdom" or is affiliated to such an organisation.[11] This definition, in excluding some organisations which English law deems to have "political purposes", such as Amnesty,[12] would seem an appropriate one to adopt in relation to constraints on public servants.

Civil Servants

In the case of civil servants the tradition of political impartiality, which dates back to the mid-nineteenth century, has been seen as a concomitant of the

[6] For a recent critique of the Lord Chancellor's position see Lord Steyn, "The Weakest and Least Dangerous Department of Government" [1997] *Public Law* 84 at 89–91.

[7] See A. W. Bradley and K. D. Ewing (eds.), E. C. S. Wade and A. W. Bradley, *Constitutional and Administrative Law* (12th edn., London, 1997 at 418 ff).

[8] *McGovern* v. *Attorney General* [1981] 3 All ER 493, 509 (Slade J).

[9] *R.* v. *Radio Authority, ex parte Bull and Another* [1997] 2 All ER 561 (CA).

[10] The Local Government Officers (Political Restrictions) Regulations 1990, SI 1990 No. 851, reg. 2.

[11] S. 33(1).

[12] See n. 9 above. In *Bull* the Court of Appeal merely held that the decision of the relevant authority under the Broadcasting Act 1990 that Amnesty's objects were "mainly political" was not unreasonable, whilst expressing some surprise at the authority's decision on the facts.

concept of a permanant civil service which serves governments of all political complexions with equal skill and expertise.[13] (Special advisers, appointed by ministers for the duration of a particular administration to provide political advice on policy questions, are an exception to this principle.) The provisions relating to political activity were avowedly intended to ensure "the continued neutrality of the Service while at the same time allowing the maximum freedom compatible with that concept".[14] Staff are divided into three categories: the "politically free"—industrial and non-office grades—who may engage in any political activity when not on duty or on official premises;[15] the "politically restricted"—Senior Civil Servants and those immediately below them—who cannot take part in national political activities and may take part in local activities only if their department or executive agency gives permission, which may be made subject to conditions;[16] and an intermediate group which may take part in either national or local activities with permission, which may be given either *en bloc* or individually.[17] "National" political activities are defined as standing as a candidate for the UK or European Parliament or canvassing on behalf of another candidate or political party; holding office in a party political organisation where this impinges on party politics in the field of either Parliament; and speaking in public or expressing views in print on matters of national political controversy. "Local" activities are similarly defined, *mutatis mutandis.*

While these definitions are mainly aimed at participation in party politics, the reference to matters of "political controversy" (local or national) seems wide enough to embrace environmental issues, such as the construction of motorways or noise control, and ethical questions, such as abortion or euthanasia. As such, their legitimacy as restrictions seems questionable. Having said that, civil servants would seem not be barred from holding office in pressure groups dealing with issues of this nature,[18] subject to their overriding duty to ensure that their duty and private interests do not conflict,[19] which might occur, for example, if they played a prominant role in

[13] See S. Fredman and G. S. Morris, *The State as Employer: Labour Law in the Public Services* (London, 1989), 216–20.

[14] The aim as expressed by the Masterman Committee, established in 1948, quoted in the *Committee on Political Activities of Public Servants*, Chairman Sir Arthur Armitage (henceforth the "Armitage Committee") (Cmnd. 7057, 1978), para. 20.

[15] Civil Service Management Code, paras. 4.4.2, 4.4.11 ff. All civil servants, regardless of grade, would need to resign to stand for the UK or European Parliament but the politically free have a right to be reinstated if not elected; for others, it is at the discretion of their department or agency: *ibid.*, paras. 4.4.6–4.4.7. It seems that there is no bar to the recruitment into the service of those who have previously been politically active: William Waldegrave, Chancellor of the Duchy of Lancaster, HC Debs., Vol. 243, col. 272, 13 May 1994, written answer.

[16] *Ibid.*, para. 4.4.9.

[17] *Ibid.*, para. 4.4.10.

[18] The Armitage Committee seemed to assume (paras. 98–99) that holding office in "pressure groups" would not be prohibited.

[19] See the Civil Service Management Code, para. 4.1.3 c.

an organisation which was attempting to influence their minister.[20] Moreover, even where civil servants are granted permission to participate in overtly political activities they remain subject to certain obligations; they must ensure that the expression of their personal political views does not constitute "so strong and so comprehensive a commitment to one political party as to inhibit or appear to inhibit loyal and effective service to Ministers of another",[21] and they must "take every care to avoid any embarassment to Ministers or to their department or agency which could result . . . from bringing themselves prominently to public notice, as civil servants, in party political controversy".[22]

In general, civil servants may join the political party of their choice; mere membership is not normally a matter of public knowledge. However it is official policy that no one should be employed on work "vital to the interests of the state" who is, or has recently been, a member of any organisation which has advocated "actions intended to overthrow or undermine Parliamentary democracy by political or industrial or violent means" or associated with any such organisation or any of its members in such a way as to raise reasonable doubts about their reliability.[23] It is likely, therefore, that individuals who have been associated with communist or fascist parties, for example, will be denied access to such posts. The bar could, however, be construed much more broadly, and is clearly wide enough to cover members of trade unions, among other groups, whose activities are considered, rightly or wrongly, to present a threat to the democratic system.[24]

The system of classifying civil service posts for the purposes of political activities has been in operation since 1953, although in 1984 the rules were relaxed pursuant to the recommendations of the 1978 Armitage Committee. In formal terms the system gives individual departments or agencies (of which there were 138 in the United Kingdom in October 1997) considerable

---

[20] See the Armitage Committee, para. 98.

[21] Civil Service Management Code, para. 4.4.13.

[22] *Ibid.*, para. 4.4.14.

[23] The Prime Minister, Mr. John Major, HC Debs, Vol. 251, cols. 764–6, 15 December 1994, written answer. Discussion of the procedures used for security vetting lies beyond the scope of this chapter. On the development of policy in this area see I. Leigh and L. Lustgarten, *In From the Cold: National Security and Parliamentary Democracy* (Oxford, 1994), ch. 6. But note the important changes introduced pursuant to the Prime Minister's 1994 statement.

[24] If a government minister certified that exclusion from a post was on grounds of national security, the individual concerned would be unable to complain of discrimination on grounds of union activity: Industrial Tribunals Act 1996, s. 10(4). The ILO Discrimination (Employment and Occupation) Convention 1958 No. 111 covers discrimination on the basis of "political opinion". However, Art. 4 exempts measures affecting an individual who is "justifiably suspected of, or engaged in, activities prejudicial to the security of the State" provided that the individual has the right to appeal to a competent body. However, somewhat curiously, where it can be established that "special conditions of reliability, integrity and loyalty for employment in given positions" are "inherent job requirements" within the meaning of Art. 1, para. 2 of the Convention such conditions may be imposed even if the requirements of Art. 4 are not met: see ILO Official Bulletin Supplement 1, Vol. LXX, 1987, Series B, para. 577.

discretion over the political activities of those in the restricted and intermediate categories (the designation of "politically free" staff requires the
approval of the Minister for the Civil Service).[25] However, departments and
agencies are directed normally to refuse permission only to individuals
employed in sensitive areas where the impartiality of the Civil Service is most
at risk.[26] Moreover, where permission is refused civil servants must be told
the reason and can appeal to the three-member Civil Service Appeal Board
(CSAB), which includes a representative from the trade union as well as the
official side. Figures are no longer kept centrally on the numbers of civil servants in each category, nor on the numbers granted permission to undertake
political activities. However, the evidence to the Armitage Committee
showed that even for staff in the politically restricted category some 90 per
cent of the applications to take part had been granted.[27] A survey in the
mid–1980s by the Cabinet Office showed that, in practice, comparatively
few civil servants sought permission[28] and since 1984 there have been only
four appeals to the CSAB on this area which have proceeded to a hearing.
The Widdicombe Committee of Inquiry into Local Authority Business
concluded that the civil service system depended for its acceptability "on the
possibility of exemptions being granted on a case by case basis and on a
reasonable consensus as to when such exemptions should be granted".[29]
Although it is impossible to say whether the existing rules deter individuals
from entering the civil service or applying for exemption, on the basis of the
numerical evidence, at least, this aspect of restrictions on civil servants'
freedom of expression does not now appear to be contentious within the
service.[30]

Local Government Employees

The position in local government could not differ more greatly. Here, too,
there has been a tradition of permanent employment, with officers serving
their council regardless of its political complexion. However, in contrast to

[25] Servants of the Crown (Parliamentary, European Parliamentary and Northern Ireland
Assembly Candidature) Order 1987.

[26] Civil Service Management Code, para. 4.4, Annex A. These include those closely engaged
in policy assistance to ministers; in the private offices of ministers or senior officials or in areas
which are politically sensitive or subject to national security; those who regularly speak for the
Government in dealings with external bodies or overseas governments; and those who have a
significant amount of face-to-face contact with members of the public who may be expected to
know of their political activities and they appear to make decisions directly affecting them personally—Inland Revenue or Benefits Agency staff, for example.

[27] Para. 76.

[28] 694 between 1984 and 1987. Letter from Cabinet Office OMCS to establishment officer,
21 Mar. 1988; quoted in Fredman and Morris, *supra* n. 13, 220.

[29] (Cmnd. 9797, 1986), para. 6.212.

[30] Before the 1984 reforms it was a prominent area of discontent: see Armitage , *supra* n. 14
para 49.

the liberalisation of restrictions in the civil service, the position of local government workers has become much more constrained in recent years. Until 1989 the sole constraint was that no one appointed by a local authority to a paid office of employment could be a member of that authority,[31] although they were free to serve in other authorities. In 1986 the Widdicombe Committee concluded that, where the duties of politically active officers involved advising councillors, there would always be "a very significant risk" that they would be "viewed with suspicion by councillors of other parties", so impairing the performance of their duties to the council as a whole.[32] The Committee therefore recommended that those whose duties routinely involved such tasks should be debarred from political activity either locally or elsewhere.[33]

The Local Government and Housing Act 1989 applied this principle in an amended form, creating a new category of "politically restricted" posts whose holders cannot be members of any local authority or of the House of Commons and whose conditions of employment are deemed to incorporate such restrictions on their political activities as the Secretary of State may by regulation prescribe.[34] The current regulations[35] prohibit a wide range of activities, including standing as a candidate for election to the UK or European Parliament or any local authority or acting as an agent, or canvassing for, another candidate; and holding any office or committee membership of a political party or branch thereof if this would be likely to involve participation in its general management or acting on its behalf in external dealings.[36] Most controversially persons holding politically restricted posts are forbidden to speak to the public at large or to a section of the public with the "apparent intention of affecting public support for a political party" and must not permit publication of any of their own written or artistic work, or work they have edited "if the work appears to be intended to affect public support for a political party".[37] The regulations state that in determining whether a person has breached these provisions regard should be had to whether the individual referred to a political party or whether the speech or work promoted or opposed a point of view identifiable as that of one political party and not of another.[38] Nevertheless, given the broad range of social, economic and other issues associated with

---

[31] Local Government Act 1972, s. 80(1). Equally a councillor, or someone who was a councillor in the last 12 months, could not be appointed as an officer of the same authority: s. 116.

[32] Para. 6.211.

[33] *Ibid.*

[34] Ss. 1–2.

[35] The Local Government Officers (Political Restrictions) Regulations 1990, SI 1990 No. 851.

[36] Sched., paras. 1, 3–5.

[37] *Ibid.*, paras. 6–7. The Government refused to exempt material which was written anonymously on the ground that the source would often in practice be known: Lord Hesketh, HL Debs., Vol. 511, col. 1040, 19 Oct. 1989.

[38] *Ibid.*, para. 4.

particular parties, the scope of restriction is potentially very extensive,[39] particularly as only "apparent" rather than actual intention need be shown. It is notable that, despite ministerial assurances during the legislation's parliamentary passage that it would not inhibit trade union activity,[40] no provision was made to this effect (in contrast to the Civil Service Management Code, which specifically exempts this[41]). This means that participation in campaigns against redundancies or the contracting-out of services, for example, may be forbidden where they involve opposition to government policy.[42] Equally an assurance that local government officers could continue writing in professional journals about local government matters,[43] which again may involve criticising party policies, was not translated into action. The regulations do leave holders of politically restricted posts free to display political posters or other documents at their homes or on vehicles or articles[44] used by them (which could presumably include bags, briefcases, etc. used at work). However there is no exception for words spoken in a social context or, indeed, at meetings of the party of which the officer is a member.[45]

For the purposes of this legislation, some posts are identified as "politically restricted", including chief officers and their deputies.[46] In addition local authorities are required to maintain a list of posts falling at or above a specified salary (as from 1 April 1997, £26,391),[47] together with any others whose duties involve giving advice on a regular basis to the authority or any of its committees or sub-committees or speaking on behalf of the authority

[39] See the argument presented by the applicants to the European Commission on Human Rights: *Ahmed et al.* v. *UK*, Appl. No. 22954/93, Report of the Commission, para. 46, noted [1997] 6 EHRLR 670.

[40] See Mr. John Selwyn Gummer, Minister for Local Government, House of Commons Standing Committee G, 2 Mar. 1989, col. 112.

[41] Civil Service Management Code, para. 4.4.16.

[42] For analogous difficulties in the context of the definition of a "trade dispute" under the Trade Union and Labour Relations (Consolidation) Act 1992, s. 244(1) see S. Deakin and G. S. Morris, *Labour Law* (London, 1995), 787–9.

[43] Mr. Gummer, House of Commons Standing Committee G, 28 Feb. 1989, col. 62.

[44] Sched., para. 7(2).

[45] The regulations are framed in terms of communication to "a section of the public", a concept which would appear not to exempt fellow party members or, indeed, fellow workers. In case law relating to the interpretation of this phrase in the context of the Race Relations Act 1968, it was held that private clubs, in providing facilities or services to members, were not providing them to "a section of the public" provided that the club's rules concerning the election of members made provision for a genuine process of personal selection of members and those rules were in practice complied with: see *Charter* v. *Race Relations Board* [1973] 1 All ER 512 (HL), where there was extensive discussion of the division between the public and private realms; *Dockers' Labour Club and Institute Ltd.* v. *Race Relations Board* [1974] 3 All ER 592 (HL). However it was emphasised in *Charter* that the meaning of this phrase depended upon its context, and the interpretation applied in one context could not automatically be applied in another; see Lord Reid at 516c; Lord Hodson at 524j; Lord Simon at 528a–c, f and 529a.

[46] Local Government and Housing Act 1989, s. 2(1).

[47] This represents point 44 on the National Joint Council pay scales for local government officers, to which restrictions are linked: the Local Government (Politically Restricted Posts) (No. 2) Regulations 1990, SI 1990 No. 1447.

on a regular basis to journalists or broadcasters.[48] Teachers or lecturers employed by local authorities are exempt from these requirements.[49] In this respect the Government followed the recommendations of the Widdicombe Committee, which concluded that there was no conflict between political activities and teachers' professional obligations,[50] a view which was apparently "almost universally welcome[d]" in consultations on the report[51].

In May 1996 there were some 40,000 holders of politically restricted posts in England and Wales.[52] Individuals who wish to contest the classification of their posts pursuant to the statutory regime may apply to an "independent adjudicator", who may grant an exemption from restriction where he does not consider that the duties of the post fall within those specified.[53] However if an authority chooses to impose restrictions in circumstances not covered by the legislation (because of the post-holder's degree of contact with the public, or in relation to head teachers, for example) no such appeal will lie,[54] although such action may constitute a violation of Article 10 of the ECHR, discussed below. Notably the government considered that local authorities could be trusted to assess their needs in imposing additional requirements but not in choosing lesser ones.[55]

As at 14 August 1997, the independent adjudicator had received 1,482 applications for exemption in England and Wales. 1,273 had been granted.[56] From the outset the adjudicator encouraged authorities not to be over-inclusive in designating posts but, even if he considers that some have been (as, indeed, happened),[57] he cannot grant exclusions unless an individual applies to him. Moreover, his discretion is tightly constrained by the terms of the legislation; he cannot exempt those whose "advice" may be purely of a technical, rather than a policy, nature, for example, and he is

[48] S. 2(2),(3). Interestingly, a third category of those "dealing on a regular basis with members of the public", initially included in the Bill, was dropped from the final version at a late stage of the parliamentary proceedings after negotiations with Opposition parties (see Lord McIntosh, HL Debs., Vol. 511, col. 1058, 19 Oct. 1989, and Lord Hesketh, *ibid.*, col. 1061; Mr. David Hunt, Minister for Local Government and Inner Cities, HC Debs., Vol. 159, cols. 718, 731, 6 Nov. 1989), despite the importance originally placed by the Government on this aspect and its centrality in the civil service provisions; cf also the Government's Response to the Widdicombe Committee of Inquiry, Cm 433, 1988, para. 5.22.

[49] S. 2(10).

[50] N. 29, para. 6.210.

[51] Lord Hesketh, HL Debs., Vol. 510, col. 886, 19 July 1987. The extent of teachers' involvement in politics was also noted: of the 16% of councillors who were local government employees, 58% were school or further education teachers: *ibid.*

[52] Mr Paul Beresford, Parliamentary Under-Secretary of State for the Environment, HC Debs., Vol. 277, col. 548, 16 May 1996, written answer.

[53] S. 3. Where a post has been listed by reference to salary alone, the authority must certify whether it considers that the post's duties fall within the specified criteria: s. 3(3).

[54] This was confirmed by Mr Gummer, House of Commons Standing Committee G, 28 Feb. 1989, col. 53.

[55] *Ibid.*

[56] Information supplied to the author by the Office of the Independent Adjudicator.

[57] See his Circular Letter No. 4, 3 Dec. 1990.

heavily reliant on a local authority's description of the duties of a post, which need not be demonstrated to have been invoked in practice.[58] Thus, unlike in the civil service, where even the politically restricted may be granted permission to participate in political activities on an individual basis, subject possibly to conditions, in this context there is no provision for examination of the merits of the individual case. In this respect, therefore, the representation that the restrictions on local government workers are less stringent than those on civil servants[59] is not entirely accurate.[60]

Although the restrictions on political activities have contractual force by statute, their enforcement is a matter for individual local authorities, creating a further opportunity for inconsistent practices. To date no proceedings for breach of these provisions have been recorded, but this does not mean that individual officers have not been adversely affected and, in the absence of any body which has the power to rule in cases of ambiguity, they are likely to operate *in terrorem*. The "chilling effect" on political speech and activity identified by William Brennan in *Sullivan* is manifestly not a phenomenon limited exclusively to the law of libel.[61]

The Challenge to the Regulations in the English Courts

In 1991 four officers who had been denied exemption by the independent adjudicator, together with their union, sought a declaration that the regulations were *ultra vires* the 1989 Act. Four major arguments were presented in support of their case, none of which found favour with either Hutchinson J or the Court of Appeal.[62]

First it was argued that the court should test the validity of the regulations by reference to the principles enshrined in Article 10 of the ECHR and ask whether they were "necessary in a democratic society". Neill LJ, giving the judgment of the Court of Appeal, afforded this argument short shrift.[63]

---

[58] One of the applicants in the proceedings before the European Commission of Human Rights, Mr Ahmed, a solicitor, was refused exemption because his employers indicated that he would be involved in giving advice to committees in the future although he had attended none in the previous 12 months.

[59] See for example Neill LJ in R. v. *Secretary of State for the Environment, ex parte NALGO and Others* (1993) 5 Admin. Law Rep. 785 at 804.

[60] A further difference is the position if post-holders resign to stand for election to the Commons. In the case of civil servants, departments and agencies may make an *ex gratia* payment equivalent to the notice to be given to the individual if the adoption process does not reasonably allow for the individual to give full notice: Civil Service Management Code, Sect. 4.4, Annex A. In the case of local government workers, notwithstanding anything to the contrary in their contract, the regulations prescribe that their appointment terminates "forthwith": Sched., para. 2.

[61] See Ch. 4 by Leonard Leigh and Ch. 5 by Ian Loveland in this volume for further discussion of the point.

[62] R. v. *Secretary of State for the Environment, ex parte NALGO and Others* (1993) 5 Admin. Law Rep. 785.

[63] For a critique of this and other aspects of the CA's judgment, see M. Hunt, *Using Human Rights Law in English Courts* (Oxford, 1997), 208–10 and 213–14.

After reviewing the judgments in *R. v. Home Secretary, ex parte Brind*,[64] he affirmed that Article 10 was not part of English domestic law and it was therefore not necessary for the minister to exercise his discretion in accordance with it. Although, where fundamental human rights were being restricted, the minister must show that there was an "important competing public interest" which was sufficient to justify the restriction, the primary judgement of whether this was so was for the minister; the courts could only make a secondary judgment by asking whether a reasonable minister, on the material before him, could make this primary judgement.[65] Moreover, in reviewing the minister's decision there was no basis for saying that the court should contain the minister's discretion within a tighter latitude when fundamental human rights were at stake. Article 10 was, therefore, of no assistance to the applicants in this case.

The union's second argument was that the regulations constituted a disproportionate interference with freedom of expression. Here Neill LJ affirmed that it was not open to a court below the House of Lords to depart from the traditional *Wednesbury* grounds when reviewing the decision of a Minister of the Crown who has exercised a discretion vested in him by Parliament. He declined to find that the regulations offended any of the criteria laid down in *Wednesbury*.

He also rejected the union's third argument: that the regulations conflicted with the policy or purpose of the Act. The union's final argument was that the minister was precluded by the doctrine of legitimate expectation from introducing regulations at variance with an undertaking given to NALGO[66] that the Act would not interfere with legitimate trade union activities. This, too, was rejected, both on the facts—there was no binding promise that the regulations would be laid before Parliament in a particular form—and as a matter of principle Neill LJ doubted whether, save perhaps in exceptional cases, an argument of legitimate expectation could be invoked to invalidate either primary or secondary legislation put before Parliament.

The Challenge to the Regulations before the European Commission

Having been refused leave to appeal to the House of Lords, the applicants submitted a complaint to the European Commission on Human Rights that the regulations infringed the Convention (Articles 10 and 11 and Article 3 of Protocol 1). Their complaint was ruled admissible and in May 1997 the Commission expressed its opinion that there had been a violation of Article 10.[67] The Commission's reasoning is analyzed below.

[64] [1991] 1 AC 696.
[65] At 798.
[66] NALGO, the applicants' union, has since merged with two other unions to form UNISON—The Public Service Union.
[67] See *supra*, n. 39.

In April 1998, the newly-elected Labour Government contested the case before the European Court of Human Rights. The Government is seeking to uphold the principle that "senior and other front-line public servants, in all their public conduct, should act in a manner which guarantees public confidence that they are discharging their official duties in a politically-impartial way".[68] In September 1997, however, the Government announced that it would conduct a review of the regulations to ensure that the detail of the restrictions imposed "is essential for the maintenance of political impartiality".[69] At the time of writing, no such proposals have been published.

In opposition, the Labour Party dubbed the proposals "an attack on the democratic rights of thousands of local government staff".[70] While it later conceded that limited restrictions on specified senior officers may be justified,[71] it maintained its opposition to restrictions on holding office in, or persuading others on behalf of, a political party.[72] It will be most interesting to see, nearly a decade on, what "New Labour" considers the appropriate ambit of restriction.

The Police

By contrast to the restrictions on civil servants and local government workers, those relating to the police apply uniformly to staff at every level. The Police Regulations 1995 (re-enacting earlier provisions) stipulate that members of a force "shall at all times abstain from any activity which is likely to interfere with the impartial discharge of [their] duties or which is likely to give rise to the impression amongst members of the public that it may so interfere; and in particular . . . [they] . . . shall not take any active part in politics". The purpose of this provision has been described as the proscription of activities "that identify those taking part with a particular interest or point of view in a way which will, or may be thought to, make it difficult for them to deal fairly with those with whom they disagree".[73] The point has not been tested, but it seems that in this context the concept of "political" would be deemed to extend beyond the party political, to cover activities in pressure groups, for example. The scope of an "active" part in politics is also unclear; it is arguable that it could preclude mere membership of political

---

[68] News release from the Department of the Environment, Transport and the Regions, 30 Sept. 1997.

[69] *Ibid.*

[70] Dr John Cunningham, HC Debs., Vol. 147, col. 177, 14 Feb. 1989.

[71] Mr David Blunkett, HC Debs., Vol. 154, cols. 746 and 748, 13 June 1989. The Bill was amended at a late stage of its parliamentary passage in the light of negotiations with Opposition parties (see *supra* n. 48) and it is notable that Lord McIntosh said that the Opposition had achieved 90% of what was wanted: HL Debs., Vol. 511, col. 1059, 19 Oct. 1989.

[72] Mr David Blunkett, HC Debs., Vol. 159, col. 715, 6 Nov. 1989.

[73] *Champion* v. *Chief Constable of the Gwent Constabulary* [1990] 1 All ER 116, *per* Lord Griffiths at 120.

organisations;[74] clearly it prevents any form of participation in their affairs.[75] The compatibility of this position with the European Convention is discussed below.

III. POLITICAL RESTRICTIONS AND THE EUROPEAN CONVENTION ON HUMAN RIGHTS, THE CANADIAN CHARTER OF RIGHTS AND FREEDOMS AND THE FIRST AMENDMENT

It is clear that restrictions on the political activities of public servants may, potentially, violate Article 10 of the ECHR, which guarantees freedom of expression, and, depending upon the form of the restriction, the right to freedom of association under Article 11.[76] Most cases to date have turned on Article 10. Until recently the European Court of Human Rights has trodden cautiously when dealing with complaints in this area. Most crucially, it has held that applications concerning the refusal of employment, or confirmation of employment, on political grounds lie outside the scope of the Convention because they concern access to the civil service. This right was deliberately omitted during the drafting process (in contrast to the Universal Declaration of Human Rights of 10 December 1948, which provides that "everyone has the right of equal access to public service in his country".)[77] On this basis, the Court reasoned in *Glasenapp* v. *Germany*[78] and *Kosiek* v. *Germany*[79] that, in dismissing the respective applicants, both of whom were probationary civil servants, because of their political views, the authorities took account of their opinions and attitude merely in order to determine whether they "possessed one of the necessary personal qualifications for the post in question".[80] However, as Judge Spielmann stated in his partially dissenting judgment in both cases:

> "while the Contracting States did not wish to commit themselves to recognising a right of access to the Civil Service . . .[they] nevertheless undertook in Article 1 of the Convention to secure "to *everyone* within their jurisdiction" the rights and *freedoms* guaranteed in the Convention. It follows that access to the Civil Service

---

[74] The Police Act 1996, s. 64, prevents the police forming or joining trade unions, a restriction which dates back to the Police Act 1919.

[75] Note also the Representation of the People Act 1983, s. 100, as amended, which makes it an offence for any member of a police force to endeavour to persuade any person to give, or dissuade any person from giving, his vote at any parliamentary election or any local government election for any electoral area wholly or partly within the police area.

[76] See, for example, *Vogt* v. *Germany*, Judgment of 26 Sept. 1995 (No. 323) (1996) 21 EHRR 205.

[77] See also the International Covenant on Civil and Political Rights of 16 Dec. 1966.

[78] Judgment of 28 August 1986 (No. 104), (1987) 9 EHRR 25.

[79] Judgment of 28 August 1986 (No. 105), (1987) 9 EHRR 328.

[80] See *Glasenapp*, para. 53 and *Kosiek*, para. 39 respectively. See also *Leander* v. *Sweden*, Judgment of 26 March 1987 (No. 116) (1987) 9 EHRR 433; *Ergul* v. *Turkey*, Appn. No. 23991/94, DR 84.

must not be impeded on grounds *protected* by the Convention (for example, freedom of opinion, freedom of expression). Taken to its extreme, the reasoning of the
majority of the Court could authorise a State to refuse to admit to the Civil Service
candidates who, while fulfilling all the requirements of nationality, age, health and
professional qualifications, did not satisfy certain criteria of race, colour or religion."[81]

This is a powerful argument. There is a considerable difference between
allowing Convention organs to scrutinise all aspects of the criteria and procedures used by Member States to select applicants for their public service,
which a meaningful right of access arguably would entail, and preventing
the exercise of a right specified in the Convention being relied upon as a
ground of exclusion, particularly as the State still has the opportunity to justify its actions under Article 10(2).

In *Vogt* v. *Germany*,[82] the Court distinguished *Glasenapp* and *Kosiek*.
Vogt was a permanent civil servant who had been dismissed from her teaching post on the ground that, by engaging in various political activities for the
German Communist Party, she had failed to comply with her duty of loyalty
to the Constitution. The Court held that although the refusal to appoint a
civil servant could not provide the basis for a complaint, this did not mean
that a person who had been appointed and dismissed could not complain if
dismissal violated a right under the Convention, given that the rights and
freedoms it guaranteed applied to "everyone".

This decision, while welcome, further emphasises the anomaly of distinguishing between dismissal and a failure to be appointed to a post; neither
is specified in the Convention but both equally constitute "penalties" for
exercising a Convention right, particularly where the applicant has under-
gone a specialist training and employment opportunities outside the public
service are negligible. The retention of the distinction may also require some
fine judgements to be made: on which side of the line would fall denial of
promotion or, in non-tenured systems, non-renewal of a fixed term contract,
for example? In a dissenting opinion in *Vogt*, Judge Jambrek stated that it
would have been preferable for the Court to have acknowledged that there
had been a change of judicial policy in this area between *Kosiek* and *Vogt*
"instead of arguing . . . that it maintained the same principle with different
results due to differences in the factual situations".[83] It remains to be seen
whether *Vogt* does, indeed, mark such a change or whether the Convention
organs will insist upon maintaining this spurious distinction.

Other cases on political restrictions have turned on whether the interference with the applicant's freedom of expression is justified within the terms
of Article 10(2). This states that the exercise of the freedoms guaranteed in
Article 10(1):

[81] *Glasenapp*, paras. 20–21; *Kosiek*, paras. 13–14.
[82] *Supra* n. 76.
[83] Para. 7.

"since it carries with it duties and responsibilities, may be subject to such formalities, conditions, restrictions or penalties as are prescribed by law and are necessary in a democratic society, in the interests of national security, territorial integrity or public safety, for the prevention of disorder or crime, for the protection of health or morals, for the protection of the reputation or rights of others, for preventing the dislosure of information received in confidence, or for maintaining the authority and impartiality of the judiciary."

The Court has emphasised that the exceptions to freedom of expression must be narrowly interpreted and the necessity for any restriction convincingly established. "Necessary" has been said to imply a "pressing social need" and the Court must look at the interference complained of in the light of the case as a whole and determine whether it was "proportionate to the legitimate aim pursued" and whether the reasons adduced to justify it are "relevant and sufficient".[84]

In relation to political activities, protection of the rights of others has proved particularly significant. A striking example is *Van der Heijden* v. *The Netherlands*,[85] where the Limburg Immigration Foundation, a private-sector body, had been granted a court order to terminate its contract with the applicant, its regional director, due to his activities in a political party hostile to the presence of immigrants in the Netherlands. The Commission found that the sanction on the applicant's freedom of expression constituted by his dismissal was necessary to protect, in particular, the rights of the staff of the Foundation and those who might approach it for assistance. It was notable in this case that there was no suggestion that the applicant had performed his duties in a discriminatory or otherwise unprofessional fashion; it was sufficient that his activities were incompatible with his employer's aims and could adversely affect its reputation.[86] By contrast, in *Vogt*, the fact that the applicant had not abused her position to indoctrinate her pupils was highly material to the Court's decision that her dismissal was disproportionate to the legitimate aim of upholding the constitutional system in Germany.

The qualification that the exercise of the right to freedom of expression is subject to "duties and responsibilities" has been important in two respects in relation to civil servants. First, it has been said that by entering the civil service individuals accept certain restrictions on the exercise of their freedom of expression (a "duty of discretion") as being inherent in their duties.[87] On this

---

[84] See for example *Lingens* v. *Austria*, (1986) 8 EHRR 407 at paras. 39–40; *Vogt supra* n. 76 para. 52.

[85] Appn. No. 11002/84, DR 41, 268.

[86] See also *X* v. *UK*, Appn. No. 8010/77, DR 16, 101 (interference with freedom of speech of a teacher who was instructed not to advertise his religious and moral beliefs on school premises necessary to protect the rights of parents); *B* v. *UK* Appn. No. 10293/83, DR 45, 41 (restriction of freedom of speech of civil servant necessary to protect the rights of his employers).

[87] See for example *Vogt*, para. 53; *B* v. *UK*, above; *Haseldine* v. *UK*, Appn. No. 18957/91, DR 73, 225.

basis it has been seen as reasonable that civil servants should be subject to at least some constraints in criticising the government, their employer, and in making use of information gained in their official capacity.[88] Secondly, the "duties and responsibilities" of civil servants have been accorded a special significance which "justifies leaving to the national authorities a certain margin of appreciation in determining whether the impugned interference is proportionate" to the legitimate aim pursued.[89]

These previous decisions make the opinion of the Commission in *Ahmed* particularly notable. The opinion centred upon examination of whether the interference with the applicants' freedom of expression constituted by compliance with the regulations was "necessary in a democratic society". The Commission had assumed, without deciding, for this purpose that the regulations pursued a legitimate aim in being designed to preserve the existence of an effective political democracy.[90] Although not crucial in the light of its other findings, it is notable that the Commission based this view upon the incorrect assumption that the regulations were designed to underpin a long tradition of abstention from active party politics on the part of local government officers, drawing an analogy between this "tradition" and the obligations of German civil servants to uphold the German constitutional system, accepted by the Court in *Vogt* as pursuing a legitimate aim in the light of pre-war German experience.[91] In this respect the Commission appears to have confused the notions of the impartial performance of their professional duties by local government officers, on the one hand, and abstention from political activities on the other. Moreover, the analogy with *Vogt* seems inappropriate; in *Vogt* the restrictions were designed to safeguard the very security of the democratic system, whereas local government officers are prevented from exercising their full rights of participation within such a system.

In looking at the questions of pressing social need and proportionality, the Commission emphasised that the Government had not given any concrete indication that the activities the individual applicants wished to pursue could give rise to fears that they were not conducting their professional duties adequately or were likely to diminish public confidence in the impartiality of local government officers generally; indeed, had this been the case, disciplinary action could have been taken against them. The Commission concluded that, "bearing in mind the applicability of the regulations to a large class of employees, within only limited possiblities of exemption, the extent of the limitations on political activity which the Regulations brought

[88] See *Haseldine* v. *UK; B* v. *UK* above.

[89] *Vogt*, para. 53. In *Ahmed*, discussed below, the Commision accepted that the applicants' roles as advisers to the local authorities carried 'duties and responsibilities', but did not accept that these could justify new statutory restrictions on normal political activity such as the applicants were persuing (para. 85).

[90] Para. 69. The Commission found that the regulations were sufficiently precise and accessible to be "prescribed by law": para. 62.

[91] *Supra* n. 75.

with them, the imposition of the Regulations by way of amendment to pre-existing contracts, and the absence of any clear need for general statutory regulation of local authority officers' political activity",[92] the restrictions went beyond the margin of appreciation and were not proportionate to the aims sought to be pursued.

In the light of its finding on Article 10, the Commission did not consider it necessary to examine the complaint that the regulations also violated Article 11. This meant that the government's argument that local government workers fell within the proviso to Article 11 allowing the imposition of lawful restrictions on the exercise of the rights it guaranteed by, *inter alia*, "members . . . of the administration of the State" went untested. In *Vogt* it was emphasised by the Court that this notion should be interpreted narrowly, in the light of the post held by the official concerned.[93] In 1988 the Commission held that workers at GCHQ came within this concept because its purpose "resembled to a large extent" that of the armed forces and the police, the other excepted groups, in that its staff fulfilled vital functions in protecting national security.[94] If the analogy with these groups is maintained, it seems highly unlikely, to say the least, that local government officers officers could be found to fall within this category.

A further argument presented by the applicants was that the regulations infringed Article 3 of Protocol 1, by which the contracting parties "undertake to hold free elections at reasonable intervals by secret ballot, under conditions which will ensure the free expression of the opinion of the people in the choice of the legislature". It has been held that this Article guarantees the right to stand for election, since a limitation of the right to stand constitutes a restriction on the choice of the legislature.[95] Moreover, although this right is subject to implied limitations, these should not be arbitrary or impair the very essence of the right; they must be imposed in pursuit of a legitimate aim; and the means employed must not be disproportionate.[96] It was argued for the applicants in *Ahmed* that the restrictions on local government workers unfairly singled out a category of persons in an arbitrary way for unfair treatment at elections and fell outside the scope of permissible limitations. In this respect the Commission's treatment of the applicants' argument was disappointing. The Commission noted that it had accepted that the need for political impartiality of local government workers was an acceptable

[92] Para. 86.
[93] Para. 67.
[94] *Council of Civil Service Unions v. UK*, App. No. 11603/85 (1988), 10 EHRR 269. See further S. Fredman and G. S. Morris, "Union Membership at GCHQ" (1988) 17 *Industrial Law Journal* 105. In *Vogt*, the Commision found that a secondary school teacher was not a member of 'the administration of the state' because the functions of the teaching profession do not resemble those of the armed forces and the police and do not involve the exercise of state authority. The Court did not decide this issue but agreed with the Commission that the concept should be interpreted narrowly.
[95] See *Mathieu-Mohin and Clerfayt v. Belgium* (1988) 10 EHRR 1.
[96] *Supra*.

concern and that the restriction was not absolute, in that there was nothing to prevent an individual from resigning his position to stand for election to the House of Commons or European Parliament.[97] It therefore concluded that there was no violation of this Article. This finding seems at odds with the finding that the regulations were disproportionate to their aim in relation to Article 10, given the importance to the democratic process that individuals have the widest possible choice of candidates and the possibility of other methods of preventing individuals from running for office on public funds, such as unpaid leave of absence.[98] Moreover, it is strongly arguable that the requirement for an individual to surrender his or her livelihood in order to stand for political office impairs the very essence of the right; it is hard to believe that democracy could still thrive if giving up a job were always the price of being a candidate.[99]

The treatment of the Local Government Regulations in *Ahmed* prompts consideration of how the restrictions on civil servants would fare in the light of the Convention. It seems much less likely that they would violate Article 10 given that they are capable of being much more flexibly applied. The provisions relating to the police are more problematic. First it could be questioned whether they are "formulated with sufficient precision to enable the citizen to regulate his conduct"[100] to satisfy the test of being "prescribed by law". Moreover, it could be argued that they are vulnerable to challenge as being over-inclusive both in terms of their application to all members of the force, regardless of their function (need a crime prevention officer be restricted, for example?) and the breadth of activity they proscribe. In relation to judges, one could attempt to argue that, because they rest purely on convention, these restrictions, too, are not "prescribed by law", although the Commission, at least, has taken account of the personal knowledge of the applicant in assessing whether this test has been met[101] and it may be somewhat fanciful to anticipate that an application could succeed on this (or any other) ground.[102]

The approach of the European Commission in *Ahmed* mirrored the approach taken by the Supreme Court of Canada in *Osborne* v. *Canada*

---

[97] Elections to local authorities are outside the scope of Art. 3; the Commission assumed, without deciding, that elections to the European Parliament were covered.

[98] Note that the regulations prevent local authorities granting individuals unpaid leave pending the result of an election (see Sched., para. 2 and *supra* n. 60).

[99] In *Gitonas and Others* v. *Greece*, Judgment of 1 July 1997 the Court held that an Article of the Greek constitution precluding holders of certain public offices from standing for election in any constituency where they had performed their duties for more than 3 months in the 3 years preceding the elections, regardless of whether they had already resigned their posts, did not violate Art. 3 of the First Protocol. This is of little relevance to *Ahmed*, given that the restrictions on local government officers are not limited in their geographical scope.

[100] *Sunday Times* v. *UK*, 2 EHRR 245, para. 49.

[101] See *Haseldine* v. *UK*, *supra* n. 87, and *B* v. *UK*, *supra* n. 86.

[102] See *E* v. *Switzerland*, Appn. No. 10279/83, DR 38, 124: restrictions on a judge who was reprimanded for distributing a political leaflet about the handling of riots in his spare time necessary to uphold the impartiality of the judiciary.

(Treasury Board)[103] where the applicants successfully sought a declaration that legislation prohibiting all public servants, regardless of their role or status, from "engag[ing] in work" for or against a candidate or political party under threat of disciplinary action[104] violated freedom of expression as guaranteed by paragraph 2(b) of the Canadian Charter of Rights and Freedoms.

The Court rejected the government's argument that the restrictions were protected by paragraph 1 of the Charter, which provides that the rights and freedoms are guaranteed "subject only to such reasonable limits prescribed by law as can be demonstrably justified in a free and democractic society" on the basis that they were not proportionate to the end to be achieved.[105] Although the restriction of partisan political activity was rationally connected to the objective of maintaining the neutrality of the public service, these provisions were over-inclusive both as to the range of activity that was prohibited and the level of public servant to whom they applied, and thus failed the test of "minimal impairment" of the freedom of expression.

In the light of *Ahmed* and *Osborne* the approach of the US Supreme Court to this issue seems particularly anachronistic. As Ian Loveland pointed out in the introductory chapter, suggestions that First Amendment jurisprudence is invariably "liberal" in orientation are quite misplaced, a point which the Supreme Court's treatment of governmental attempts to curb the political activities of public employees makes very clear.

In the 1973 landmark case of *United States Civil Service Commission et al* v. *National Association of Letter Carriers, AFL-CIO, et al.*,[106] the plaintiffs challenged the validity of the Hatch Act prohibition against federal employees taking "an active part in political management or in political campaigns".[107] The majority of the Supreme Court reaffirmed its earlier decision in *United Public Workers* v. *Mitchell*[108] that plainly identifiable acts of political management and political campaigning on the part of federal employees may constitutionally be prohibited in order to secure an efficient public service. In the words of White J, who gave the Court's judgment:

[103] [1991] 2 SCR 69.

[104] Public Service Employment Act, RSC 1985, s. 33(1).

[105] It was conceded in this case that the governmental objective of preserving the neutrality of the civil service was "of sufficient importance to warrant overriding a constitutionally protected right or freedom", the first element required to satisfy the "reasonable limit" test: *R* v. *Oakes* [1986] 1 SCR 103 at 138, *per* Dickson CJ.

[106] (1973) 413 US 548.

[107] As prohibited before 19 July 1940 by determinations of the Civil Service Commission: para. 9(a), codified in 5 USC para. 7324(a)(2). See R. G. Vaughn, "Restrictions on the Political Activities of Public Employees: The Hatch Act and Beyond" (1976) 44 *The George Washington LR* 516 for a discussion of the background to this legislation. The Hatch Act Reform Amendments of 1993 permitted federal employees to participate actively in most activities that had previously been prohibited to them: for a concise summary of the present position see M. Stein, "The Hatch Act Do's *(sic)* and Don'ts: Political Activities for Federal Employees" (1996) 43 *The Federal Lawyer* 16.

[108] (1947) 330 US 75.

"Such a decision on our part would no more than confirm the judgment of history, a judgment made by this country over the last century that it is in the best interest of the country, indeed essential, that federal service should depend upon meritorious performance rather than political service, and that the political influence of federal employees on others and on the electoral process should be limited."[109]

In both this case and *Broadwick* v. *Oklahoma*,[110] which concerned a challenge to similar state legislation,[111] the court rejected the argument that the provisions were unconstitutionally vague and over-broad.[112] It was notable that the majority of the Court did not, in either case, address itself to the implications of the uniform application of the restrictions to all employees, irrespective of their grade or function. By contrast, in his powerful dissenting judgment in *Broadwick*, Douglas J emphasised that these restrictions affected over thirteen million people at Federal and state level, including scrubwomen, janitors, typists, filing clerks, chauffeurs, messengers, nurses, orderlies, policemen and policewomen, night watchmen, telephone and elevator operators, as well as those doing some kind of administative, executive, or judicial work".[113] In his view, the exercise of First Amendment rights was "as important in the public sector as . . . in the private sector";[114] those working for the Government did not have "watered-down constitutional rights" and the provisions, both Federal and state, were unconstitutional.[115]

While Douglas' views have yet to command a majority on the Court, it would nonetheless be unduly hasty to dismiss the First Amendment as an insufficiently sophisticated source of legal principle in respect of this particular issue. Despite the decision of the majority in *Letter Carriers* and *Broadwick*, Supreme Court jurisprudence does have crucial lessons for other systems in this area. First, the Court has unequivocally rejected its earlier view that public employment could be made conditional upon the surrender of constitutional rights which could not be abridged by direct government action.[116] In this respect it compares favourably with the jurisprudence of

---

[109] At 557.

[110] (1973) 413 US 601.

[111] Although here there was no reference to decisions of the Civil Service Commission, a difference regarded by Brennan, Stewart and Marshall JJ as "fundamental" in considering the arguments on vagueness and over-breadth.

[112] For a pithy critique of these decisions, see "Developments in the Law—Public Employment" (1984) 97 *Harvard Law Review* 1611 at 1656–60.

[113] At 620.

[114] At 621.

[115] In *Letter Carriers*, Douglas J's dissent, with which Brennan and Marshall JJ concurred, centred around the "chilling effect" of the "vague and generalised provisions" (at 596) and the notion that it was no concern of the government what an employee did in his spare time "unless what he does impairs efficiency or other aspects of his job"; his "political creed, like his religion, is irrelevant" (at 597). As noted above, the British legislation controlling the political activities of local council employees can readily be presumed to have a similar impact.

[116] See *Keyishian* v. *Board of Regents of the University of the State of New York et al.* (1967) 385 US 589 at 605–6; cf *Adler* v. *Board of Education* (1952) 342 US 485.

the European Court of Human Rights, which effectively permits the State to require individuals to waive the rights it guarantees. Secondly, the Court's reasoning carries a salutary message in emphasising that "mere knowing membership without a specific intent to further the unlawful aims of an organisation"—and *a fortiori* "guilt by association"[117]—is not a constitutionally adequate basis for exclusion from public employment .[118]

Lastly, there is an important affirmation of the free speech principle in *Pickering* v. *Board of Education of Township High School District 205, Will County Illinois*.[119] Pickering, a teacher, challenged the constitionality of his dismissal for writing a letter to a local newspaper about a proposed tax increase which criticised the way in which the Board of Education had handled past proposals to raise new revenue for schools. The evidence showed that, although erroneous, these statements had not impeded his proper performance of his daily duties, nor had they interfered with the operation of the schools in general (nor was his position such that there was a great need for confidentiality or the relationship with those he criticised "of such a close and intimate nature" that his working relationship with them had been seriously undermined).[120] The Court concluded that "the interest of the school administration in limiting teachers" opportunities to contribute to public debate is not significantly greater than its interest in limiting a similar contribution by any member of the general public".[121] An approach of this kind could leave open to challenge those aspects of the civil service procedure which restrain comment upon issues of national or local political controversy.[122]

IV. CONCLUSION

The importance of freedom of expression in democratic societies cannot be overstated. Brennan's comments in *Sullivan* as to the centrality of free political discussion have been alluded to earlier in this book.[123] In the next chapter, Sir John Laws examines in some depth the impact that Alexander Meiklejohn's similarly forthright advocacy of an expansive interpretation of First Amendment freedom might have if applied to the United Kingdom's

---

[117] *Keyishian*, at 606.

[118] At 607. However in *United States* v. *Robel* (1967) 389 US 258 the Supreme Court recognised (at 266–8) that different considerations may apply in relation to sensitive positions in defence facilities.

[119] *Supra* n. 1.

[120] The Court noted that significantly different considerations would be involved in such cases without intimating how they would impact in practice: at 570 n. 3.

[121] At 573.

[122] For recent discussions of the issues surrounding "whistleblowing" see L. Vickers, *Protecting Whistleblowers at Work* (London, 1995); D. Lewis, "Whistleblowers and Job Security" (1995) 58 *Modern Law Review* 208.

[123] At 53–55.

regulation of political expression. But it is not difficult to identify *Sullivanesque* sentiments informing the jurisprudence of the European Court of Human Rights. That Court has made it quite clear that it regards freedom of expression as "one of the essential foundations of a democratic society and one of the basic conditions for its progress and each individual's self-fulfillment".[124]

In the context of the specific free-speech issue addressed in this chapter, such grand sentiments might readily be thought to sustain a legal principle which requires that all citizens have equal rights to participate in political activities, and that any restrictions placed on particular employees should be justified by specific reference to the functions the individual performs and the nature of such restrictions proportionate to the aim sought to be achieved. On this basis it may be thought justifiable to restrict the activities of those involved in law enforcement or high-level policy formation, but this should be done only after close and specific scrutiny of the activities involved in the employment and the reasons why the exercise of freedom of expression may inhibit their proper performance. It follows that in conducting such a task it is anachronistic to ground the need for restrictions upon the legal status of the employer; a variety of functions traditionally associated with local or central government may, overnight, be privatised or contracted out to private-sector operators whose workforces perform identical tasks to their public sector counterparts. Indeed, a profitable starting-point in considering whether restrictions are truly necessary may be to ask whether a service is deemed capable of being contracted out and, if so, whether any existing restrictions on political expression would be imposed upon any private sector workers who performed it.

Applying this test to two of the primary reasons traditionally invoked for restricting public servants' political activities produces interesting results. First, it is said that elected representatives could not rely upon policy being impartially formulated and executed. However, central and local government regularly seek external legal and other professional advice upon a range of issues and presumably do not consider that the quality of such advice may be vitiated by the political activities of those providing it; indeed, it is unlawful for local authorities to make restrictions of this nature a condition of service for those with whom they deal.[125] Thus, had Mr Ahmed been a partner in a local solicitor's firm which tendered to advise the Council his political activities could not lawfully have been considered relevant. On this basis it is anomalous and unjustifiable to require it in the public sector. A second argument has been the perception that administrative discretions may be influenced by political considerations. However, the fact that individuals are prohibited from public expression of their views and allegiances does not mean such views and allegiances do not exist; indeed, it is para-

[124] See for example *Lingens* v. *Austria*, *supra* n. 84, para. 41.
[125] See the Local Government Act 1988, s. 17.

doxical that in relation to freemasonry, whose prevalence within the criminal justice system has been a cause for concern, the appropriate way forward was recently thought by the Home Affairs Select Committee to be public disclosure of membership rather than a ban.[126] In relation to the exercise of discretion greater transparency and accountability in the decision-making process, including a duty to give reasons, would do more to secure public confidence than attempting to eliminate only one of a range of possible causes of bias.

Finally it is argued that the political machine may be corrupted if the political preferences of staff are known. This, too, can also be countered by a transparent system of appointments and promotions, with provision for reasons to unsuccessful applicants and the opportunity for appeal to an independent body; in this, and in other areas relating to the award of contracts, central government has been protected from legal scrutiny for too long.[127] Indeed, political allegiances should normally be irrelevant in all sectors of employment. It is arguable that the ECHR already requires protection of workers in both the public and the private sectors against discrimination on grounds of their political activities once employed;[128] and the logic of the US Supreme Court[129] suggests that this should also be the case as regards access to employment. The introduction of a remedy of general application would also bring this country into line with the ILO Discrimination (Employment and Occupation) Convention 1958 (No. 111), according to which signatory States undertake to take appropriate measures to eliminate discrimination in relation to access to, and terms and conditions of, employment on grounds, *inter alia*, of "political opinion", which has been interpreted to embrace the expression or demonstration of such opinions,[130] although it exempts distinctions based upon the "inherent requirements" of a job.[131] A test of this nature would permit, on rare occasions,

---

[126] Home Affairs Committee: Third Report, *Freemasonry in the Police and the Judiciary: Volume I*, House of Commons Session 1996–7, 192–I, para. 56.

[127] See for example D. Oliver, "Is the *Ultra Vires* Rule the Basis of Judicial Review?" [1987] *Public Law* 543; S. Arrowsmith, "Judicial Review and the Contractual Powers of Public Authorities" (1990) 106 *Law Quarterly Review* 277 and "Government Contracts and Public Law" (1990) 10 *Legal Studies* 231.

[128] See A. Clapham, *Human Rights in the Private Sphere* (Oxford, 1993), especially 222–44.

[129] See *Rutan* v. *Republican Party of Illinois* (1990) 497 US 62, where the Supreme Court held that unless "patronage practices", including hiring, are "narrowly tailored to further vital government interests" they encroach on First Amendment freedoms (see Brennan J at 74). See also *Elrod* v. *Burns* (1976) 427 US 347 and *Branti* v. *Finkel* (1980) 445 US 507. The scope of application of the exception to the general principle is, of course, crucial; see Scalia J's dissenting judgment in *Rutan*, especially at 111 ff.

[130] This is the conclusion of the Committee of Experts on the Application of Conventions and Recommendations. See *Equality in Employment and Occupation* (ILO, Geneva, 1996) paras. 45–47 and 192ff.

[131] This requires strict interpretation so as not to result in undue limitation of the protection which the Convention is intended to provide: *supra* para. 194. Where requirements of a political native are set for a particular job they must be strictly limited to the characteristics of the post (specific and definable) and in proportion to its inherent requirements; para. 196.

restrictions in the private sector; thus, an organisation concerned with work with refugees may legitimately require its workers not be active supporters of repatriation; Conservative Central Office may lawfully choose to exclude from its administrative team a member of the Liberal Democrats.

The fallacy of continuing to rely upon a divide between the public and the private sectors has been exposed in many areas of administrative and employment law in recent years; re-examination of the traditional assumptions which have operated in the area of freedom of expression is long overdue in order to allow an approach to be constructed which is more attuned to the reality of the organisation of the delivery of services in the contemporary State. As was suggested earlier in this book, one of the most valuable lessons that First Amendment jurisprudence offers to comparative lawyers is that the public core of ostensibly private activities can quickly be uncovered with no more than a little intellectual digging. An enhanced awareness of this line of judicial reasoning may assist both the English Courts and the European Court of Human Rights in examining the legitimacy of restrictions on the political activities of public servants, when they find themselves faced with a rather more subtle question—namely the extent to which the common law or Article 10 ECHR lends an inviolably "private" character to what are most certainly the very "public" activities of indisputably "public" employees.

7

Meiklejohn, the First Amendment and Free Speech in English Law

SIR JOHN LAWS

I. INTRODUCTION

In this chapter I propose to consider how far the views of Dr Alexander Meiklejohn about the First Amendment to the Constitution of the United States may inform or enlighten the development of free-speech jurisprudence in England. Meiklejohn was not a lawyer; he was an academic philosopher. He was most certainly recognised as a leading commentator on the First Amendment. I wish that academic philosophers in England took more interest in the substantive law, as opposed to the largely arid question, what law *is*.

II. THE MEIKELJOHN PERSPECTIVE

I will start with a discussion of the First Amendment and of Meiklejohn's view. Out of my own ignorance of American jurisprudence, this section is largely derivative. The text of the Amendment, so far as material for my purpose, is as follows:

> "Congress shall make no law . . . abridging the freedom of speech, or of the press, or the right of the people peaceably to assemble, and to petition the Government for a redress of grievances."

Brennan J's paper "The Supreme Court and the Meiklejohn Interpretation of the First Amendment",[1] written shortly after the seminal case of *New York Times* v. *Sullivan*[2] was decided, contains a masterly summary of the differing views of the First Amendment expressed in opinions of the Supreme Court. He refers first to:

> "the so-called 'absolute' view which holds that the amendment's words mean precisely what they say: 'Congress shall make no law' absolutely prohibits Congress . . . from making laws abridging the freedoms secured by the amendment.

---

[1] (1965) 79 *Harvard LR* 1.
[2] (1964) 376 US 254. *Sullivan* is discussed in greater detail in the chapters by Leigh and Loveland in this volume.

Probably Mr Justice Black has been the most eloquent and persuasive proponent of this view."[3]

Secondly, however:

"the absolute view has not prevailed within the Court. A majority of the Justices from time to time have recognised contexts in which government has power to curb speech as such. One view is that the first amendment renders immune from regulation only speech that has "redeeming social importance". The stated ground of this view is that, although all ideas having even the slightest redeeming social value—unorthodox ideas, controversial ideas, even ideas hateful to the prevailing climate of opinion—have the full protection of the guarantees, implicit in the history of the first amendment is the rejection of speech that is utterly without redeeming social importance."[4]

Thirdly:

"Another limiting test of the scope of the first amendment is expressed in Mr Justice Holmes's words: 'The question in every case is whether the words used are used in such circumstances and are of such a nature as to create a clear and present danger that will bring about the substantive evils that Congress has a right to prevent. It is a question of proximity and degree'."[5]

Fourthly:

"Still another limiting test is the so-called balancing test, whose articulate spokesman among my colleagues is Mr Justice Harlan. Professor Emerson of Yale has defined it as follows: 'The formula is that the court must, in each case, balance the individual and social interest in freedom of expression against the social interest sought by the regulation which restricts expression'."[6]

These differences of view are very stark. On the face of it concerned with interpretation of the First Amendment, in fact they represent contrasting perceptions about a question which has little to do with the measure's language. That question is a much broader one: what, if any, are the limits upon freedom of expression which the law ought in principle to recognise?

A difficulty inherent in written constitutions is that they tend to conflate two fundamentally different judicial processes: the elaboration of legal principle and the construction of statutes. It is possible to discern this in the literature on the First Amendment. However, it is not merely that judicial administration of a written constitution melds interpretation with the elaboration of principle. More deeply, the task of ascertaining a constitution's meaning *systematically* involves an ordering of ideals which cannot be done by resort only to the text. Plainly, if a constitution (or the part under consideration) is capable of more than one interpretation, the "right" inter-

---

[3] Brennan, *op cit*, at 3
[4] *Ibid.*, at 5.
[5] *Ibid.*, at 8.
[6] *Ibid.*, at 9.

pretation cannot be got out of the language alone. But there will always be more than one interpretation: the document's core provisions will inevitably be cast in general terms, and, no less inevitably, they will seek to uphold or vindicate more than one value—for example, political freedom and national self-preservation—such that the values sought to be upheld are in potential conflict. If a constitution purported to uphold only one value, it would be a recipe either for insecurity and anarchy or for dictatorship.

Imagine a State in which everything else were subordinated to free speech on the one hand, or national self-preservation on the other. The legal and organisational needs of civilised society are not unitary or monolithic. They consist in a series of different principles which are in constellation with each other. Here is an important paradox: these principles are at the same time interdependent and mutually repugnant. In a sophisticated State you cannot have freedom without order, nor *vice versa*; but the requirements of order constrain freedom, and order is diminished by the requirements of freedom. These reflections will possess some significance when I come to measure Meiklejohn's perceptions of the First Amendment in the context of the law of England.

I will take Meiklejohn's own views from passages in his 1961 article, "The First Amendment is an Absolute":[7]

"The First Amendment does not protect a 'freedom to speak'. It protects the freedom of those activities of thought and communication by which we 'govern'. It is concerned, not with a private right, but with a public power, a governmental responsibility."[8]

"the First Amendment, as seen in its constitutional setting, forbids Congress to abridge the freedom of a citizen's speech, press, peaceable assembly, or petition, whenever those activities are utilized for the governing of the nation. In these respects, the Constitution gives to all 'the people' the same protection of freedom which, in Article I #6(1), it provides for their legislative agents: 'and for any speech or debate in either House, they shall not be questioned in any other place'. Just as our agents must be free in their use of their delegated powers, so the people must be free in the exercise of their reserved powers."[9]

"In my view, 'the people need free speech' because they have decided, in adopting, maintaining and interpreting their Constitution, to govern themselves rather than to be governed by others. And, in order to make that self-government a reality rather than an illusion, in order that it may become as wise and efficient as its responsibilities require, the judgment-making of the people must be self-educated in the ways of freedom. That is, I think, the positive purpose to which the negative words of the First Amendment gave a constitutional expression . . . I believe . . . that the people do need novels and dramas and paintings and poems, 'because

---

[7] [1961] *Supreme Court Review* 245.
[8] *Ibid.*, at 255.
[9] *Ibid.*, at 256.

they will be called upon to vote'. The primary social fact which blocks and hinders the success of our experiment in self-government is that our citizens are not educated for self-government. We are terrified by ideas, rather than challenged and stimulated by them. Our dominant mood is not the courage of people who dare to think. It is the timidity of those who fear and hate whenever conventions are questioned."[10]

The landmark decision of the Supreme Court in *Sullivan*, to which I have referred in passing, may be seen as a vindication of Meiklejohn's views, though the Court does not mention them. Meiklejohn considered it an "occasion for dancing in the streets".[11] As is well known the case concerned a defamatory attack on the conduct of a public official, an Alabama Commissioner of Police, made without malice. The Court held that no action would lie in such circumstances. Brennan J, who delivered the Court's opinion, says in his aforementioned article:

> "The first amendment question was whether its protections nevertheless limit a state's power to apply traditional libel law principles, since the statements were made in criticism of the official conduct of a public servant. In other words, the case presented a classic example of an activity that Dr Meiklejohn called an activity of 'governing importance' within the powers reserved to the people and made invulnerable to sanctions imposed by their agency-governments. The Court held that Alabama's use of its civil libel law in this context violated the constitutional guarantees. . . .
>
> The Court examined history to discern the central meaning of the first amendment, and concluded that that meaning was revealed in Madison's statement 'that the censorial power is in the people over the Government, and not in the Government over the people'. This, the Court said, was the lesson taught by the great controversy over the Sedition Act of 1798. . . .
>
> [The Act] had been roundly condemned . . . as patently unconstitutional in a broadside attack joined in by Jefferson and Madison. The attack was founded upon their claim that the Government established by the Constitution was powerless to impose sanctions for criticism of Government or Government officials. The New York Times opinion concludes that this view carried the day in the court of history."[12]

Brennan J proceeds to cite this passage from the judgment:

> "Madison prepared the Report in support of the protest. His premise was that the Constitution created a form of government under which 'The people, not the government, possess the absolute sovereignty'. The structure of the government dispersed power in reflection of the people's distrust of concentrated power, and of

[10] [1961] *Supreme Court Review* at 262.
[11] Brennan, *supra* n. 2, 17, referring to a conversation between Meiklejohn and Professor Kalven of the University of Chicago Law School. In his book *Make No Law—the Sullivan Case and the First Amendment* (New York, 1991), Anthony Lewis, who covered *Sullivan* as a reporter and who at the time of his book's publication was the James Madison Visiting Professor at Columbia University, has written a fascinating and learned account of the case.
[12] *Supra* n. 2, 14–15.

power itself at all levels. This form of government was 'altogether different' from the British form, under which the Crown was sovereign and the people were subjects."[13]

The materials I have cited demonstrate a number of features which it is useful to identify in seeing how far Meiklejohn's approach to the First Amendment may have lessons for the development, in our own unwritten legal order, of free speech principles. I will summarise them as follows:

(1) Meiklejohn's position rests on a political ideal, the sovereignty of the American people, which, founding both on history and on the text of the Constitution, he holds to have been delegated only in part to the agencies of government.
(2) His view of the First Amendment's force is intimately connected with this ideal, and accordingly ascribes a limitation to the Amendment's scope: its purpose is to maximise the value and effectiveness of self-government by the people.

In analysing this second point, Professor Eric Barendt says:

"[Meiklejohn] thought the primary purpose of the First Amendment is to protect the right of all citizens to understand political issues so as to be able to participate effectively in the working of democracy."[14]

In fact I think Meiklejohn would more likely have asserted that it was to protect (or to help fulfil) the *duty* of the people to understand and take part in the political process. Lee Bollinger, in *The Tolerant Society,* says this:

"Quite clearly, Meiklejohn was of the view that the only interest cognizable under the principle of free speech was the public, or collective, interest and not any individual interest of the speaker."[15]

If, as seems right, this was Meiklejohn's view, I consider it to be very deeply misconceived, for reasons I will explain below.

(3) In light of this it is obvious that Meiklejohn's position is, as Barendt says; "firmly utilitarian or consequentialist in spirit."[16]

Meiklejohn's work has been subject to important criticisms, some of which I will touch on briefly. Here is Barendt:

"Unlike the case for free speech based on its relationship with fundamental human rights, this argument [that is, Meiklejohn's approach] does not appear necessarily to trump counter-arguments that the exercise of free speech may in particular situations be contrary to the public welfare. . . .
   This difficulty is one aspect of the central weakness of the Meiklejohn position. If the maintenance of democracy is the foundation for free speech, how is one to

---

[13] *Ibid.,* at 15. The original citation is at (1964) 376 US at 274.
[14] *Freedom of Speech* (Oxford, 1985), 20. Professor Barendt offer a more broadly based critique of traditional First Amendment orthodoxies in Ch. 3 of this collection.
[15] (Oxford, 1986), at 153.
[16] *Supra* n. 14, 20–1.

argue against the regulation or suppression of that speech by the democracy acting through its elected representatives?"[17]

Lee Bollinger, in *The Tolerant Society*, asks:

"Why should a theory of free speech, which envisions its purpose as serving the
system of self-government, lead to the conclusion that a self-governing society
cannot choose to prohibit speech that advocates the end of self-government
itself?"[18]

However what Bollinger goes on to say is important for the views I shall
develop shortly in relation to English law:[19]

"The 'theory' of free speech is not really theory in the usual sense of the word . . .
but part of an overall rhetorical effort to persuade us to become the sort of people
Meiklejohn would like us to be . . .
    The task of the free speech enterprise was not simply to guard against a regime
of seditious libel, but the far more difficult one of creating a kind of democratic
personality . . .
    What is being taught is much more grand than when to employ legal coercion
against speech . . .
    The end being sought is not just wise decisions but a more general identity.
Meiklejohn offers the possibility of being capable of self-control, a matter always
in some doubt and therefore positively established by the insistence that even the
most worthless speech never be foreclosed, by oneself or by others. This is the
image that would become so attractive to later scholars,[20] who would sense in
Meiklejohn's argument the possibility of being an 'autonomous' person. . . .
    For Meiklejohn, true self-government was conducted according to a certain
intellectual standard by which all citizens think and vote in terms beyond themselves, objectively and in pursuit of the general, collective welfare. . . .
    Thus, for Meiklejohn, the First Amendment embodies an intellectual life in the
broadest sense, one to which we aspire under the tutelage of the Supreme Court.
    . . .
    For speech that attacks and challenges community values, the act of toleration
serves to both define and reaffirm those values; the act of tolerance implies a contrary belief and demonstrates a confidence and security in the correctness of the
community norm. Through toleration, in short, we create the community, define
the values of that community, and affirm a commitment to and confidence in those
values."

These ideals, I think, recall Pericles' funeral oration in honour of the
Athenian dead who fell early in the Peloponnesian War, as it is given in Book
II of Thucydides' *History*:

[17] *Freedom of Speech* (Oxford, 1985), 21.
[18] *Supra* n. 15, 153.
[19] *Ibid.*, 154–8.
[20] Bollinger refers to Scanlon W., "A Theory of Freedom of Expression" (1972) 1 *Philosphy
and Public Affairs* 204.

"An Athenian citizen does not neglect the state because he takes care of his own household; and even those of us who are engaged in business have a very fair idea of politics. We alone regard a man who takes no interest in public affairs, not as a harmless, but as a useless character; and if few of us are originators, we are all sound judges of a policy. The great impediment to action is, in our opinion, not discussion, but the want of that knowledge which is gained by discussion preparatory to action, For we have a peculiar power of thinking before we act and of acting too, whereas other men are courageous from ignorance but hesitate upon reflection."[21]

If Bollinger's description of Meiklejohn's true concerns is accepted, there is on the face of it a degree of philosophical discomfort in the combination of a theory of the First Amendment which rests on its utility as a servant of democratic government with the idea that free expression promotes Man's self-fulfilment as an autonomous being, however much it may be protested that he is only to be fulfilled in the matrix of the community of which he is a member. It fails to confront these two inconsistent propositions: that democracy is an end in itself, and that democracy is only a means (maybe a necessary means) towards the achievement of man's potential as a free and rational being. The second proposition seem to me to be plainly true. With these reflections, I turn to the law of England.

III. FREEDOM OF SPEECH AS A CONSTITUTIONAL PRINCIPLE IN ENGLISH LAW

In this section, I will explain my perception of the nature of a constitutional right in English law, and will refer in particular to the possession by free speech of such a place. The endeavour requires me to give some account of the idea of constitutional principle in our unwritten legal order.

Since English law knows no sovereign text, the idea of a constitutional right has to be forged in the common law. The backdrop to any such idea must first be the general rule of the common law, as it applies to private individuals, which is that everything which is not forbidden is allowed. Any elaboration of the notion of distinct constitutional rights must not forget this cardinal principle. It is contrary to the spirit and letter of the common law that we should contemplate a scheme where private actions have to be justified by positive law.

Secondly, however, the law relating to public bodies, as opposed to private individuals, is opposite. For them, everything that is not allowed is forbidden.[22] This is no less a general principle. It is necessary for the avoidance

---

[21] Jowett's translation.

[22] This, I think, is the true view, and I ventured to express it in *Ex parte Fewings* [1995] 1 All ER 513, 524. (There is not, I apprehend, any additional or contrary reasoning on the point in the judgments in the CA in the same case.) Put so broadly, however, it is not consistent with *Malone* [1979] Ch. 344 or *Hibbit & Saunders* [1993] COD 326: see Professor Dawn Oliver's valuable discussion in "The Underlying Values of Public and Private Law", in M. Taggart (ed.),

of arbitrary government. These two principles may be called *first order* constitutional principles, so that they may be distinguished from other, *second order*, principles whose subject-matter is specific.

But they are silent as to *what* may in the one case be forbidden, in the other allowed, by the State. In particular they say nothing about the protection of individual rights. So long as we adhere to the doctrine of parliamentary legislative supremacy, the State may in theory forbid or allow anything: and under our present constitutional arrangements, the sovereignty of Parliament is also a *first order* principle. But Parliament cannot secure the legal protection of constitutional rights; it can offer no protection against itself.

The reason, upon traditional doctrine, is because of its own supremacy. The problem is, of course, the old chestnut of *entrenchment*. Because sovereignty entails (or perhaps consists in) the proposition that Parliament cannot bind its successors, legislation which purports to entrench rights (or any other legal state of affairs, for that matter) cannot succeed in doing so: not only because a future Parliament may expressly repeal the rights enacted, but also because of the doctrine of implied repeal, whereby a later Act whose provisions on its true construction are inconsistent with the terms of an earlier statute is taken to repeal the latter *pro tanto*. However implied repeal is a common law doctrine, and the common law changes.

In *Factortame*[23] the House of Lords had to consider part of the Merchant Shipping Act 1988, which was inconsistent with certain rights guaranteed by Community law. Community rights are to be read into English law, and have overriding effect, by virtue of section 2 of the European Communities Act 1972. On the conventional doctrine, the relevant provisions of the 1988 Act would have *pro tanto* repealed section 2. But the House of Lords took no such line; nor did the government argue it. The House held that the 1988 Act had to be read as if subject to a proviso to the effect that any provisions inconsistent with Community rights were to be set aside. Sir William Wade thinks that the decision in *Factortame* was contrary to principle.[24] Might it be said, however, that the *Factortame* approach may offer a means whereby fundamental rights may after all be protected by Parliament, if for example it were to be applied to statutes enacted after the incorporation of the European Convention?

The Province of Administrative Law (London, 1997). It is, however, consistent with Sir William Wade's opinion that for a public body there is no such thing as an unfettered discretion: see W. Wade and C. Forsyth, *Administrative Law* (7th edn., Oxford, 1995), 391–3; a passage which (as it appeared in the 6th edn.) was approved by the HL in *Ex parte Chetnik Developments Ltd.* [1988] AC 858 at 872.

[23] [1990] 2 AC 85, in particular at 140B–C, *per* Lord Bridge of Harwich.
[24] See "Sovereignty—Revolution or Evolution?" (1996) 112 *LQR* 568; and Wade and Forsyth, *supra* n. 22, 30–1. Cf P. Craig, *Administrative Law* (3rd edn., London, 1994), 188–93. In his Hamlyn Lectures, *Constitutional Fundamentals* (London, 1980), Sir William expressed the view that the means by which legislation protecting fundamental rights might be entrenched in the British constitution would be by changing the judicial oath.

As is of course well known the present government is promoting legislation intended to incorporate the Convention.[25] The Bill in its current form in fact contains its own mechanisms for dealing with later statutes held by judicial declaration to be inconsistent with Convention rights, and so it is difficult or impossible to see any place for the doctrine of implied repeal in a case where a later Act violates any of the rights sought to be protected. But it is important to have in mind the elementary legal fact that the Human Rights Act will not possess the status of an over-arching constitutional text. It will be subject to the power of express repeal or amendment. Nothing in it alters, or could alter, the supreme power of Parliament to change the law. It will offer *legal*, but not *constitutional*, guarantees of basic rights, including of course freedom of expression: Article 10 of the Convention. (It is obviously yet to be seen how the courts will approach their task of applying Article 10, and its relationship with Article 8 which guarantees the right to private and family life[26]).

Accordingly, while incorporation will be a fact—an achievement—of major legal and social importance, it remains the case that Parliament, paradoxically by the very fact of its own sovereign power, is as I have said incapable of providing any assured constitutional guarantees of fundamental rights.

Now, the common law is logically prior to statute; the supremacy of Parliament, indeed the duty to obey Parliamentary legislation, are creatures of the common law. The very concept of statute *as law* is, ultimately, given by the courts. The common law sets the framework for the status of legislation. Without a sovereign text to which other Acts are subordinate, our constitution is and remains a construct whose nature and content are given by history, convention and the common law. If, then, some areas of human activity ought to receive special protection from State interference, the common law must in the last analysis afford it. It does so by means of a series of presumptions. The content of such presumptions will amount to the *second order* constitutional principles. They will provide that in the area covered individual freedom of action may not be abrogated by Parliament save by express words. This is in large measure the nature of constitutional rights under the common law, at the present stage of its evolution.

For the common law to establish constitutional rights by means of presumptions is characteristic of its method: it gives a new name to an old process. Some such rights are perfectly clear. No one would suggest that any public authority might enjoy the legal power to take a man's life, or to incarcerate him, without the clearest possible statutory words. And the

---

[25] The Government's Bill is going through Parliament; it was published with the White Paper, *Rights Brought Home—The Human Rights Bill* (1997, Cm 3782).

[26] I discuss these issues in "The Limitations of Human Rights", a forthcoming paper to be published in *Public Law*, based on the Gabriele Ganz Public Law Lecture which I gave at Southampton University in 1997.

requirement of express provision has been insisted on in other contexts, such as the compulsory acquisition of a person's land[27] and the denial of access to the Queen's courts.[28] Such protections may be, and often are, referred to as vindications of the rule of law, and there is no clearly elaborated distinction between applications of the rule of law and constitutional rights in the law of England.[29] The problem for both, however, is to set limits.

In particular, the use of discretionary power by government may very plainly override individual rights, and be antipathetic to the rule of law, unless it is controlled according to clear principles well known in advance; and Parliament, the source of such power, again cannot achieve it. There is nothing to prevent the legislature from conferring apparently unfettered authority to act in the field in question, and it has very often done so. The use of such power is limited by the common law: by the *Wednesbury*[30] rule, the requirements of procedural fairness and legitimate expectations, and the *Padfield*[31] rule. All this is elementary enough. The difficulty is to find the *reach* of such a principle as *Wednesbury*, so as to allow the elected government its proper democratic authority. And in relation to constitutional rights, the question will be: what are the areas of a citizen's activity which call for the special protection of a presumption which will not allow its infringement save on the faith of express words used by Parliament?

As other chapters in this volume have suggested,[32] the incorporation of the Convention will make a major contribution to this task of definition or delineation. It will shape and buttress the second order principles. Free speech, very plainly, is one of the rights calling for special protection. However, the presumptions contained in the second order principles will not suffice on their own. The reason is that governmental interference with free expression is almost always done in the exercise of discretionary power. The main statute may be clear enough to pass the presumption's test. It may, for example, authorise the prohibition of broadcast material if the delegated decision-maker concludes that it would be injurious to public feeling, or to national security. In such a case there is no doubt that the power exists to censor, conferred by express provision: it passes the second order test. The

---

[27] *Prest* v. *Secretary of State for Wales* (1983) 81 LGR 193, *per* Lord Denning MR at 198.

[28] *R.* v. *The Lord Chancellor, ex parte Witham* [1997] 2 All ER 779 (Div. Ct.).

[29] There would be if we adopted a *formal* as opposed to *substantive* theory of the rule of law. Potential difficulties with the latter are crisply summarised by Craig, *supra* n. 24, at 22–3. Since I think that the common law is necessarily an ethical construct, and that even a formal concept of the rule of law reflects the moral good of anarchy's rejection, I doubt the validity of the distinction; any theory of the rule of law involves substantive values. But it is too big a subject to go into here.

[30] [1948] 1 KB 223.

[31] [1968] AC 997. I think that the *Padfield* rule is an aspect of the principle of reasonableness—of *Wednesbury*; but this is not consistent with Lord Bridge's reasoning in *Ex parte Hammersmith and Fulham LBC* [1991] 1 AC 521, 597C–D, where it is described as a function of illegality.

[32] See particularly Morris on the question of the political activities of public officials in Ch. 6; Leigh on political libels in Ch. 4; and Warbrick on obscenity in Ch. 9.

real question in such a case will be whether the decision-maker has advanced a sufficient justification for the power's use. His statutory discretion is subject to the court's control on *Wednesbury* and other public law grounds. But the test of rationality is not enough for the protection of free expression. The rule should be that the decision-maker should advance substantial reasons in the public interest why his decision to censor should prevail. As much was recognised by Lord Bridge in the *Brind*[33] case, when he said:

> "But I do not accept that this conclusion [viz. that there is no presumption that a statutory discretionary power must be exercised within European Court of Human Rights limits] means that the courts are powerless to prevent the exercise by the executive of administrative discretions, even when conferred, as in the instant case, in terms which are on their face unlimited, in a way which infringes fundamental human rights. Most of the rights spelled out in terms in the Convention, including the right to freedom of expression, are less than absolute and must in some cases yield to the claims of competing public interests. Thus, article 10(2) of the Convention spells out and categorises the competing public interests by reference to which the right to freedom of expression may have to be curtailed. In exercising the power of judicial review we have neither the advantages nor the disadvantages of any comparable code to which we may refer or by which we are bound. But again, this surely does not mean that in deciding whether the Secretary of State, in the exercise of his discretion, could reasonably impose the restriction he has imposed on the broadcasting organisations, we are not perfectly entitled to start from the premise that any restriction of the right to freedom of expression requires to be justified and that nothing less than an important competing public interest will be sufficient to justify it. the primary judgment as to whether the particular competing public interest justifies the particular restriction imposed falls to be made by the Secretary of State to whom Parliament has entrusted the discretion. But we are entitled to exercise a secondary judgment by asking whether a reasonable Secretary of State, on the material before him, could reasonably make that primary judgment."[34]

Here, I think, we can uncover a requirement for a *third order* constitutional principle. Where the right in question may be potentially infringed by the use of discretionary power granted by statute which itself is cast in express terms, so as to override the presumption contained in the second order principle, the decision-maker must nevertheless offer a compelling public interest justification for the power's use. As Gillian Morris indicated in the previous chapter, this approach is akin to that taken by the European Court of Human Rights in requiring the demonstration of a "pressing social need" if a right such as that of free expression enshrined in Article 10 of the Convention is to be diminished or abrogated.[35]

Here, too, incorporation will provide muscular support to the third order principles. As likely as not the courts will directly adopt the "pressing social

---

[33] [1991] 1 AC 696.
[34] At 748F–749B.
[35] See also the *Sunday Times* case (1979) 2 EHRR 145.

need" test, although the extent to which the Strasbourg jurisprudence will be followed is not clear-cut. Clause 2(1) of the Government's Bill requires the national court to "take into account" the judgments of the European Court of Human Rights and opinions of the Commission, and the White Paper[36] adds in a parenthesis the words "although these will not be binding".

I have referred to first order, second order and third order principles. Between them they crystallise the nature of constitutional government in the United Kingdom. Before returning to Meiklejohn in part three of this chapter, I must say more about them.

First, the common law rules contained in *Wednesbury, Padfield*, the duty of fairness, the absolute prohibition of illegality (in Lord Diplock's sense),[37] and the requirements of legal certainty and equality (a function, for my purpose, of *Wednesbury*: treating like cases alike is demanded by the rule of reason), have also to be seen as *first order* principles, because they constitute a series of necessary conditions for the judicial supervision of all and any public power; none could be abrogated, generally or in any context, without express authority given by main legislation. But neither these principles, nor the other first order principles relating to private individuals or public bodies, could be abandoned save at the price of transforming the British State from an open society subject to the rule of law into a State governed by arbitrary power.

And here lies the true limit at the present time of the doctrine of Parliamentary supremacy, which I have described as a further first order principle. It possesses that status for reasons of history, three hundred years and more. It cannot without revolution inflict any gross curtailment upon the freedoms of the British people; and in that case, it would deny the rule of law. Its sovereign power might now be seen—in contexts other than day-to-day legislation in which the government seeks, with every democratic justification, to enact the policies for which it was elected—not as an absolute; but as a residual right to modify the application of other principles of the Constitution in circumstances of emergency or pressing national importance.

Any such modification, however, would be subjected to the courts' most anxious scrutiny.[38] The difference between the view that Parliamentary sovereignty ought in principle to be curtailed, on grounds that Parliament must be subject to the rule of law and is obliged to satisfy fundamental constitutional rights,[39] and the view that its power, though theoretically absolute,

---

[36] *Supra* n. 25, para. 2.4.

[37] *Council for the Civil Service Unions v. Minister for the Civil Service* [1985] AC 374 at 410F.

[38] To borrow a phrase from Lord Bridge in *Bugdaycay* [1987] AC 514, 531G. See further Ian Loveland's introductory ch., *supra*, at 2–3.

[39] A view I have expressed myself: "Law and Democracy" [1995] *Public Law* 72.

cannot in truth (and without contradicting its own democratic credentials) be exercised so as to abrogate the other principles of our constitution is, perhaps, a difference between *de jure* and *de facto* approaches to the same reality.

The present power of the British Parliament to modify our constitutional arrangements as they are to be found in the first, second and third order principles which I have described may be regarded as akin to the power of amendment of a written constitution, where that is provided for, though it lacks such safeguards as special procedures and qualified majorities; and that is a weakness. On the other hand, having no sovereign document, we are not trammelled by the philosophical slippage between interpretation and the development of principle which seems to me to have agonised the Supreme Court. It is instructive, I think, to see how Lord Keith's reasoning in *Derbyshire County Council* v. *Times Newspapers,*[40] in which the House of Lords denied a right of action in defamation to a local authority complaining of attacks on its governmental competence, was developed, referring both to *Sullivan* (as well as much other authority)[41] and to the European Convention:

> "[After citing earlier authority] These propositions were endorsed by the Supreme Court of the United States in . . . *Sullivan*. . . . While these decisions were related most directly to the provisions of the American Constitution concerned with securing freedom of speech, the public interest considerations which underlaid them are no less valid in this country. What has been described as 'the chilling effect' induced by the threat of civil actions for libel is very important".[42]

And:

> "My Lords, I have reached my conclusion upon the common law of England without finding any need to rely upon the European Convention. My noble and learned friend, Lord Goff of Chieveley, in [*Spycatcher (No. 2)*] expressed the opinion that in the field of freedom of speech there was no difference between English law on the subject and Article 10 of the Convention. I agree, and can only add that I find it satisfactory to be able to conclude that the common law of England is consistent with the obligations assumed by the Crown under the Treaty in this particular field."[43]

IV. CONCLUSION

I return to Meiklejohn and the First Amendment. I have said earlier that I consider that Meiklejohn's view that the free speech principle is a collective, and not an individual, interest is deeply misconceived. I take him as meaning

---

[40] [1991] AC 534.
[41] Ian Loveland discusses and questions the use of this authority *supra* in Ch. 5.
[42] At 548D.
[43] At 551F–G.

that the right of free expression is a servant of the democratic form of government, in particular the ideal of self-determination in which the sovereign people have delegated a part, but not the whole, of their right to govern themselves. The right of free speech ought not to be a function of any particular form of government, and certainly must not be defined as such. It may in practice be largely incapable of fulfilment without democracy; but its virtue is not, or not only, a democratic virtue. Behind it lies the value of free thought, the moral birthright of every person, in whatever polity he has to live.

There is as it happens a provision remaining in the law of England which forbids free thought: it is the Black Rubric, which is one of the instructions appended to the Order for Holy Communion in the Book of Common Prayer. It is in these terms:

> "Whereas it is ordained in this office for the Administration of the Lord's Supper, that the Communicants should receive the same kneeling . . . yet, lest the same kneeling should by any persons, either out of ignorance and infirmity, or out of malice and obstinacy, be misconstrued and depraved: It is here declared, that thereby no Adoration is intended, or ought to be done, either unto the Sacramental Bread or Wine there bodily received, or unto any Corporal Presence of Christ's natural Flesh and Blood . . .".

The Rubric was written by Archbishop Cranmer for his second Prayer Book of 1552. It requires the communicant to kneel; but forbids him to worship the bread and wine as if it were Christ's flesh and blood. It is intended to regulate what happens in his head while he is on his knees. Queen Elizabeth I had the Rubric removed; as Sir Francis Bacon tells us, "[s]he would not make windows into men's souls". But it was restored in the 1662 Prayer Book, and has been the law of the land ever since. Queen Elizabeth, a great sovereign, was of course no democrat. But in this respect at least, she would not demand conformity in her subjects' beliefs. Free speech is ultimately an imperative put upon by us by the destiny of our freedom of thought. It is not a creature of democracy, or of self-government. Very likely it will not flourish without them; but it is our freedom that demands democracy, and not the converse. Here, then, Meiklejohn was wrong. Nor is the American constitution, or any constitution, a *definiens* of the good life. As I have said, no constitution, save one which is anarchic or tyrannical, can be interpreted without appeal to principles that are logically and morally prior to it. Maybe a written text inclines to obscure this truth.

But Man's nature as a free and rational being is not solipsistic. It means nothing save in his relation to others of his kind. Meiklejohn's ideal of the educated citizen reflects it. He serves to point up the necessity that morality is the reconciliation of self and other. But self and other are individuals. Their moral fulfilment is not the suppression, but the expression, of self. The value of the individual gives value to everything else; but the individual whose throne has his fellows at its feet ceases to be an individual; he becomes a thing.

Meiklejohn's views of the First Amendment are thus both a warning and a lesson for the British constitution, and the place it must give to free expression. It is an imperative which is not utilitarian, nor a mere function of a form of government, and so far as he asserted otherwise Meiklejohn was wrong. But it is a necessity for the fulfilment of free individuals living in community, and so far as he asserted that, he was right. It is integral to any form of good government, so that no good government, seeing itself as the trustee and the servant of the people, can deny it save on pain of self-contradiction. In particular, no sovereign Parliament may so deny it. In the British State, we must read Meiklejohn's lesson free of the First Amendment's words which gave rise to it. Doing so, the first order principles of our constitution are (as regards free speech) conformable with one another, and the second and third order principles will be in gear with them, so as to serve the freedom of the individual and the tranquillity of the State.

In America the sovereign text, here the sovereign legislature, have by force of history come to possess an iconic quality. But both are servants, not masters. The force of history is dynamic, not static. The respect which is its due demands that each generation think for itself, affirm and refine the ideals of freedom and democracy which have been bequeathed to us. We must not forget that majorities may be tyrannous; that fashionable ideas may be false; that every individual is an end not a means; that freedom rests in the alchemy of self-respect and mutual co-operation. It is the task of succeeding ages to reconcile collective authority with individual rights, and to transform these notions into a constitutional law that is both comfortable and challenging.

8

Content Neutrality

DAVID FELDMAN*

I. INTRODUCTION

Should the legal systems of the UK adopt a fundamental principle that governmental restrictions on free speech are permissible only to the extent that they do not discriminate between speeches by reference to content? The First Amendment jurisprudence of the USA has such a doctrine, providing (along with other doctrines) extensive constitutional protection for freedom of speech and the press, and thereby disabling governmental action against a wide range of expressive activities. The Human Rights Act 1998, which introduces the principles of the European Convention on Human Rights to the domestic legal systems of the UK, is unlikely to have that effect. The jurisprudence of the European Court and Commission of Human Rights allows some content-based restrictions on speech so long as they fall within the justifications for interfering with expression set out in Article 10(2) of the Convention.[1] While domestic courts are not bound by ECHR jurisprudence under the 1998 Act, it is likely to be highly persuasive. Would a departure from it in the direction of a more rigid content-neutrality rule be desirable?

This chapter assumes that one should always treat with suspicion controls on speech which are not neutral as to content. Nevertheless, it argues that the UK would be unwise to adopt an absolute rule prohibiting non-neutral interferences with expression, for three reasons. First, such a rule is too rooted in the USA's distinctive political and constitutional ethos to be readily transplantable to the UK. Secondly, the rule fails to give sufficient weight to the full range of situations and constraints to which a conscientious legislator can properly have regard. Thirdly, it does not sufficiently distinguish

* I am very grateful to many people who have influenced my thinking on this subject: Christopher McCrudden, whose criticism of my earlier work encouraged me to think more carefully about the subject; Jane Hanna, Laurence Lustgarten, Joseph Magnet and Frederick Schauer for thought-provoking discussions; Andrew Halpin for his constructive comments on a draft of the ch.; those who attended the conference in 1996 which gave rise to this vol.; participants in postgraduate seminars on comparative human rights in the University of Oxford in 1997; and students in the University of Birmingham who have tolerated my preoccupations and challenged my assumptions. Few (if any) of them agree with me, and none is responsible for what follows.

1 See *Jersild* v. *Denmark* (1994), Series A, No 298, Eur Ct HR.

between four different senses of "content", each of which has weight which may vary in different contexts: the subjects chosen to speak about; narrative or argumentative thread and factual assertions; the viewpoint advanced; and the form of the expression.

The first substantive section of the chapter argues that the high degree of protection which the First Amendment jurisprudence affords to speech is a resolution of political, cultural and philosophical tensions which are special to the USA and are not replicated in the UK. It argues that a notion rooted in a distinctively American view of the social compact should be treated with reserve by societies with different histories, traditions and values. In particular, the Americans' characteristically profound suspicion of government and the whole-hearted belief in the socially beneficial effects of unfettered economic freedom and individual endeavour have never dominated UK politics (except perhaps among certain groups during the period of the Thatcher governments, 1979–90). These distinctively American traits will be shown to have generated a model of the role of the state which precludes government and courts from offering protection against certain significant forms of social and personal harm. While it would go too far to suggest that the First Amendment provides blanket protection for racist speech and action,[2] it does not follow that all relevant interests and harms are adequately recognised under First Amendment jurisprudence.

The second section illustrates this by examining the American content-neutrality rule, particularly in the context of racist speech. It concentrates on the controversial decision of the Supreme Court in *RAV* v. *City of St. Paul, Minnesota*,[3] and argues that American First Amendment jurisprudence has been insufficiently sophisticated in its analysis of content-neutrality, in that it does not distinguish between the four different elements of the content of speech noted above. As a result, the content-neutrality requirement is incoherent. It is unsatisfactory even in the conditions prevailing in the USA, and would not fit the very different system of values which dominates in the UK. This does not mean that the approach to such issues adopted in the UK is wholly satisfactory. I have argued elsewhere that our law governing the regulation of public order, for example, is profoundly unsatisfactory, combining as it does an historical reluctance to define speakers' rights (which may change when the Human Rights Act 1998 comes into force), very wide and weakly structured official discretion, and a lack of effective accountability for the way that discretion is exercised.[4] However, a constitutional content-neutrality requirement would do little to improve the position, since the rel-

---

[2]   See I. Loveland, "The Criminalisation of Racist Violence", in I. Loveland (ed.), *A Special Relationship? American Influences on Public Law in the UK* (Oxford, 1995).

[3]   (1992) 112 S Ct. 2538; 120 L Ed. 2d. 305.

[4]   See e.g. D. Feldman, "Protest and Tolerance: Legal Values and the Control of Public-Order Policing", in R. Cohen-Almagor (ed.), *Liberal Democracy and the Limits of Tolerance* (Ann Arbor, Mich., 1998).

evant rules (such as they are) already take a broadly consequentialist and content-neutral form.[5] As Dr Christopher McCrudden has written in an illuminating phrase, while content-neutrality could be regarded as "a useful barium meal (helping us to identify previously unnoticed elements in one's own jurisdiction's approach), it is a doubtful litmus test for the acceptability of our approach".[6]

The third section examines the implications of those arguments about content-neutrality for the scope of rights generally and free-speech rights in particular. It argues that the strength of claims to rights varies according to the range and value of the social as well as individual interests which the exercise of a right serves, and that communal interests can justify governmental action to restrict speech on the basis of non-neutral rules if that is demonstrably important in order to maintain the mutual respect and social responsibility on which a functioning democracy (at least in the UK's tradition) depends.

II. THE DESCRIPTIVE AND NORMATIVE TENSIONS UNDERLYING FIRST AMENDMENT JURISPRUDENCE

Despite the famously absolutist rhetoric of Mr Justice Hugo Black, the protection which judges offer to expression under the First Amendment to the Constitution of the USA has always been qualified to some extent. Some categories of expression were, and to some extent remain, privileged. For example, attempts to regulate political expression are permissible only if the expression gives rise to a clear and present danger of national harm, and such regulation is subjected to close scrutiny by the judges. There are kinds of expressive action (sometimes called "speech-plus") which, if political in intent, attract judicial protection similar to that offered to pure speech. Conversely, some categories of speech, despite being expressive, have traditionally been regarded as having insufficient social value to justify such protection. The categories of "fighting words", untruths, child pornography and obscene publications which lack redeeming social value have accordingly attracted relatively little protection.

Yet free speech as a constitutional value has been idealised in the USA. This is partly because of trust in the outcome of a trade in ideas between individuals, and the consequential need to protect individual expression against government interference. Even people whose expression falls in the category of fighting words or aggressive action are treated as being entitled

---

[5] See D. Feldman, *Civil Liberties and Human Rights in England and Wales* (Oxford, 1993), 812–13.

[6] C. McCrudden, "Freedom of Speech and Racial Equality", in P. Birks (ed.), *Pressing Problems in the Law Volume 1: Criminal Justice and Human Rights* (Oxford, 1995), at 129. The paper includes a critique of the passage in Feldman, *Civil Liberties and Human Rights*.

to some protection from the judges under the First Amendment. In particular, they have long benefited from the due-process requirement that legal restrictions on expression must be formulated in language which is not too vague, and from the rule against over-breadth, a requirement of balance or proportionality which forbids restrictions on rights which go beyond what is needed to advance a compelling state interest. The First Amendment is so much a part of America's self-image, so central to Americans' perceptions of their commitment to ideals of tolerance and liberal democracy, that it resonates deeply and symbolically in the culture and society of the United States. It is part of a particular attitude to democracy, which presupposes that citizens are "courageous, self-reliant men, with confidence in the power of free and fearless reasoning applied through the processes of popular government".[7] People who have this faith in the intellectual and moral capacity of citizens and governments see little reason to impose controls on expression beyond what is needed to protect people who are known to be currently incapable of participating as an informed and rational trader in the market-place of ideas. However, we would do well to maintain a healthy scepticism in the face of exhortations to subscribe to a blind faith in the capacity of an heroic citizenry and the market-place of ideas to weed out the bad ideas and allow only the good to flourish. Such a capacity depends on prevailing social conditions, and is thus subject to geographical and temporal change. In any case, markets are unreliable guides to the value of ideas.[8] Furthermore, as Professor Schauer has argued,[9] where a society adheres to an ideal of free speech to the point where it becomes an ideology (by which he means "a prevailing idea existing within an environment in which adherence to the idea is more or less required, and challenge to the idea is more or less discouraged"[10]) it may become difficult to subject free speech to the kind of critical evaluation which the commitment to free speech itself requires.

The highly protective attitude to speech under the First Amendment attempts to hold in balance several tensions which run through twentieth-century First Amendment jurisprudence, reflecting the condition of American society, and to generate prescriptive norms which (like American society) pull in different directions. There are four of these tensions, which are inter-related.

First, American society has been increasingly challenged to maintain a national identity in the face of increasing recognition of cultural heterogeneity. There is a tension between pressure towards assimilation and demands for respect for group pluralism. This presents particular problems

---

[7] *Whitney* v. *California* (1927) 274 US 357 at 377 *per* Brandeis J, in a concurrence which, as H. Abraham and B. Perry, *Freedom and the Court: Civil Rights and Liberties in the United States* (6th edn., New York, 1994), 161, point out, "in effect, reads like a dissent".

[8] See T. Campbell, "Rationales for Freedom of Communication" in T. Campbell and W. Sadurski (eds.), *Freedom of Communication* (London, 1994), at 24–5.

[9] F. Schauer, "The First Amendment as Ideology" (1992) 33 *William and Mary LR* 853.

[10] *Ibid.*, at 855.

in the USA, which faces the task of nation-building in a society formed largely of immigrants from many different places. The tension has presented itself in its starkest form in the flag-saluting and flag-burning cases: demanding respect from all for a symbol of nationhood is important in establishing the existence of the nation. While celebrating difference in some areas (notably in the impact of religious diversity[11]), the Supreme Court has tended to adopt an individualist approach, protecting freedom of individual expression rather than the sensitivities of groups or communities at whom expression is directed. There is a brand of pluralism which demands that members of ethnic or cultural groups should be treated with respect. This approach led Lord Scarman, in *R. v. Lemon*,[12] to advocate the extension of criminal liability for blasphemy to scurrilous attacks on any set of religious beliefs (not only those of the established church). It is an increasingly prevalent European attitude to setting the bounds of free speech in a multicultural society. For example, the recent *Report: Independent Review of Parades and Marches 1997*[13] stressed the importance of understanding and accommodating the very different aspirations of various parts of the divided community of Northern Ireland when developing laws and practices to avoid conflict during the "marching season". However, this consideration cut no ice with the Supreme Court in *Cantwell* v. *Connecticut*,[14] where (as Professor Robert Post has pointed out) the focus was on the freedom of the individual Jehovah's Witness to express religious beliefs rather than on the right of the Catholic addressees of the expression to be free from it. For the Court, Post argues, respect for diversity involves protecting the ability of individuals to create or opt for membership of particular religious or other communities, rather than protecting those who consider themselves to be inescapably members of pre-existing communities.[15] This is important, because (as the *Skokie* cases[16] demonstrated) it makes it very difficult for a court or legislature to justify giving special protection to particularly vulnerable or threatened communities.[17] The desire to protect individual freedom of speech clashes with the search for equal respect for groups. In the United States, suggests Professor Post, equality is seen as an important collectivist value in relation to constitutional rights such as that to equal protection of the laws, as to which:

[11] *Cantwell* v. *Connecticut* (1940) 310 US 296; *Wisconsin* v. *Yoder* (1972) 406 US 205.
[12] [1979] AC 617, HL.
[13] Stationery Office, Belfast, 1997 (Chairman: Dr. Peter North).
[14] (1940)310 US 296.
[15] R. Post, *Constitutional Domains: Democracy, Community, Management* (Cambridge, Mass., 1995), 104–5.
[16] See *National Socialist Party* v. *Village of Skokie* (1977) 432 US 43; *National Socialist Party* v. *Village of Skokie* (1977) 434 US 1327; *Collin* v. *Smith* (1978) 578 F 2d. 1197, 7th Cir., stay denied (1978) 436 US 953; certiorari denied (1978) 439 US 916.
[17] As Post demonstrates, n. 15 above, 108–16, the same reluctance to permit action to protect the dignity of women (another group in plural society) hampers attempts to make arguments for control of non-obscene pornography compatible with the First Amendment.

"the federal government has for forty years aggressively sought to inculcate particular national values of equality. But legal imposition of these values acquires democratic legitimacy precisely because the First Amendment has already established an arena of public discourse within which they can be freedly embraced or rejected."[18]

This may be overstating the case. It is true that democratic processes legitimise legislation such as Title VII of the Civil Rights Act, but it is far from clear that they legitimise the judicial interpretation of the "equal protection" clause in the Fourteenth Amendment which held sway in the school desegregation cases. Nevertheless, Post argues that the First Amendment jurisprudence is distinctively and properly based on individual autonomy rather than protection for communal values, for reasons which the other areas of tension in First Amendment jurisprudence help to make clear.

Secondly, while the power of the First Amendment is based in significant part on the contribution it makes to democratic political discourse, there is a tension between individual autonomy and collectivism in models of democracy. Professor Alexander Meiklejohn presupposed a model of political discourse in which citizens had to identify policy objectives and decide how best to achieve them.[19] The institutions and procedures for doing this were assumed to be in place, and constraints on free speech could be justified in order to permit the decision-making process to function efficiently. Professor Post has shown how this leads to the incoherent notion of the "public forum", in which speech is specially protected within limits set by reference to what he describes as a "managerial" decision-making structure.[20] We in the UK are no strangers to the incursion of managerialism into the structures of public discourse: the Public Order Act 1986, as amended, allocates high levels of discretion to public authorities (particularly the police) to control assemblies, processions and other expressive public behaviour in the pursuit of public order.

Even more significantly for present purposes, Post's meticulous analysis of Meiklejohn's approach has demonstrated how Meiklejohn's freedom of speech theory is designed to safeguard the collective decision-making process, rather than individual autonomy. However, individual autonomy is essential to the notion of participative democracy. Without it, the outcomes of the deliberative process lack legitimacy. The ideal of national or local *self-government* by a community requires, at the very least, that people choose to accept the process as conferring authority on decisions, and directly or by way of representatives exercise choice between views expressed in the forum

---

[18] n. 15 above, 278.

[19] A. Meiklejohn, *Free Speech and its Relation to Self-Government* (New York, 1946) and *Political Freedom: The Constitutional Powers of the People* (New York, 1965). See the critiques by W. J Brennan, "The Supreme Court and the Meiklejohn interpretation of the First Amendment" (1965) 79 *Harvard LR* 1, and by Sir John Laws in Ch. 7 of this volume.

[20] Post, n. 15 above, ch. 6.

for political discourse.[21] This presupposes that freedom of political speech will be theorised on the basis of individual autonomy most of the time. Collective self-determination is a problematic goal, since (as J. S. Mill saw clearly) in a majoritarian democracy it amounts to domination of the individual citizen by other citizens in a way which may be entirely incompatible with individual autonomy. Yet since democratic legitimacy requires and presupposes individual autonomy, Professor Post concludes that collectivist or communitarian notions of free speech should be employed "when it is truly necessary to sustain the enterprise of self-governance, or when we need standards to govern the regulation of speech of public functionaries. But these circumstances should be the exception rather than the rule. . . ."[22] This makes it hard to reconcile free-speech rights, particularly in respect of political speech, with legal protection for the sensitivities of diverse cultures.

Thirdly, there is a tension between the idea of communal *self*-government and the way in which free speech theory conceives of the position of governments. In what Professor Lee Bollinger has described as the "fortress model" of the First Amendment, the threat to free speech comes from overmighty government, which has the capacity by regulating speech to subvert both individual self-fulfilment and the foundations of the democratic process from which government draws its legitimacy.[23] It has been particularly influential in the development of the requirement of content- or viewpoint-neutrality and its limitations,[24] of which more will be said shortly. However, this postulated opposition between government and the community, which ill fits the model of democratic self-governance, also obscures the demonstrable, empirical truth that governmental interference with speech in America in this century has usually been a response to a popular will for such interference. As J. S. Mill warned, the main threat to freedom of thought and speech in the Anglo-American tradition has usually come from intolerant fellow-citizens, not big government. Joseph McCarthy's anti-Communist crusade was an expression of popular opinion, not something imposed on the general population by government. Free speech theory, therefore, should be a means of protecting speech against interference by intolerant groups (majorities and influential minorities), individuals and corporations within society, as much as against regulation by intolerant governments. Indeed, it should be recognised that government may play a

[21] See P. Kahn, *Legitimacy and History: Self-Government in American Constitutional Theory* (New Haven, Conn., 1992).

[22] N. 15 above, 289.

[23] L. Bollinger, *The Tolerant Society: Freedom of Speech and Extremist Speech in America* (Oxford and New York, 1986).

[24] In *RAV* v. *City of St. Paul, Minnesota* (1992) 120 L. Ed. 2d. 305 at 320, the majority limits its interpretation of the First Amendment as prohibiting content discrimination because; "[t]he rationale of the general prohibition . . . is that the content discrimination 'rais[es] the specter that the Government may effectively drive certain ideas or viewpoints from the marketplace,' *Simon & Schuster*, . . . 116 L Ed. 2d. 476 . . . But content discrimination among various instances of a class of proscribable speech often does not pose this threat".

positive role in helping to maintain the conditions for civil co-existence. Those conditions include mutual respect, or at least forbearance, between those who adhere to divergent cultural traditions. This is only weakly institutionalised in First Amendment case law, with its predominantly individualistic, rather than communitarian, attitude to speech.

Fourthly, there is a tension between (a) a process which seems to respect individual autonomy, and (b) the outcomes which people regard as appropriate. Evaluating the outcomes produced by rules and principles can contribute to the evaluation of the rules and principles themselves. Central to Professor Rawls's great book *A Theory of Justice*[25] is the idea that seeking to bring intuitions about acceptable principles and intuitions about acceptable outcomes into a "reflective equilibrium" is a valuable method of moral reasoning. There is, within First Amendment jurisprudence, a place for outcomes, but the "clear and present danger" test effectively limits regulation of speech unless there is an imminent threat of serious damage to an important governmental interest (such as state security or public order), or of real harm to an identifiable individual. Those threats, or harms, which count for this purpose are established by reference to a theory of harm similar to that espoused by J. S. Mill and H. L. A. Hart. There is little room, if any, for government to regulate speech to forestall threats of ideological harm or group injuries.

Such harm is real and appreciable, but the First Amendment is blind to it. This causes judges who simply accept the established categories of harm to individuals and the state to be unhappy, sometimes, at the results of their decisions. Professor Bollinger draws attention to the discomfort which judges in the *Skokie* case expressed with regard to the outcome. There is a tendency in the First Amendment to allow general principles free rein without regard to the desirability or otherwise of the outcomes. Such an approach ultimately threatens free speech rights by bringing them into disrepute. There is a danger that the individualism of the 1930s has put the First Amendment into a strait-jacket which makes it hard to adapt to the needs of modern (or post-modern) social conditions and theories of justice.

The distinctive positions adopted by the Justices of the US Supreme Court in relation to these tensions are illustrated by their views of content-neutrality, with which the next section is concerned.

III. TYPES OF CONTENT-NEUTRALITY AND THE US SUPREME COURT

It has long been established in several contexts in US constitutional law that governmental regulation of protected speech would not be tolerated unless it was "content-neutral". For example, the idea that the state should not

---

[25]   (Oxford, 1972).

discriminate between the expression of different points of view, particularly in relation to politics, underpinned the decision to allow a march by Nazi sympathisers through a Jewish area in the Skokie case, *Collin* v. *Smith*.[26] Content-neutrality is a cluster concept. It comprises at least four elements, which need to be unpacked. First, there is the idea that the state should not discriminate between speakers or speeches on the basis of the topic with which the expression is concerned. This can be justified by reference to autonomy, democracy, market-place-of-ideas and truth theories of free speech. Curiously, there is a move towards making the desirability of free speech itself a no-go area for discussion,[27] but this has not yet been supported by the courts. Nevertheless, there is a recognition that some subjects (particularly expression on political and governmental matters) merit particularly strong protection, not least because of their importance to keeping a check on Professor Bollinger's "fortress state". Secondly, at a more concrete level there is the principle that controls should not discriminate on the basis of the substantive content of the expression so far as it is made up by the factual claims or narrative content of the expression. Again, this freedom can be justified by reference to autonomy, democracy, market-place and truth theories of speech, but is sometimes treated lightly by the Supreme Court. Most obviously, obscenity and false statements have attracted reduced levels of protection against regulation because of their substantive content. Thirdly, there is a claim that the state should be neutral as between the many forms or modes of expression. Sometimes this claim is given considerable weight, not least because it is not always possible to separate the form of expression from its substantive content. Vigorous and offensive verbal or non-verbal expression may be protected as political speech (most famously in *Cohen* v. *California*,[28] where a jacket carrying the words "Fuck the Draft" was protected, and in cases of symbolic speech such as the flag-burning case, *Texas* v. *Johnson*[29]). On the other hand, regulation by reference to the time, place and manner of speech is usually permissible, and words which are purely aggressive in meaning, so-called "fighting words", are proscribable. This is usually said to be because fighting words do not convey ideas, but (as will be discussed further below) it is probably better to regard them as proscribable because their substantive content is anti-social and aggressive, as is the form in which they are conveyed. Fourthly, it can be argued that the state should not be permitted to discriminate between expressive acts in protected categories by reference to the viewpoint which the speaker adopted in respect of the matter in question. This principle, particularly in relation to political speech, is essential to the maintenance of a strong democracy.

---

[26] (1978) 578 F 2d. 1197.
[27] See Schauer, n. 9 above, at 859 ff.
[28] (1971) 403 US 15.
[29] (1989) 109 S Ct. 2533.

The idea that content-neutrality should be a fundamental principle of free-speech jurisprudence thus encompasses a range of different claims to state neutrality with regard to speech. Underlying them are a number of competing values. They emerge clearly from the earlier discussion of the tensions in American First Amendment jurisprudence, and include in particular the tension between the desirability of free expression with the desirability of taking steps to secure so far as possible social structures in which all citizens feel equally respected by the state, so that they have as much right to their views and values as those who disagree with or despise them. A free market-place of ideas needs careful management to prevent abuse of power by those who can apply money or physical force to demean or drive out others. The US Supreme Court has been slow to recognise the deleterious effect which allowing the market to be dominated by money or power has on free speech. The generally individualist ethic underpinning First Amendment jurisprudence is not conducive to market regulation.[30] *RAV* v. *City of St. Paul, Minnesota*[31] provides an interesting case-study of the way in which the Court deals with the different kinds of neutrality outlined above, and how the Court's treatment of neutrality affects outcomes for the people involved.

RAV v. *City of St. Paul, Minnesota*

In *RAV*, five members of the US Supreme Court held that a rule restricting an interest protected by the First Amendment would be unconstitutional if the rule distinguished between permissible and impermissible expression by reference to the content of the expression. The facts alleged in *RAV* were depressingly simple and familiar. A number of youths had allegedly burned a crude cross (made out of chair-legs taped together) within the fenced front-yard of a black family in St. Paul, Minnesota. Cruciform pyromania invokes the potent symbolism of the racism of the Ku Klux Klan. The city of St. Paul had an ordinance specially constructed to combat such activity, the Bias-Motivated Crime Ordinance of 1990, which provided:

> "Whoever places on public or private property a symbol, object, appellation, characterization or graffiti, including, but not limited to, a burning cross or Nazi swastika, which one knows or has reasonable grounds to know arouses anger, alarm or resentment in others on the basis of race, color, creed, religion or gender commits disorderly conduct and shall be guilty of a misdemeanour."[32]

The youth RAV was charged with (*inter alia*) a misdemeanour under the Ordinance. At trial, he moved to dismiss this count, arguing that it was

---

[30] See F. Schauer, "The Political Incidence of the Free Speech Principle" (1993) 64 *University of Colorado LR* 935 especially at 949 ff.

[31] (1992) 120 L. Ed. 2d. 305.

[32] St. Paul, Minnesota, Legislative Code § 292.02.

invalid under the First Amendment because it was (a) overbroad, and (b) impermissibly content-based. The trial court agreed, but on appeal the Minnesota Supreme Court reversed the decision, interpreting the Ordinance as applying only to "fighting words" which, as established by the US Supreme Court in *Chaplinsky* v. *New Hampshire*,[33] are not entitled to full First Amendment protection. The US Supreme Court granted certiorari, and reversed the decision unanimously, but on sharply divergent grounds. A bare majority held that the Ordinance was impermissibly content-based. The other four Justices disagreed, but reached the same result because they considered (unlike the majority) that the Ordinance was overbroad:

> "The mere fact that expressive activity causes hurt feelings, offense, or resentment does not render the expression unprotected. . . . Although the ordinance reaches conduct that is unprotected, it also makes criminal expressive conduct that causes only hurt feelings, offense, or resentment, and is protected by the First Amendment. . . . The ordinance is therefore fatally overbroad and invalid on its face."[34]

Scalia J delivered the majority opinion, in which Rehnquist CJ and Kennedy, Souter and Thomas JJ concurred. They used the notion of content-neutrality to rationalise previous decisions under the First Amendment in a new and controversial way. Scalia J argued that the content-neutrality requirement made it unacceptable to distinguish between categories of fully protected and unprotected speech. Any speech was protected, but might be restricted by reference to a clear and present danger, or regulated to advance a compelling state interest in ways which were within the powers of the governmental agency concerned. Categories of speech such as obscenity, defamation and "fighting words" were not, as had previously been thought, wholly outside the protection of the First Amendment. The defamatory or obscene content of speech was constitutionally proscribable. In the case of "fighting words", the exclusion of First Amendment protection could be ascribed to "a 'non-speech' element of communication".[35] The Court had long recognised the legitimacy of "time, place, or manner" restrictions on speech, where the restrictions were not imposed by reference to the content of the speech. "Fighting words" restrictions were constitutionally acceptable because they were of the "time, place, or manner" kind. Yet such words (or actions) still had the expressive quality of speech, and that is entitled to First Amendment protection. "Our cases surely do not establish the proposition that the First Amendment imposes no obstacle whatsoever to regulation of particular instances of such proscribable expression, so that the courts 'may regulate them freely'."[36]

---

[33] (1942) 315 US 568.
[34] 120 L Ed. 2d. at 338–9, White J, with whom Blackmun, O'Connor and Stevens JJ joined.
[35] 120 L Ed. 2d. at 319.
[36] *Ibid.*, at 318, quoting from the opinion of White J.

According to the majority, it was constitutionally impermissible to regulate even "fighting words" in a way which discriminated between speeches or speakers on the ground of the content of the speech. "The government may not regulate use based on hostility—or favoritism—towards the underlying message expressed."[37] Such regulation is "presumptively invalid", although it may be justified by the special risk of fear of violence and consequent disruption following from particular fighting words (e.g. those directed against the President), or an enhanced risk of fraud or other criminal activity from allowing unbridled speech in a particular setting or profession.[38] Since the Ordinance purported to criminalise "fighting words" only if the distress caused was "on the basis of race, color, creed, religion or gender", it attempted to use the law to express hostility towards offensive speech of that kind only. This was unconstitutional: "[t]he politicians of St. Paul are entitled to express that hostility — but not through the means of imposing unique limitations upon speakers who (however benightedly) disagree."[39]

This reasoning makes it impossible to control generally, by law, expressions of repulsive political views on the ground of their repulsiveness alone, or to adopt regulations which have the effect of restricting the expression of one view on a matter more than another. It is at least potentially true to the heroic belief in the market-place of ideas, and the capacity of free citizens to choose the best of those on offer, but it does not recognise the difference between the various elements of content-neutrality identified above. It is proper to be suspicious of attempts to interfere with First-Amendment rights on the strength of the subject-matter dealt with by the speaker. Such restrictions can impoverish public debate. But they do so only if the speech in question contributes to that debate. Three Justices (White, Blackmun and O'Connor JJ) seem to have considered that some categories of expression, including child pornography and obscenity, do not contribute to public discourse in any useful way, and therefore could be regulated on account of their evil content.[40] As the Court had held in *Chaplinski* v. *New Hampshire*[41] they "are no essential part of any exposition of ideas, and are of such slight social value as a step to truth that any benefit that may be derived from them is clearly outweighed by the social interest in order and morality".

This judgment about the social value of expression depends on an evaluation of one particular aspect of the content of that expression, namely its narrative content. A similar argument could be made in respect of defama-

---

[37] 120 L Ed. 2d. at 320.
[38] 120 L Ed. 2d. at 321.
[39] *Ibid.*, at 326.
[40] 120 L Ed. 2d. at 315, *per* White J, joined by Blackmun and O'Connor JJ, citing *New York* v. *Ferber* (1982) 458 US 747 at 763.
[41] *Chaplinsky* v. *New Hampshire* (1942) 315 US 568 at 571–2.

tion, which is controllable partly because of the limited social value of its narrative or factual assertions and partly because of its impact on the victim. However, this ought to lead to an approach to regulation which pays close attention to the contribution which speech makes to the core values of freedom of expression (including democratic discourse, the pursuit of truth, and personal identification with values or causes[42]) in the context in which the speech is made. It is evident that this requires legislators and regulators to pay careful attention to the content of the speech, in the sense of narrative and factual assertions. To speak of controls of this sort being content-neutral is nonsense. The more extensively regulation would intrude on speech which, given its content and context, contributes to the core values of freedom of expression, the more difficult it is to justify allowing the state to interfere with expression on the basis of its own judgement as to what is essential to the exposition of ideas, or what ideas are valuable.

For example, when one looks at the category of fighting words it becomes clear that the conditions and context for the speech, and sometimes even the manner of the exposition, cannot always be separated from the views or claims expressed. It cannot be said that fighting words are devoid of any message, or that controls on fighting words are directed to a "non-speech" element in the communication. The contentious element in both non-proscribable symbolic or "speech-plus" expression such as flag-burning and proscribable fighting words is the the manner in which the message is expressed, which has symbolic and rhetorical force which is inseparable from the message. Messages have qualities of both meaning and forcefulness which influence their reception. Those qualities are affected by factors such as argumentative persuasiveness, rhetorical force, historical and symbolic resonance, and the communicative traditions through which the message is transmitted. All these form part of the message, and cannot be separated from it or from each other. As Mr Rabinder Singh has written of another Supreme Court decision, *Clark* v. *Community for Creative Non-Violence*[43]:

> "the Court makes the assumption that one can detach 'the' information being transmitted from the particular channel chosen by the speaker herself or himself. This assumption is contradicted not only by the evidence of socio-linguistics,[44] but also by the Court's acknowledgment, on an earlier occasion, that the medium is often the message: '. . . much linguistic expression serves a dual communicative function: it conveys not only ideas capable of relatively precise, detached exposition, but otherwise inexplicable emotions as well'."[45]

[42] See Campbell, n. 9 above; J. Raz, "Free Expression and Personal Identification", in W. J. Waluchow (ed.), *Free Expression: Essays in Law and Philosophy* (Oxford, 1994), ch. 1.
[43] (1984) 468 US 288.
[44] H. Tajfel and C. Fraser (eds.), *Introducing Social Psychology* (Harmondsworth, 1978), ch. 5.
[45] Rabinder Singh, *The Future of Human Rights in the United Kindom: Essays on Law and Practice* (Oxford, 1997), 69–70, quoting Harlan J in *Cohen* v. *California* (1971) 403 US 15 at 26.

An argument about relationships between races published in the language appropriate to a scholarly paper is a different message, not merely different in form, from that expressed by RAV burning his crudely constructed cross outside the home of a black family. Any attempt to categorise kinds of speech inevitably turns on some aspect of the content of the speech.

Would a consequentialist approach work better than categorising speech? The majority in *RAV* v. *City of St. Paul* argued that speech may be regulated because of the harmful consequences of its content. An Ordinance could ban outdoor fires, and if a flag-burner were prosecuted under it the Ordinance would not violate the content-neutrality requirement. The "non-speech" element in fighting words could be regulated, although the "speech" element could not.[46] Control of obscene publications was said to be justifiable because of their harmful consequences, rather than because of their intrinsic evil or social value.

This is attractive to some extent. It helps to explain why we are inclined to accept the legitimacy of the clear-and-present-danger and compelling-state-interest tests for the constitutionality of interference with speech. It also explains why someone who shouts "Fire!" in a crowded theatre where there is really no fire can be liable to those who are injured in the rush for the exit. Yet in the end it does not offer a convincing global principle, because sometimes (perhaps often) it is either superficial or disengenuous to distinguish between content and consequences of these kinds of speech. The person shouting "Fire!" in the theatre can be made liable because of the foreseeable consequence of people hearing the factual assertion which formed the substance of the speech, in the situation in which it was asserted. Fighting words are likewise calculated to provoke fear and violence. One cannot sever the link between the content of the speech, the context in which it takes place and the social dangers to which it is intrinsically likely to give rise.

The majority concentrated on content-neutrality, in the sense of the tendency of an ordinance to favour one viewpoint over another, while ignoring the other aspects of the content of speech (subject-matter, factual or narrative content, and manner of expression) which are sometimes inextricably linked to the content. Although White, Blackmun and O'Connor JJ were sympathetic to the social and historical context, their category-based approach to identifying unprotected speech seems not to be a very sensitive instrument for taking account of it. Nevertheless, they pointed out, along with Stevens J, that one very powerful reason for excluding fighting words from First Amendment protection was that such words are likely to have a special impact on groups which "have historically been subjected to discrimination".[47] In other words, even so far as it can be said to be genuinely consequentialist, the approach of the majority in *RAV* does nothing to

[46]   120 L Ed. 2d. at 319.
[47]   *Ibid.*, at 334.

improve the weakness of First Amendment jurisprudence in taking account of certain socially important social interests and values. In particular, as seen earlier, it has systematically under-valued non-material and collective group interests.[48] Although the Court accepted that the state has a compelling interest in protecting the rights of members of historically disempowered groups, the majority held that compelling state interest to be subject to a content-neutrality requirement in which the different elements in the content of speech, and the importance of context, were poorly understood.

The City of St. Paul and Stevens J had a clearer view of, and would have given greater weight to, the immediate context. The argument for St. Paul asserted:

"the 'content' of the 'expressive conduct'. . . is no less than the first step in an act of racial violence. It was and unfortunately still is the equivalent of [the] waving of a knife before the thrust, the pointing of a gun before it is fired, the lighting of the match before the arson, the hanging of the noose before the lynching. It is not a political statement, or even a cowardly statement of hatred. It is the first step in an act of assault. It can be no more protected than holding a gun to a victim['s] head."[49]

Stevens J accepted that a message was being communicated, but denied it much social value:

"The cross-burning in this case—directed as it was to a single African-American family trapped in their home—was nothing more than a crude form of physical intimidation. That this cross[-]burning sends a message of racial hostility does not automatically endow it with complete constitutional protection."[50]

Stevens J also accepted that the Ordinance interfered with the youth's message, but denied that it did so in a way which discriminated by reference to viewpoint, since opponents of racism were subject to precisely the same restrictions as were its proponents[51]:

"In a battle between advocates of tolerance and advocates of intolerance, the ordinance does not prevent either side from hurling fighting words at the other on the basis of their conflicting ideas, but it does bar *both* sides from hurling such words on the basis of the target's 'race, color, creed, religion or gender. . . .' It does not, therefore, favor one side of any debate."[52]

---

[48] In *Beauharnais* v. *Illinois* (1951) 343 US 250 the Sup. Ct. held that speech calculated to hold up ethnic or religious groups to "contempt, derision, or obloquy" was unprotected by the First Amendment. However, that decision proceeded on the basis that such speech was a form of libel, and that libel fell outside First Amendment protection, whereas it is now clear from *Philadelphia Newspapers, Inc.* v. *Hepps* (1986) 475 US 767 that it does not. See Post, n. 15 above, at 113.

[49] Quoted by Stevens J, 120 L Ed. 2d. at 350, n. 8.

[50] *Ibid.*, at 350.

[51] *Ibid.*, at 350–1.

[52] *Ibid.*, at 352.

The rule against threats of violence in race-related debate was directed to the factual and narrative content of speech (the violent threat), in a context (racial disharmony) in which such threats resonated historically and socially in ways which were particularly damaging to the dignity and sense of worth of those attacked. The Ordinance did not embody viewpoint-based discrimination merely because the creed to which protagonists of one point of view adhere made them more likely than their opponents to resort to violence in word or deed. Were it otherwise, it would often allow people who are prepared to use violent but expressive behaviour to dictate the shape of the law governing violence.

Such considerations call for a contextual approach to First Amendment adjudication. Ultimately, however, as Stevens J appreciated, real contextual flexibility may make it impossible to formulate rules for the constitutionality of interferences with speech. In grasping this nettle, Stevens J argued that both the majority's search for viewpoint-discrimination and the commitment of White, Blackmun and O'Connor JJ to maintaining established categories of unprotected speech were flawed: "[t]he concept of categories fits poorly with the complex reality of expression. Few dividing lines in First Amendment law are straight and unwavering, and efforts at categorisation inevitably give rise only to fuzzy boundaries."[53] Instead, an approach was needed which could take account of the social and historical context in which speech took place. He identified four factors as having properly influenced the Court previously when assessing the constitutionality of regulation of speech[54]:

(a) the subject-matter (political speech rates more protection than commercial speech or sex films);
(b) the distinctive setting in which speech takes place (such as a university or secondary school,[55] or the captive nature of the audience[56]);
(c) the nature of the restriction (prior restraint being presumptively invalid,[57] and restrictions based on viewpoint being regarded as more pernicious than restrictions based on subject-matter, and requiring special scrutiny[58]); and
(d) the scope of the restrictions (for example, merely restricting where adult films can be shown, or address the particular problems of broadcast material, limiting the times when kinds of offensive speech could be broadcast[59]).

[53] Quoted by Stevens J, 120 L Ed. 2d. at 346.
[54] 120 L Ed. 2d. 305 at 348–9. For a rather different, but equally contextual, list of factors which should be regarded as relevant, see Singh, n. 46 above, 74–8.
[55] *Widmar* v. *Vincent* (1981) 454 US 263 at 277–80, Stevens J, concurring; *Hazelwood School District* v. *Kuhlmeier* (1988) 484 US 260.
[56] *Lehman* v. *City of Shaker Heights* (1974) 418 US 298 at 302.
[57] *Bantam Books, Inc.* v. *Sullivan* (1963) 372 US 58 at 70.
[58] *Texas* v. *Johnson* (1988) 491 US 397 at 414.
[59] *Young* v. *American Mini Theatres* (1976) 427 US 50 at 71; *FCC* v. *Pacifica Foundation* (1978) 438 US 726 at 748–50.

This makes a good deal of sense as both a rationale (albeit *ex post facto*) and a justification for many First Amendment decisions of the Court, although it represents as radical a departure from *stare decisis* as the approach of Scalia J and the majority. It has the advantage over other approaches of allowing judges to be highly sensitive to historical and social context. However, even Stevens J did not sufficiently recognise in paragraphs (a) and (c) that he was dealing with different elements in content or subject-matter discrimination. Once that is recognised, it becomes possible to distinguish between more and less objectionable interferences on the ground of subject-matter, and see how those distinctions justify different approaches to the social context of the expression and the kinds and extent of interferences which should be regarded as constitutionally permissible.

There are, in fact, two different but related questions to be answered. First, did the Ordinance discriminate between speakers by reference to a preferred viewpoint, or to some other aspect of the content of their speech? Secondly, to what level of constitutional protection is the speech entitled in respect of that aspect of its content, in the circumstances prevailing? If one were to conclude, with the majority, that the speech in question was entitled to some level of constitutional protection, it does not follow automatically that it was entitled to "complete constitutional protection". Some aspects of the content of speech are more important than others to maintaining democratic discourse, freedom of personality and the pursuit of truth. Maintaining as far as possible a free market-place of ideas requires people to refrain by and large from behaving or expressing themselves in ways which deter others from entering or taking advantage of the market-place. For this reason, restrictions on the topics of expression are unacceptable; those on factual claims and narrative content may be acceptable if their effect is to deter or demean others; "time, place or manner" restrictions are acceptable in the same circumstances; while controls imposed by reference to viewpoint are generally unacceptable, because they skew the intellectual market-place. The elements of content which are most central to the purposes for speech which make it valuable should enjoy particularly strong constitutional protection. Others can be accorded a lower level of protection. But when the message as a whole is one of hostility and intimidation, its weakness as a contribution to debate and its harmful impact on its audience in the circumstances ought to lead to a very low level of constitutional protection indeed.

Analytically, the approach of the majority in *RAV* did not distinguish adequately between the different values of the narrative content, the manner, and the viewpoints at which the Ordinance was aimed and which RAV was expressing. This led to an approach which was insufficiently sensitive not only to social context, but also to the meaning of the speech in question, seen in its social and historical context. The judges generally ignored the significance of the distinction between narrative assertions and viewpoints. The latter are entitled to great respect and strong constitutional protection. The former too will often deserve strong constitutional support, but not when the narrative amounts to an incitement to or threat of violence. To exclude from consideration the impact of the narrative assertions of the speech and the manner of it on the target of it[60] fails to take seriously the claims of members of other groups to respect for their collective ethnic, religious or cultural traditions and sensitivities. As Blackmun J said:

> "I see no First Amendment values that are compromised by a law that prohibits hoodlums from driving minorities out of their homes by burning crosses on their lawns, but I see great harm in preventing the people of Saint Paul from specifically punishing race-based fighting words that so prejudice their community."[61]

Treating the content of such expression as deserving of constitutional protection, and moreover of the same level of protection as political speech,[62] displays an absurd level of tolerance for threats of lawless violence masquerading as political expression.

Placing the reasoning of the majority in the framework of the four tensions in First Amendment jurisprudence outlined in the previous section, the majority concentrated on the position of the individual "speaker" rather than that of the people (collectively or individually) "spoken to"; adopted Bollinger's "fortress" model of free speech which tended to reduce the ability of the government to use its democratic decision-making process to strike what they considered to be a proper balance the interests of social groups; and failed to recognise the impact of the cross-burning on the householders and their community as a serious and constitutionally cognizable harm.

IV. THE EUROPEAN CONVENTION ON HUMAN RIGHTS ARTICLE 10

In Europe things are done differently.[63] Respect for state action in the regulation of expression is reflected in the drafting of Article 10 of the European Convention on Human Rights, which will form part of domestic law in the UK under the Human Rights Act 1998:

> "1. Everyone has the right to freedom of expression. This right shall include freedom to hold opinions and to receive and impart information and ideas without interference by public authority and regardless of frontiers. This Article shall not prevent States from requiring the licensing of broadcasting, television or cinema enterprises.

---

[60] 120 L Ed. 2d. at 325, relying on *Boos* v. *Barry* (1988)485 US 312.
[61] 120 L Ed. 2d. at 339.
[62] See Stevens J, joined by White and Blackmun JJ, *ibid.*, at 344, n. 4.
[63] See E. Barendt, "Freedom of Speech in an Era of Mass Communication", in Birks (ed.), n. 6 above; D. J. Harris, M. O'Boyle and C. Warbrick, *Law of the European Convention on Human Rights* (London, 1995), chs. 8, 11 and 12.

2. The exercise of these freedoms, since it carries with it duties and responsibilities, may be subject to such formalities, conditions, restrictions or penalties as are prescribed by law and are necessary in a democratic society, in the interests of national security, territorial integrity or public safety, for the prevention of disorder or crime, for the protection of health or morals, for the protection of the reputation or rights of others, for preventing the disclosure of information received in confidence, or for maintaining the authority and impartiality of the judiciary."

The right covers expression of unpopular as well as popular ideas. As the European Court of Human Rights said in *Handyside* v. *United Kingdom*[64]:

"Subject to paragraph 2 of Article 10, it [Article 10(1)] is applicable not only to 'information' or 'ideas' that are favourably received or regarded as inoffensive but also to those that offend, shock or disturb the state or any sector of the population. Such are the demands of pluralism, tolerance and broadmindedness without which there is no 'democratic society'."

Nevertheless, the emphasis on the duties and responsibilities of those who exercise the right to free expression is notably different from the approach which prevails under the First Amendment in the USA. Article 10(2) has a wide reach, but (unlike most of the judges of the US Supreme Court in *RAV*) it neither defines categories of speech which attract lesser levels of protection nor adopts an entirely consequentialist approach to evaluating controls on expression. Instead, it defines the interests or purposes for which state interference may be legitimate, and leaves it to the Court to decide whether particular examples of interference are (*inter alia*) "necessary in a democratic society" for one of the legitimate purposes listed in Article 10(2). The nature and extent of the interference must be compatible with the essential notion of a democratic society, so the Court closely scrutinises any interference with speech and associated activities (particularly those of the press and broadcasters) which may advance democratic participation or accountability or the free market of ideas. In addition, any interference must be directed to a "pressing social need", proportionate to the legitimate aim pursued.[65]

In assessing proportionality the Court pays great regard to the assessment of the national authority and the rights of others, and may well permit a state to convict someone of a crime for speech defined by reference not only to its narrative (e.g. obscenity or blasphemy[66]) but even to its viewpoint, where the effect of the speech may be (for example) to encourage racism.[67] The Court has regard to other international treaties, including Article 20 of

[64] Series A, No. 24, para. 49 of the judgment, reiterated many times since (e.g. in *Oberschlick* v. *Austria* (1991) Series A, No. 204, (1991) 19 EHRR 389).

[65] *Sunday Times* v. *United Kingdom* (1979) Series A, No. 30; *Lingens* v. *Austria* (1986) Series A, No. 103; *Observer and Guardian* v. *United Kingdom* (1991) Series A, No. 216; *Vereinigung Demokratische Soldaten Österreich and Gubi* v. *Austria* (1994) Series A, No. 302; *Vereniging Weekblad* Bluf! v. *The Netherlands* (1995) Series A, No. 306–A.

[66] See *Handyside* v. *United Kingdom*, Series A, No. 24; *Otto-Preminger-Institut* v. *Austria* (1994) Series A, No. 295–A; *Wingrove* v. *United Kingdom* (1996) 24 EHRR 1.

[67] *Jersild* v. *Denmark* (1994) Series A, No. 298.

the International Covenant on Civil and Political Rights, which impose a positive obligation on states to criminalise racist and some other speech on the basis of its viewpoint.[68]

This makes it clear that the prevailing balance of values on free speech in Europe is very different from that which obtains in the USA. It leads to rules which are less individualistic, more concerned with minority rights and less rigid than those under the First Amendment, which leading scholars of free speech have recognised is by no means self-evidently right or universally acceptable.[69] In the UK the emphasis is even more heavily on public interests and public order rather than rights to free speech. Although on the whole there is a tendency to interference on value-neutral grounds,[70] the amount of discretion exercised by officials makes the soil hardly seem fertile for the seed of American First Amendment jurisprudence.

Even in its own constitutional context the decision in *RAV* has had difficulty in taking root, as shown in subsequent cases where courts have attempted to apply it. In his opinion in *RAV* Blackmun J drew attention to the possibility that the decision:

> "will not significantly alter First Amendment jurisprudence, but, instead, will be regarded as an aberration—a case where the Court manipulated doctrine to strike down an ordinance whose premise it opposed, namely, that racial threats and verbal assaults are of greater harm than other fighting words".[71]

Since 1992, where the decision has been considered, it has generally been distinguished. Two examples will suffice. First, it has become clear that a state's obligation to comply with the Establishment Clause of the First Amendment, as applied to states by the Fourteenth Amendment (the government "shall make no law respecting an establishment of religion") is a sufficiently compelling state interest to justify content-based regulation of or restrictions on freedom of speech.[72]

Secondly, in *Wisconsin* v. *Mitchell*[73] the Court unanimously held that the First Amendment did not prevent a state from enacting a "hate-crimes" statute providing for longer-than-usual sentencing maxima in cases where an offender intentionally selects a victim by reason of the victim's race, religion, colour, disability, sexual orientation, national origin or ancestry. The

---

[68] Art. 20 ICCPR provides: "1. Any propaganda for war shall be prohibited by law. 2. Any advocacy of national, racial or religious hatred that constitutes incitement to discrimination, hostility or violence shall be prohibited by law." See also International Convention on the Elimination of All Forms of Racial Discrimination, Art. 4.

[69] See e.g. Schauer, n. 9 above, at 857–8: E. Barendt, "Importing United States Free Speech Jurisprudence?" in Campbell and Sadurski, n. 8 above.

[70] Feldman, n. 5 above, esp. chs. 12, 17.

[71] (1992) 120 L Ed. 2d. at 339.

[72] *Lamb's Chapel* v. *Center Moriches Union Free School District* (1993) 124 L Ed. 2d. 352; *Capital Square Review Board* v. *Pinette* (1995) 132 L Ed. 2d. 650 at 651.

[73] (1993) 124 L Ed. 2d. 436. For a more extensive treatment of *Mitchell* see Loveland, n. 3 above.

Wisconsin statute[74] increased the maximum penalty for aggravated assaults from two to seven years' imprisonment where the perpetrator was motivated by such hatred. The accused, Todd Mitchell, was a young black man who had been convicted of aggravated assault on a young white boy in the course of a racially-motivated revenge attack. Mitchell had been sentenced to four years' imprisonment. He challenged the constitutionality of the statutory provisions on First Amendment grounds. The Supreme Court of Wisconsin, reversing the Court of Appeals, held that the statute was unconstitutional, because it punished motive rather than conduct. The Court felt bound by *RAV* to hold that the Wisconsin legislature had unconstitutionally attempted to "criminalise bigoted thought with which it disagrees".[75] On certiorari, the US Supreme Court reversed the decision and remanded the case for further proceedings not inconsistent with the Court's opinion.

The unanimous Supreme Court accepted[76] that a sentencing judge may not take account of a defendant's abstract beliefs, however obnoxious.[77] Nevertheless, it had been held that evidence of racial animus towards the victim could be taken into account in determining whether to impose the death sentence for murder, because such animus could be relevant to a number of factors which could legitimately be regarded as aggravating.[78] Motive had also been held to be a constitutionally acceptable ground for laws prohibiting employment discrimination *because of* race, colour, religion, sex or national origin.[79] Yet, on the face of it, there seem to be difficulties in reconciling this with *RAV*.

In attempting to reconcile the decisions, the Court first noted[80] that the plurality in *RAV* had accepted that Title VII would be an example of a permissible content-neutral regulation of conduct. However, this is unconvincing in the context of the Wisconsin statute. The plurality in *RAV* v. *St. Paul* had sought to save Title VII on the ground that:

> "a particular content-based subcategory of a proscribable class of speech can be swept up incidentally within the reach of a statute directed at conduct rather than speech. . . . Thus, for example, sexually derogatory 'fighting words', among other words, may produce a violation of Title VII's general prohibition against sexual discrimination in employment practices. . . . Where the government does not target conduct on the basis of its expressive content, acts are not shielded from regulation merely because they express a discriminatory idea or philosophy."[81]

However, in the sentence-enhancement case, the very target of the legislation was intentional, racially motivated criminal acts. It is hard to see how

---

[74] Wis. Stat. §§ 939.05 and 940.19(1m) (1989–90).
[75] (1992) 485 NW 2d. 807 at 815.
[76] (1993) 124 L Ed. 2d. at 445–6.
[77] *Dawson* v. *Delaware* (1992) 117 L Ed. 2d. 309.
[78] *Barclay* v. *Florida* (1983) 463 US 939.
[79] Title VII, 42 USC § 2000e–2(a)(1); *Hishon* v. *King & Spalding* (1984) 467 US 69 at 78.
[80] (1993) 124 L Ed. 2d. 436 at 446.
[81] (1992) 120 L Ed. 2d. 305 at 322.

such intention could have been formed except as an expression of a background "discriminatory idea or philosophy".

Was there, then, any better argument for distinguishing *Mitchell* from *RAV*? In *Mitchell*, the Court wrote that *RAV*:

> "involved a First Amendment challenge to a municipal ordinance prohibiting the use of 'fighting words' that insult, or provoke violence, 'on the basis of race, color, creed, religion or gender'. . . . Because the ordinance only proscribed a class of 'fighting words' deemed particularly offensive by the city—i.e., those 'that contain . . . messages of "bias-motivated" hatred' . . . we held that it violated the rule against content-based discrimination. . . . But whereas the ordinance struck down in R.A.V. was explicitly directed at expression (i.e., 'speech' or 'messages'), . . . the statute in this case is aimed at conduct unprotected by the First Amendment."[82]

In other words, fighting words are protected speech (*pace* the disagreements of the Justices wedded to a categorisation of such words as outside First Amendment protection) at least in as much as they are protected against *explicit* regulation on the ground of their content. Legislation against conduct, even conduct motivated directly by ideas deemed by the government to be particularly offensive, need not be content-neutral. It is not easy to appreciate the practical difference between the categories of behaviour distinguished by the Court in *Mitchell*. The harm caused by the aggressive, intimidatory, and racially motivated cross-burning in *RAV* is different in degree, but not in kind, from the aggressive, intimidatory, and racially motivated assault committed by the defendant in *Mitchell*. The distinction between expression and conduct in this context is jejune: the fighting words in *RAV* were conduct expressive of and motivated by repulsive ideas, as was the almost wordless fighting in *Mitchell*. The attempt to distinguish the cases indicates that the content-neutrality requirement is ultimately impossible to combine with most socially worthwhile restrictions on freedom of expression.

If one turns to see how the *RAV* decision has affected the jurisprudence of the various circuits of the federal Court of Appeals, one finds that its impact is very limited. Three main lines of argument have been used to uphold different kinds of regulation of expressive conduct. First, the level of scrutiny applied to legislation designed to protect people from intimidation is intermediate, i.e. asking whether the basis for the legislation was reasonable, rather than strict. In other words, unlike the "compelling state interest" test which is applied where legislative or executive action affects interests which are regarded as fundamental or falls into a suspect category such as race, legislation which regulates threatening action on grounds of colour is constitutionally legitimate if it is within the powers of the legislature and has a rational basis.[83] The courts are thus concerned primarily with

---

[82] (1993) 124 L Ed. 2d. 436 at 446–7.

[83] *American Life League, Inc.* v. *Reno* (1995) 47 F 3d. 642 (US CA 4th Cir.), one of a number of cases concerned with the Freedom of Access to Clinic Entrances Act, passed by Congress to control intimidation by anti-abortion protestors of patients entering clinics. The Act has been

the reason for legislative or executive action. They have therefore upheld injunctions which create buffer zones round clinics by excluding anti-abortion protestors, where the purpose of the injunctions are to give a breathing space to vulnerable patients, rather than to prevent expression,[84] although the decision was partly reversed by the Supreme Court on appeal, on the ground that the injunctions imposed a greater burden on free speech in the public forum of the street than was necessary in pursuit of the substantial state interest of protecting patients.[85] Secondly, in the same spirit courts stress that the evil which the *RAV* decision attacks is viewpoint discrimination rather than subject-matter discrimination, so rules which differentiate by reference to content but not viewpoint survive scrutiny. In *Ethredge* v. *Hail*[86] an order promulgated by the US Air Force forbidding (*inter alia*) bumper-stickers embarrassing or disparaging the Commander in Chief (then President Reagan) survived First Amendment scrutiny, because the order permitted critical bumper-stickers as long as they did not embarrass or disparage the President. Thirdly, it has been accepted in a cross-burning case, *United States* v. *Stewart*, that the decision in *Mitchell* "clearly limited the impact of *R.A.V.* on statutes . . . which are aimed at conduct as opposed to expression".[87] In *Stewart*, members of the Ku Klux Klan had burned a cross outside the home of a black family. The pyromaniacs were charged with (*inter alia*) conspiracy to deprive the family of their civil right to own a dwelling-house, conspiracy to interfere with their rights by reason of colour and conspiracy to intimidate and injure. The perpetrators of these forms of conduct were held to be unprotected by the First Amendment against criminal liability under rules regulating the conduct by reference to its intended effects on victims, even when framed partly in terms of colour. Similarly, the making of direct threats against a judge has been held to be a form of conduct which does not attract First Amendment protection,[88] and legislation which prohibits pre-recorded telephone calls (a common means of communicating racist group-libels) was held to impose a permissible time-place-manner restriction on free speech.[89] This means that the effect of *RAV* can be easily circumvented if legislation is drafted and prosecutions

held to be within the powers of Congress under the Commerce Clause: see *United States* v. *Dunwiddie* (1995) 76 F 3d. 913 (US CA 8th Cir.).For a clear explanation of the distinction between strict judicial scrutiny, intermediate scrutiny and cases in which there is a presumption of constitutionality, see H. Abraham and B. Perry, *Freedom & the Court: Civil Rights and Liberties in the United States* (6th edn., New York, 1994), 14–16.

[84] *Pro-Choice Network of Western New York* v. *Schenck* (1995) 67 F 3d. 377 at 391–2 (US CA 2d. Cir.).

[85] *Schenck and Saunders* v. *Pro-Choice Network of Western New York* (1997) 137 L Ed. 2d. 1.

[86] (1995) 56 F 3d. 1324 at 1327 (US CA 11th Cir.), concerning a bumper-sticker proclaiming "Hell with Reagan" on a car at Robins Air Force base.

[87] *United States* v. *Stewart* (1995) 65 F 3d. 918 at 929 (US CA 11th Cir.).

[88] *United States* v. *Bellrichard* (1995) 62 F 3d. 1046 (US CA 8th Cir.).

[89] *Moser* v. *FCC* (1995) 46 F 3d. 970 (US CA 9th Cir.).

framed in ways which concentrate on the conduct of the accused and the effect on the victim's interests. Although, as the discussion of *RAV* above indicated, this is not an easy line to draw convincingly, the courts do not seem to have followed the lead of the Supreme Court in minutely scrutinising legislation for any possible hint of viewpoint discrimination when the overriding object is clearly to protect victims' rights, and may (as *Ethredge v. Hail* seems to indicate) actively strive to avoid finding viewpoint discrimination even when there is no immediate victim.

The argument of this chapter so far has been that the decision in *RAV* shows the values underlying the First Amendment to be flawed, and illustrates the incoherence and dangers which would be imported if the UK were to enact freedom of expression rights modelled on the First Amendment. However, if as this section has suggested the shortcomings of the decision in *RAV* have had far less practical impact than might have been expected, it might indicate that the dangers have been overstated, and that a sensible judiciary would be able to ignore or sideline decisions which give excessive weight to the value of free speech and too little to the interests of victims and society at large. Supreme appellate tribunals sometimes make mistakes, and may make the law incoherent, but (it might be said) lower courts are well able to keep their eyes on the main issue and repair the damage done to fundamental values. Surely isolated errors, even by the highest courts, cannot undermine the value of recognising worthwhile rights to free speech?

That argument is powerful, but on the reading of First Amendment jurisprudence offered in this chapter the approach adopted in *RAV* is not an aberration. The decision flowed directly from the tendency, fostered if not necessitated by the terms of the First Amendment, to treat free speech as a fundamental right, without reference to the social responsibilities which under a less absolutist European (or at any rate, non-US) jurisprudence, exemplified by Article 10(2) of the European Convention on Human Rights and Article 19(3) of the International Covenant on Civil and Political Rights, would accompany it. It is of the very essence of the First Amendment (at least as it has been interpreted in this century) to treat individuals' freedom of speech as being so important to the individual and to the particular kind of society established in the USA that legislatures, executives and judges are required to cast about anxiously for compelling reasons to restrict it. An individualistic vision of society has made the First Amendment what it is; it was even suggested in the early part of this chapter that the individualism of the First Amendment helped to make American society what it is.

In *RAV*, the majority failed to find adequate reasons to temper concern for individual freedom with concern for vulnerable people whom the exercise of that freedom may harm. Whether the failure was due to lack of imagination or to the demands of the internal logic of the First Amendment is not for an outsider to say, but the outcome was not an aberration. It was a statement of faith in a set of values and a way of life, like the Skokie case. Such values could not, and should not, be comfortably accommodated in a society which (as I think, rightly) places value on social responsibility as an essential part of making individual rights worthwhile. United Kingdom society values responsibility. It does not compel people to tolerate the intolerable, merely to enable people to indulge their freedoms. The First Amendment cannot be planted here successfully without changing both law and society, and changing it for the worse. To make clear the basis for that evaluative claim it is necessary to say something about the conditions under which freedom of speech is valuable and compatible with social responsibility.

V. FREEDOM OF SPEECH AND THE RESPONSIBILITIES OF CITIZENS IN A CIVIL SOCIETY

Any discussion of the proper extent of a right to freedom of expression, such as the one above, assumes that free speech is sufficiently valuable to justify imposing duties on state agencies and on other citizens, limiting their powers and liberties. Because of its value, one can require people and institutions to tolerate speech even when it inflicts some harm on them. A right to toleration only of speech which does not cause any harm would not be a right in any meaningful sense: it could not outweigh an injury to a competing interest, which is the essence of a right. Yet the value of free speech is not absolute. There will be limits both to the harms which others can be expected to bear and to the circumstances in which different harms are considered tolerable. It was argued earlier in this chapter that the relative weights of free-speech and other interests or rights will inevitably be assessed in the light of a society's history and its prevailing political and social morality. This is particularly true in relation to a constitutional right to free speech, as the symbolic and practical significance of the constitution which embodies a right will itself vary between societies and over time. As no two societies have quite the same history and values, the boundaries to free speech will be drawn in different places, will mean something different, and will be policed in different ways, in each society.

Of course, this is true of all rights, not only freedom of speech. Every society must establish for itself the scope of rights, decide how they rank in relation to each other, and settle the conditions under which they can be restricted or interfered with. The solution must be one which generally accords with citizens' judgements about the value of rights, as otherwise they will not be willing to respect other people's freedoms. Such respect requires people to tolerate some injury to interests which they consider to some degree valuable. The level of tolerance required is especially high if one not only strongly disagrees with the way the freedom is being used, but considers either that it causes significant harm or makes society a worse place to live. In deciding whether citizens should be compelled to tolerate the exercise of freedoms in particular ways which impose costs on individuals or society, citizens, legislators and judges must decide how valuable the freedom is, and whether toleration itself has independent value in a democracy and, if so, how much. The weight of the considerations favouring tolerance must then be set against the cost imposed by the exercise of freedom in question.[90] Attempts to provide individualistic philosophical underpinnings for freedom of expression, such as those of J S. Mill, H. L. A. Hart or Joel Feinberg, can be seen as different approaches to the task of assessing when the boundaries of tolerance have been overstepped.

Leaving aside for present purposes the question of the independent value of toleration, there are essentially three social levels at which a right may be valuable. First, an individual may value it for the contribution it makes to his or her opportunities for self-fulfilment and personal identification with favoured groups or causes. Secondly, groups may value it for the way it allows the group to give effect to their values (whether they be Muslims, Freemasons, or academic lawyers). Thirdly, the freedom might be valuable to society as a whole, enabling it to advance shared goals or permitting it to be the sort of society in which its members typically want to live. These are not mutually exclusive. A general right to education, or to free expression on matters of political or governmental concern, confers benefits of all three kinds. All these kinds of benefits should be recognised, but societies may attach different weights to them. For example, in the previous section it was noted that the USA's First Amendment jurisprudence tends to attach greater value to rights at the first, individual, level than to the second or third level, while the approach adopted in international human rights law (and particularly under the European Convention on Human Rights) typically attaches a higher value than does US constitutional law to the impact of rights at the second and third social levels.

The maintenance of rights in a liberal democracy requires a high level of toleration based on concern for the second and third, social, levels from which rights obtain their value. Democratic politics and social pluralism both presuppose that every citizen will be willing to tolerate (at least to some extent) values, opinions and ways of life which are not just different from his or her own, but opposed to them. The citizen must believe that his or her own views are important (as otherwise there would be no particular reason for that citizen or others to take them seriously), but must accept that the maintenance of a liberal democratic polity has a value which is greater than that of any one citizen's views. The citizen must be prepared to see his or her ideals sacrificed (temporarily or permanently) to the greater good. This is not an easy mindset to establish, as is clear from the relatively small number of societies in which a functional democracy flourishes.

---

[90] See F. Schauer and R. Zeckhauser, "Cheap Tolerance" (1994) 18 *Synthesis Philosophica* 439.

The commitment to toleration as a general principle is most severely tested in situations where it produces results which appear to be entirely unacceptable.[91] In such circumstances, the state, through law, must either limit freedom to avoid the effects which are judged intolerable, coerce citizens into acquiescence in the exercise of the freedom notwithstanding the effects or offer incentives for toleration. Rationally self-interested people will want evidence that there is something significant to be gained, and nothing overwhelmingly important to be lost, by tolerating others' freedoms which threaten interests which we hold dear. If the conditions which a rationally self-interested person would lay down for being tolerant are not maintained, tolerance will be contra-indicated in relation to expression or behaviour which significantly inconveniences, annoys, harms or threatens the person.

This does not in any way undervalue selflessness or altruism, since the incentive for toleration will often be a social rather than individual benefit. What it does is to point to the importance of giving weight to the social value of rights in order to explain why it might be in the interests of individuals to agree to respect other people's rights. If respect for a right confers a benefit on society or a social group, as well as on the individual who is exercising it in the particular case, it gives a reason (although not always an overriding reason) for people to accept some detriment to their interests flowing from the exercise of it.

The social benefit which freedoms confer is thus an important element in justifying claims to rights against the state and other individuals. It goes further than merely providing a reason for people to tolerate such rights. It suggests that the social benefits and costs, if any, which flow from a particular exercise of a right should be taken into account both in defining the scope of the right in the abstract and in weighing the value of that right in a concrete instantiation and in particular circumstances against countervailing interests. Freedoms do not carry a great deal of value in the abstract. Their value mainly depends on the way in which a particular freedom is used, in general or in a specific case. We need to apply social values to assess the persuasive strength not only of a claim to a general right and a particular instantiation of that right but also of incursions on the right. This is so because, as Dr Halpin has pointed out, "[t]he acceptance of a possible instantiation of an abstract right cannot be determined by the existence of the abstract right alone, although that does give a reason to ask why the instantiation is not accepted."[92] This means that one can justify restricting freedom to prevent a threatened social harm, as in the American "clear-and-present-danger" test. Such restrictions have caused some problems for traditional liberals, who seek to elevate fundamental freedoms above competing claims to social

[91] See D. Raphael, "The Intolerable", in S. Mendus (ed.), *Justifying Toleration: Conceptual and Historical Approaches* (Cambridge, 1988), at 139.

[92] A. Halpin, *Rights and Law Analysis and Theory* (Oxford, 1997), 122.

(rather than freedom-based) benefits. Professor Schauer has drawn attention to the fact that such theorists typically assert that normal rules do not apply to catastrophes, but do not deal with the far more common case where allowing the freedom to operate imposes costs on individuals or society generally which are not catastrophic but are hugely and disproportionately greater than any benefits likely to flow from its exercise.[93] It is surprising (to me, at least) that anyone suggests that society is always obligated to tolerate speech which imposes such costs on someone other than the speaker. Treating social interests as capable of generating limitations on rights allows one to justify restricting a right to protect a non-right interest of another person.

It might seem odd for someone with a concern for rights to allow exceptions to right-instantiating rules to be created simply in order to protect non-right interests. However, any apparent oddity disappears once one appreciates first the need for social acceptance of right-creating rules and social tolerance of the exercise of rights, and secondly the relationship between rules and exceptions to the rules. As suggested above, social interests are essential when instantiating rights and defining their scope in a legal rule. Where part of that rule is expressed in the form of an exception to a more general part of the rule, it makes no logical or structural difference whether one treats the exception as a derogation from the general rule or as part of its definition. Structurally, exceptions are part of the definition of the rule, and expressing them as exceptions to rights rather than part of the definition of them is usually designed to clarify such matters as the burden of proof rather than being a statement of substantive values or political principle.[94]

Much has been written about the importance of toleration as a social ideal, sometimes even as one which gives special social value to free speech.[95] There is also sometimes an acknowledgment among liberals of the importance of maintaining the conditions under which it is fair to demand tolerance or reasonable to exercise it.[96] Legal and constitutional rights derive their authority ultimately from acceptance by society or a legislative or judicial body acting on its behalf. When rights conflict with other rights or interests, it does not demean the rights to suggest that in weighing them against competing rights or interests any exercise of freedom is more valuable if it improves the lot of people other than, or in addition to, the individual who is exercising the freedom. In the same way, a freedom which is exercised in a way which has anti-social consequences is less valuable, and when exercised in that way deserves less protection, than one which has no

---

[93] F. Schauer, "A Comment on the Structure of Rights" (1993) 27 *Georgia LR* 415.

[94] F. Schauer, "Exceptions" (1991) 58 *University of Chicago Law Review* 871.

[95] See D. Richards, *Toleration and the Constitution* (New York, 1986); "Free Speech as Toleration", in Waluchow (ed.), n. 42 above: Bollinger, n. 23 above.

[96] For examples, see Rawls *op. cit.*; J. Raz, *The Morality of Freedom* (Oxford, 1986).

anti-social consequences, or confers benefits on people.[97] Often it is relatively easy to see when individuals suffer harm, but (as the Skokie litigation and the *RAV* case show) it may be less clear when the state should take cognizance of harm which is inflicted on society as a whole or groups within it. Nevertheless, if a society's prevailing social morality accepts that social harms may be significant enough to justify restraint on rights, that society is entitled, and may be bound, to protect itself against having the fundamental constitutional value of toleration under conditions of social cohesion undermined.

How does this apply to freedom of expression and content-neutrality in the sort of regulation of speech exemplified by the *RAV* case? Several of the grounds which support freedom of expression are concerned with collective rather than individual goods: for example, it is assumed that society as a whole will benefit from a growth in knowledge, whether or not the speaker or hearer would benefit personally. The effect of the position outlined above is that a claim to freedom of expression in specified circumstances is stronger if the claimant can show empirically that accepting a general rule which instantiates the freedom claimed, or authorises the particular exercise of free expression, would produce more rather than fewer of the various benefits which are said to justify freedom of expression in principle, and that the direct and indirect benefits outweigh the direct and indirect social costs.

Thus a claim which can call in aid an identifiable benefit from the expression or rule to society as a whole, or to an identifiable group within society as well as to an individual will be more powerful than one which is calculated to confer only individual benefits. There may be an exception to this if the benefits to the individual in the particular case are shown to be particularly great or important. Even then, the benefits fall to be assessed according to standards provided by society, not purely by the individuals involved. If A's free-speech right conflicts with B's free-speech right, or with B's right not to be spoken to in specified ways, the relative weights of these rights should be assessed by reference to the range of social and individual interests which they respectively serve, the value of those interests, and the contribution of the rights to advancing those interests in the particular case.

Conversely, in a civilised society citizens are presumptively entitled to insist on being protected against intimidation and harassment. The arguments which favour free expression carry relatively little weight when the expression puts people of reasonable firmness in fear. As Professor Wojciech Sadurski puts it, when faced by:

"verbal assaults, motivated by racial hatred in face-to-face situations, when the victim has no (or little) opportunity to avoid the assault, and where the point of such a 'message' is not to persuade anyone towards the speaker's views about the

---

[97] For an application of this argument to privacy, see D. Feldman, "Privacy-Related Rights and their Social Value" in P. Birks (ed.), *Privacy and Loyalty* (Oxford, 1997).

group depicted in the statement . . . we have no right to be protected from knowing that others have a low opinion of us (or of a larger class to which we belong);
indeed, we are *entitled* to know of the fact that some people hate our race, religion, sexual orientation, etc., and government suppression of hate speech deprives
us of this important, even if distressing, knowledge. On the other hand, however,
we have a right to be protected from assaults which provoke us to fight or which
intimidate us."[98]

VI. CONCLUSION

In view of the social nature of rights, then, the question is not whether content-based regulation of speech should be permitted. Other things being
equal, a content-based restriction on freedom of speech should permissible
under the following conditions.

First, expressive action is proscribable if it intimidates people or groups, or
if by reason of any aspect of its content (subject-matter; narrative, argument or factual assertion; viewpoint; form) in its social context it gives rise
to a real risk of violence or serious damage to a compelling state interest.
Secondly, expression is proscribable if the manner of it requires members of
the audience to respond if they are to avoid the likelihood of being taken
to agree, where their forbearance can be interpreted as a speech-act in its
own right with a meaning which the person would find morally repulsive.
Thirdly, the proscription must go no further than necessary to prevent the
harm, and where the risk of harm arises from one aspect of the content
the proscription must not go beyond that aspect. Thus one cannot
absolutely ban the expression of a viewpoint, but one can legitimately regulate the circumstances in which a thoroughly offensive viewpoint can be
expressed.

Not only are there are circumstances when content-based regulation
should be permitted; as has already been observed, all regulation of speech
involves, at some level, that judgments be made about the value of the
speech in its context.[99] The real issues are, first, how it should be regulated,
and, secondly, what decision-making procedure should be adopted to identify situations in which regulation is required.[100]

[98] W. Sadurski, "Racial Vilification, Psychic Harm, and Affirmative Action" in Campbell
and Sadurski, n. 8 above, 88.

[99] Halpin, n. 92 above, 162–3, rightly criticises me for having failed to recognise that the
idea of content-neutrality is misconceived, since whenever speech is proscribed "the viewpoint
of those whose speech is being curtailed is being judged differently from the viewpoint of those
who wish to see such speech prohibited" and civil libertarian anxieties about exceptions to
rights "can be met not by neutral justification but by the particular justification of different concrete rights".

[100] That demands a new inquiry. For my initial attempts to embark on it see "Protest and
Tolerance: Legal Values and the Control of Public-order Policing", in Cohen-Almagor (ed.),

While content-neutrality is a useful test for the need to seek justifications for interference with freedom of speech, I suggest that it can serve as a determinative test for the legitimacy of speech restrictions only if one accepts the presuppositions on which the majority reasoning in *RAV* is implicitly based. Those are the primacy of individual autonomy over community goods; the idea that the harm inflicted by racist speech is not an adequate ground for interfering with free speech, in the absence of a clear and present danger of physical or psychological injury to identifiable individuals or serious harm to the State; and suspicion of government intervention in the market-place of ideas. These may form part of the prevailing social and constitutional ethos of the USA, but (as noted earlier) it is unlikely that they are as powerful in the UK or Europe. There are very distinct reasons why the UK in particular should not give too much weight to any First Amendment case law.

First, while individualism has grown in popularity as an ideology over the past twenty years, it is far from clear that it constitutes an essential part of our national and constitutional identity. There are signs that government increasingly recognises the value of social networks, and relies on them, for example, to underpin social services and health care, undertake neighbourhood watch and provide school governors. Our policing arrangements take account (imperfectly, it is true) of the need for local consultation. Many of the fora for our most active political discourses lie in communities and reflect the views of communities, such as in the trees around Newbury or in the peace camps at Greenham. Groups of one sort or another (particularly in Northern Ireland, but also on the mainland) are increasingly significant in politics.

Our legal system has responded. The collectivist work of the Equal Opportunities Commission and the Commission for Racial Equality has been recognised and empowered by recent judicial decisions, particularly in the equal pay area. Individualism is seen to be desirable up to a point (as Professor Post observed), but insufficient for a functioning polity. It may overstate the case to say, as one American observer has done, that the reason "perhaps why the English are more comfortable than we in using pluralist principles to regulate speech [is that] categories of group identity have in England been made so much more definite by history and tradition".[101] Nevertheless, it is undoubtedly true that one of the benefits of our historical refusal to adopt an absolutist approach to freedom of speech (or any other freedom) is that it has left open the opportunity to pay attention to collective goods.

Secondly, the approach to democracy in the United Kingdom has, until now, tended to be more experimental and radical than that in the USA. The

---

n. 4 above; and "Achieving Transparency and Accountability in Public-Order Decision-making: an Evaluation of the North Report on Parades in Northern Ireland" (1998) 18 *Holdsworth LR* forthcoming.

[101] Post, n. 15 above, 114.

doctrine of parliamentary legislative supremacy gives Parliament a considerable—perhaps unlimited—capacity to interfere with rights of all sorts. Our legal freedoms depend on the good sense and balance of parliamentarians and public agencies. They are not merely able, but expected, to balance individual freedoms (including freedom of expression) against other social benefits. This is true, also, of the European Convention on Human Rights. Article 10 permits municipal legislatures a wide (probably over-wide) margin of appreciation when deciding how to limit freedom of expression, as long as the interference with the freedom is in accordance with the law and calculated to achieve one of the social objectives identified as legitimate within the Article itself. This is not something with which we feel uncomfortable.

What is more, in the UK context there has been relatively little concern that government has been censoring expression. Instead, there is more concern about the excessive powers of media magnates to influence opinion. The law is criticised as often for failing to secure equality of access to the media of mass expression and information as for interfering with press freedom. Our courts would be unlikely to strike down legislation designed to equalise access to publicity at election time, as the High Court of Australia (perhaps unduly influenced by US First Amendment case law) did in *Australian Capital Television Pty. Ltd.* v. *The Commonwealth*.[102]

Thirdly, our system recognises the harms which speech can do, without necessarily enumerating them. Discretionary powers (or duties with a discretion as to how to execute them) have long existed to prevent reasonably apprehended and imminent breaches of the peace, and incidentally form one of the important respects (in theory, if not in everyday practice) in which ordinary citizens are required to shoulder responsibilities for peace-keeping within their communities. The task of balancing the value of free expression of ideas with the desire for quietude and freedom from annoyance has been left to the discretion of local agencies (the constabulary in particular) which are generally subject to supervision within the local community. This leads to problems for the principles of the Rule of Law, and perhaps inadequately protects the Article 10 right to freedom of expression, but it recognises (and perhaps gives too much weight to) the social interest in not being spoken to in certain ways.

Whence does this interest come? It is not purely a matter of protecting individuals against offence or psychological harm. Instead, we understand that people's dignity is partly established by reference to the regard in which the communal circles in which they move are held by others. Defaming groups devalues their members. In addition, we feel, perhaps subconsciously, that certain kinds of speech exact a price from all of us. We cannot conscientiously allow offensive speech to go unchallenged in situations

---

[102] (1992) 66 ALJR 695. See the ch. by Leonard Leigh in this volume.

where silence might be thought to signify either moral weakness or lack of commitment to the opposite point of view. As Professor Bollinger has pointed out:

> "The trouble with speech behaviour . . . is that it very often demands a response from those who know of it. It compels us to act in response, and in that sense it exerts a controlling power over other people's behavior. It is agenda-setting, for without any response, messages different from those we want to be communicated are communicated. . . . The entire subject of interaction between speakers and listeners is, therefore, a matter of considerable complexity. We trivialize the problems speech behavior can pose for any individual or community by speaking simply of the risk of the speaker's persuading some weaker minded listeners or of the offense that some listeners will experience at the speech, as something equivalent to a momentary pain one feels from a cut or a stubbed toe."[103]

Silence in the face of such speech has meaning.[104] Where speech is of a kind which, in the circumstances, is particularly likely to make its audience feel obliged to respond at the peril of being thought to assent to the views expressed, there are powerful reasons for restricting it in order to safeguard the rights of the audience. For freedom of expression, as is well understood both in the USA and under the ECHR, includes the freedom not to be forced to express a position, and that freedom is threatened by people who flaunt their offensively immoral views before those most likely to be shocked by them. The International Covenant on Civil and Political Rights, Article 20, demands legislation against hate-speech, and the Human Rights Committee in its General Comment has treated this as quite compatible with the right to freedom of expression under Article 19. The Committee is right, as long as we do not insist on too individualistic a view of freedom of expression. Freedoms have added value if they are used responsibly. Their value is reduced when they are used irresponsibly. There can be no more irresponsible use of a freedom than one which both puts individuals in fear and wantonly strikes at the social cohesion of the varied communities which together constitute modern, pluralist states. Rights to freedom of expression, or anything else, are conferred by society. They rely on self-control and tolerance on the part of all social groups. Hate speech threatens to undermine the conditions of security which sustain the commitment of groups to tolerating ideas or behaviour of which they disapprove. Apart from being uncivil and bad manners, it is an abuse of the right conferred generously by society. It is a form of anti-social behaviour against which any self-respecting society is entitled protect itself.

---

[103] Bollinger, n. 23 above, 64–5.
[104] For an examination of the implications of this for free-speech theory, see P. Pettit, "Enfranchising Silence: An Argument for Freedom of Speech" in Campbell and Sadurski, n. 8 above.

9

"Federalism" and Free Speech: Accommodating Community Standards—the American Constitution and the European Convention on Human Rights

COLIN WARBRICK*

I. INTRODUCTION

As Ian Loveland noted in the introductory chapter to this volume, the concept of obscenity has presented the Supreme Court with one of its most difficult First Amendment problems. Those difficulties have stemmed in part from the elusive nature of an "objective" definition of obscenity, a characteristic which is also evident in British obscenity law. However, the Supreme Court's problem has been compounded by its need to accommodate the concept of obscenity to the federal structure of the US constitution, a structure which invited the assumption that the meaning of obscenity will vary not just chronologically but also geographically. This Chapter charts the Supreme Court's attempts to resolve this difficulty, and suggests that its efforts to do so provide a valuable comparator against which to measure the adequacy of the way in which the European Court of Human Rights has addressed this question.

II. THE UNITED STATES SUPREME COURT AND COMMUNITY STANDARDS

In *Miller* v. *California*, Burger CJ said:

"Under a national Constitution, fundamental First Amendment limitations on powers of the States do not vary from community to community, but this does

* I have examined the institutional and policy differences between the American constitutional system and the international arrangements of the European Convention on Human Rights in C. Warbrick, " 'Federal' Aspects of the European Convention on Human Rights" (1989) 10 *Michigan Journal of International Law* 698. As to the use of "federal" with respect to the Convention, see n. 11 *infra*. I have used "speech" when dealing with American Law and "expression" when dealing with the Convention.

not mean that there are, or should, or can be, fixed, uniform national standards of precisely what appeals to the 'prurient interest' or is 'patently offensive'. These are essentially questions of fact, and our nation is simply too big and too diverse for this Court to reasonably expect that such standards could be articulated for all 50 States in a single formulation, even assuming the requisite consensus exists. . . .

It is neither realistic nor constitutionally sound to read the First Amendment as requiring that the people of Maine or Mississippi accept public depiction of conduct found tolerable in Las Vegas or New York City. People in different states vary in their tastes and attitudes, and this diversity is not to be strangled by the absolutism of imposed uniformity."[1]

It is impossible to imagine that the same tolerance of local differences would have been acceptable to the Court if the subject-matter of the contested expression had been of a political nature. Flag-burning appeared to arouse quite as great a degree of outrage among its opponents as obscenity but the Court remained resolute in the protection of the message the demonstrators wished to convey.[2]

The treatment of obscene expression is an example, an exceptional one if not the only one,[3] of the Court reacting to what is undoubtedly "speech" in the ordinary sense on the ground of its content. The government may impose controls on an obscene publication or on its distribution because of what it says or what it shows, without further regard to considerations of "time and place" or whether it so incites to immediate action to be "fighting words" or whether it represents a "clear and present danger" to important public interests. It is enough that the authorities show a rational state interest for their action.[4] Because the States may choose to act, they may choose to act differently or not at all. It is something of an irony that diversity is respected by the Court establishing a national test of obscenity which, by taking obscene speech out of the First Amendment understanding of "speech", allows for its differential regulation by the states.

Before going on to examine *Miller*, it is necessary to make brief reference to another aspect of the interpretation of the First Amendment. Besides protecting freedom of speech, it provides also that "Congress shall make no law respecting an establishment of religion, or prohibiting the free exercise thereof . . ."[5] The Supreme Court has interpreted this to mean that the government may not penalise speech on the ground that it is contrary to the tenets of one religion or another.[6] This position—"[t]he law knows no heresy . . ."[7] has a long tradition. It eliminates the possibility of a law of

[1] (1973) 413 US 15, at 30, 32.
[2] *Texas* v. *Johnson* (1989) 491 US 397; K. Greenawalt, *Fighting Words: Individuals, Communities and Liberties of Speech* (Princeton, NJ, 1995), 28–46.
[3] See H. Kalven, Jr., *A Worthy Tradition: Freedom of Speech in America* (New York, 1988), 23–73.
[4] *Paris Adult Theatre I* v. *Slaton* (1973) 413 US 49.
[5] United States Constitution, First Amendment.
[6] *Epperson* v. *Arkansas* (1968) 393 US 97.
[7] *Watson* v. *Jones* (1872) 13 Wall. 679, 728.

blasphemy consistent with the Constitution and reaches other attempts to impose adverse consequences on speakers who offend the doctrines of any religion.[8]

The test of obscenity in *Miller* is this:

(a) Whether the average person applying contemporary community standards, would find the work, taken as a whole, appeals to the prurient interest,

(b) whether the work depicts or describes in a patently offensive way, sexual conduct specifically defined by the applicable State law,

(c) whether the work, taken as a whole, lacks serious, literary, artistic, political or scientific value.[9]

Questions (a) and (b) are for the jury, but question (c) is an objective matter upon which the Supreme Court may have the last word.[10] What was this "community" to whose standards the jury was expected to defer? It was not the jury members' own predilections. As part of the test he had laid down for excluding obscenity from constitutional protection, Brennan J, doubtless aware of the danger of local and repressive decision-makers widening out what he had intended as a narrow category, maintained that it was the "national community".[11] In *Miller* and later cases, this was rejected as requiring a search for an undiscoverable or non-existent benchmark. In *Miller*, a state-wide community was considered adequate[12] and in *Jenkins* v. *Georgia*, the Court said that it was not even necessary for state law to stipulate what was the "community" whose standards were to be decisive.[13] Recourse to a community standard appears not to have been based on federalism or diversity grounds, as such, but rather on the nature of the jury function once it had been decided that the determination of constitutional obscenity (or part of it) were a jury question.

It might be asked why there should be a national test at all for obscenity, at least with respect to state criminal laws. The answer lies in the "nationalisation" of individual rights by the Supreme Court during the 1950s and 1960s, though it is a rather incidental part of the process. Indeed, speaking for the majority in *Miller*, Burger CJ said:

---

[8] See L. Levy, *Blasphemy: Verbal Offence Against the Sacred, from Moses to Salman Rushdie* (New York, 1993), 522–33.

[9] *Supra* n. 1.

[10] *Pope* v. *Illinois* (1987) 481 US 497, 500. Scalia J, concurring, thought that an objective assessment was impossible of "at least literary or artistic value" and that *Miller* needed reconsideration: *ibid.*, 504.

[11] *Roth* v. *United States* (1957) 354 US 476, 484; *Jacobellis* v. *Ohio* (1964) 378 US 184, 197—"It is, after all, a national Constitution we are expounding".

[12] *Supra* n. 1, 31.

[13] (1974) 418 US 153; also *Hamling* v. *United States* (1974) 418 US 87.

"To equate the free and robust exchange of ideas and political debate with commercial exploitation of obscene material demeans the grand conception of the Free Amendment and its high purposes in the historic struggle for freedom."[14]

The power of the Court to impose uniform, national standards of rights on the states was vested in the Fourteenth Amendment, which the Court interpreted as requiring at least the core of the national Bill of Rights to be respected by the states. The question still waits definitive resolution: is the "pith and substance" of the Bill of Rights the limit of the states' obligations or is the Bill of Rights incorporated "bag and baggage"?[15] While it was accepted for speech that there was a uniform standard to be applied to the states, not all judges were prepared to say that it was identical to the standard applicable to the Federal government. Harlan J put the reason for any difference specifically in Federalism terms.[16] Nonetheless, the national standard was so strongly against interference with speech that any room for manœuvre for states, even under Harlan's test, would have been very limited. Whereas previous essays on the nationalisation of rights had been founded on the "privileges and immunities" clause, now attention shifted to equal protection and due process. The initiatives of the Court were driven by failures of Federalism, the failure of the states to protect the rights of minorities. From *Brown* v. *Board of Education*[17] onwards, evidence was brought of the way state laws and policies disadvantaged blacks—in criminal justice and the prisons, in voting,—and those who sought to help them.[18] The judgment in *Sullivan*,[19] which constitutionalised part of states' laws of defamation, was based on the recognition that more plaintiff-friendly rules were being used against out-of-state newspaper reports which sought to give an account of excesses of law enforcement and the indignities heaped upon blacks in some of the states in the South. Huge damages awarded by local juries to local figures against out-of-state corporations were perceived to be capable of putting a chilling effect on a particularly important exercise of freedom of speech.[20]

Besides such high purposes, the activities of those who wished to disseminate obscene materials looked rather insignificant. The difficulty was that laws directed against obscenity were often drawn widely or relied on tests that were extremely vague—defects which the Court was assiduous in strik-

---

[14] *Supra* n. 1, 34; also R. Kimball, "Uncensored and Unashamed" [1996] *Index on Censorship* 128.

[15] L. Tribe, *American Constitutional Law* (2nd edn., Mineola, New York, 1988), 769–80.

[16] *A Book Named "John Cleland's Memoirs of a Woman of Pleasure"* v. *Attorney General of the Commonwealth of Massachusetts* (1966) 383 US 413, 456–8, Harlan J dissenting.

[17] (1954) 347 US 483.

[18] For a brief account of this process, see R. McCloskey, *The American Supreme Court* (2nd edn., revised by S. Levinson, Chicago, 1996), 148–73.

[19] *New York Times* v. *Sullivan* (1964) 376 US 254.

[20] A. Lewis, *Make No Law* (New York, 1991).

ing down in other instances.[21] These other cases placed a high premium on toleration, a toleration which was now claimed by those with less laudable aims. The dangers of the traditional approaches to obscenity was that the legal standards relied on too great an identity between the description of depiction of sexual activity and obscenity. Accordingly, the reach and uncertainty of some laws meant that some worthy expression, notably works of art, could be caught by the criminal law.[22] The approach eventually sustained by the Supreme Court sought to avoid Stewart J's "I know it when I see it",[23] test but did so at the cost of adopting the restrictive, though exclusionary, test of obscenity considered above. In particular, the third leg of "merit" is assessable against constitutional standards, giving the Court the means to prevent the thin end of the wedge being driven in too far. In this way, strong local demands for the regulation of obscenity could be accommodated without infecting the whole of First Amendment jurisprudence. It was further argued that such an approach had the functional advantage that contested speech might be available somewhere in the United States, even if prohibited elsewhere, whereas a Federal rule of prohibition would have had a blanket effect[24]—the alternative, that the Federal rule should be as permissive as it was for other kinds of expression was not, of course, entertained by those who made this point.

The Mapplethorpe Exhibition in Cincinnati

The approach of the Court was effective and the controversy about obscene speech was largely put to rest. One notable exception was the attention given to the exhibition of photographs taken by Robert Mapplethorpe.[25] The exhibition, "The Perfect Moment" was a retrospective of Mapplethorpe's work and galleries were obliged to show the collection in its entirety. It included the "X, Y and Z Portfolios", which contained sadomasochistic portraits, pictures of flowers and figure studies, some of them of young children. Not without considerable controversy in Washington, the exhibition had been shown at various museums across the country. When it reached Cincinnati, where it was to be shown at the Contemporary Arts Center, the police inspected the photographs and eventually a prosecution

---

[21] *Gooding* v. *Wilson* (1972) 405 US 518 (overbreadth); *Stromberg* v. *California* (1931) 283 US 359 (vagueness).

[22] See Brennan J dissenting, on the dangers of overbreadth of obscenity statutes in *Parish Adult Theatre I, supra* n. 4, 83–93.

[23] Referring to "hard-core pornography" in *Jacobellis, supra* n. 11 at 197.

[24] Harlan J, concurring in *Miller, supra* n. 1.

[25] See W. Steiner, *The Scandal of Pleasure: Art in an Age of Fundamentalism* (Chicago, 1995), 9–59; D. Banks, "Conservatism in the 1980s: Art and Obscenity in Cincinnati, the Beauty and the Conflict" (1991) 34 *Howard LJ* 439; O. Fiss, "State Activism and State Censorship" (1991) 100 *Yale LJ* 2087.

was brought against the gallery director and the Arts Center for pandering obscenity and illegal use of a minor in nudity-orientated material. Seven photographs were extracted from the exhibition to form the basis of the charges. They were the only evidence presented by the prosecution. The defence called a large number of expert witnesses to speak to the status and value of Mapplethorpe's photographs as works of art. The jury was selected from the greater Cincinnati area, rather than the metropolitan centre, from where, it was suggested, the defence might have obtained a more sympathetic jury.[26] No matter: the jury acquitted on all charges.

It is not possible to identify exactly why the members of the jury decided as they did[27] (or, for that matter, if they had decided differently, whether the verdict could have withstood constitutional challenge[28]). The constitutional rule allowed for local decision-making and these local decision-makers decided in favour of publication. Did they so decide because the photographs did not "appeal to the prurient interest in sex" or that they did not portray sexual conduct in "a patently offensive way" or because they had "serious artistic value"? If it were the last, were the members of the jury persuaded by the experts or did they "know art when they saw it"? The fact is that the prosecutor's strategy—not putting evidence that the photographs had no serious artistic value—required the jury to say that some things can never be art. The verdict appears to have rejected that for these photographs, at least. If this were the case, the display of materials which shock and disturb will have been protected. Art may (or may not) be that which is displayed in museums and galleries but that which is displayed in galleries will be protected.[29] The national standard of the third part of the *Miller* test does limit the damage that local determinations of the first two tests might have appeared to threaten.

This outcome becomes more important as the pressure for content-based restrictions on speech mount.[30] If speech is valued for its instrumental ends rather than for its foundational quality, the possibility is open for legitimate attacks on speech because of the (disproportionate) damage that it causes to other interests. The tests of what is acceptable become more nuanced and the identity of the decision-maker more significant. In a recent article, Professor White has pointed out that there never has been an all-embracing and universally endorsed theory of the First Amendment, though certain

---

[26] Steiner, *supra* n. 25, 32.

[27] Though see *ibid.*, 33–4, saying that the jurors thought the photographs were "art" and should be protected.

[28] Amongst the reasons for constitutional challenge would have been the trial judge's decision to allow the prosecution to select seven photographs from the exhibition on which to base the charges, in defiance of the *Miller* requirement that a work should be judged "as a whole": Banks, *supra* n. 25, 442.

[29] See Steiner, *supra* n. 25, 52–9.

[30] D. Allen and R. Jensen (eds.), *Freeing the First Amendment: Critical Perspectives on Freedom of Expression* (New York, 1995).

versions have enjoyed a fashionable ascendancy.[31] Now, he notes the paradox of free speech theory, caught between, on the one hand, attempts to identify that which is *truly* valuable and that which is not, with the risk that the latter will reduce the range and eventually diminish the status of speech, and, on the other, acceptance of a libertarian understanding of speech, sufficiently valuable simply because the speaker wishes to speak, which, he says, reduces speech to "noise".[32] Of course, for artists, their work is valuable precisely and sufficiently because they wish to "speak". The jury's decision in the *Mapplethorpe* case avoided the need for an appellate court to apply the third limb of *Miller* and decide whether, in Mapplethorpe's case, it was enough that this was the way he chose to "speak". So far, it seems that the Court has stayed faithful to the libertarian perspective.[33] The "content neutral" test for any interference with speech is a pervasive feature of its jurisprudence.

The Communications Decency Act

The importance of the Court holding to this line increases as it inclines towards a view of judicial federalism more favourable to the states—more willing to challenge Congressional action on federalism grounds, more deferential to state choices,[34] demonstrated, among other ways, by being less willing to impose national standards of individual rights on the States.[35] If speech could be properly subject to a wider range of interferences and if state determinations of the propriety of interference were to enjoy a preferred status, the national standard which has characterised First Amendment jurisprudence since the beginning of the twentieth century would be vulnerable. The latest indication from the Court is that it is not going to retreat. Striking down a (admittedly federal) statute, accompanied by a series of judgments in other cases which acknowledged an increasing degree of state autonomy on other matters, the Court has recently affirmed the strong weight it gives to speech. The case was the *Internet* case—*Reno* v. *ACLU*.[36] The constitutionality was challenged of two provisions of the Telecommunications Act 1996, part of which, Title V (known as the "Communications Decency Act") was to protect minors from "indecent"[37] and

---

[31] G. White, "The First Amendment Comes of Age: The Emergence of Free Speech in Twentieth Century America" (1996) 95 *Michigan LR* 299.

[32] *Ibid.*, 390–2.

[33] *American Booksellers Association* v. *Hudnut* (1985) 771 F. 2d 323, (1986) 106 S Ct 1172; *RAV* v. *City of St. Paul* (1992) 112 S Ct 2538.

[34] *United States* v. *Lopez*, 115 S Ct 1624; S. Gardbaum, "Rethinking Constitutional Federalism" (1996) 74 *Texas LR* 795.

[35] This has been notably in the field of criminal justice, see, for example, *New York* v. *Quarles* (1984) 467 US 649; *Oregon* v. *Elstad* (1985) 470 US 298.

[36] *Reno v ACLU* (1997) 117 S. Ct. 2329.

[37] 47 USCA $223 (a) (Supp. 1997).

"patently offensive"[38] transmissions over the Net. The challenge of the ACLU was based on considerations of over-breadth and vagueness, defects which, it was maintained, contravened the First and Fifth Amendments. The Supreme Court resolved the case under the First Amendment alone. The Court distinguished all the authorities on which the government cumulatively relied to support the legislation. In *Gibsberg*,[39] the Court had upheld the constitutionality of a state statute which prohibited selling of narrowly defined material, obscene as regards children even if not adults, to persons under 17. Compared to that state law, the Court noted, *inter alia*, the absence of definition of the term "indecent" in the Communications Decency Act and any requirement that patently offensive material also lacks serious literary, artistic, political or scientific value. *Pacifica*[40] was distinguished on grounds of the ease of access of children to the medium (there, daytime radio broadcasts) compared to items on the Net, and because the interference there was an administrative sanction imposed by the FCC with respect to a specific item in a single programme. It found *Renton*[41] not to be determinative because it was concerned with the secondary effects of speech—adult cinemas in residential areas (a "time and place" restriction), whereas the Communications Decency Act was a content-based, blanket interference.

The Court was concerned about the vagueness of the proscription (it gave examples of matters about which one could not be certain whether they fell within the Act or not) and its criminal quality, which raised fears of a "chilling effect" and discriminatory prosecution. It reiterated the *Miller* test for obscenity. *Miller* denied constitutional protection to a certain category of speech. That category was cabined by the combined effect of the three point test. In particular, the "lack of serious literary, artistic, political or scientific value" test:

> "Allows appellate courts to impose some limitations and regularity on the definition by setting, as a matter of law, a national floor for socially redeeming value."[45]

The Communications Decency Act potentially reached adult communications, primarily sexual expression, which were not obscene. Even if these were "indecent", they were protected and could not be regulated merely because some persons would find them offensive.[43] The conclusion was ringing:

> "As a matter of constitutional tradition, in the absence of evidence to the contrary, we presume that the governmental regulation of the content of speech is more

[38] 47 USCA $223 (d).
[39] *Ginsberg* v. *New York* (1968) 390 US 629.
[40] *FCC* v. *Pacifica Foundation* (1978) 438 US 726.
[41] *Renton* v. *Playtime Theatres* (1986) 475 US 41.
[42] *Supra* n. 36.
[43] Defects of vagueness and over-breadth undermined the government's claim that the statute was constitutional because it was aimed at the protection of minors: *ibid.*

likely to interfere with the free exchange of ideas than to encourage it. The interest of encouraging freedom of expression in a democratic society outweighs any theoretical but unproven benefit of censorship."[44]

It has been contested whether Federalism has as an objective at all the protection of individual rights.[45] However, rights must be protected within a federal system.[46] In some cases, that may mean giving priority to national standards of rights over the divergent interests of the constituent states. The clearer the national standard and, therefore, the less the room for different interpretations and applications of it, the less there is anything for the states to decide. Adhering to the national standard is a criterion for participation in the federal whole. Of all the individual rights in the Bill of Rights, freedom of speech as understood by the Supreme Court is the strongest and clearest national standard. It demands tolerance. It does not allow the government to intervene to protect those who are offended[47] or even those who are put in fear[48] by reason of what is being said.[49] Among the supporters of the strong rule there are those who say that freedom of speech not only promises good government but delivers it too.[50] Where diversity has been permitted, as it has with respect to obscene speech, the Court has, nonetheless, taken steps to make sure that the opportunity for pursuing it is limited and kept under its control.

III. THE EUROPEAN COURT OF HUMAN RIGHTS AND COMMUNITY STANDARDS

Interfering with Expression to Protect Morals or the Rights of Others

If one must tolerate speech that is offensive which is said to one's face or appears on one's television, offence or even outrage that expression is available to others, even if one can readily avoid contact with it oneself, does seem an even more dubious basis for the State to interfere with the rights to freedom of expression of the producer and consumer of the controversial materials. In a system which values tolerance, as well as expression, the "damage" done may be thought to be minor or, even if serious and genuine,

[44] *Ibid.*
[45] J. Choper, *Judicial Review and the National Political Process* (Chicago, Ill., 1980), 244. W. Norman, "Towards a Philosophy of Federalism" in J. Baker (ed.), *Group Rights* (Toronto, 1994), 79–100, deals with federalism only as a means of protecting collective rights.
[46] J. Blumenstein, "Federalism and Civil Rights: Complementary and Competing Paradigms" (1994) 47 *Vanderbilt LR* 1251; K. Scheppele, "The Ethics of Federalism" in H. Scheiber and M. Feeley (eds.), *Power Divided: Essays on the Theory and Practice of Federalism* (Berkeley, Cal., 1989), 51.
[47] *Forsyth County* v. *Nationalist Movement* (1992) 505 US 123.
[48] *RAV, supra* n. 33.
[49] See D. Richards, *Toleration and the Constitution* (New York, 1986), 189–95.
[50] See S. Walker, *Hate Speech: The History of an American Controversy* (Lincoln, Nebraska, 1994).

to be borne.[51] There is language in the judgments of the European Court of Human Rights which suggests that this is the case under the Convention. As it said in *Handyside*:

"Subject to paragraph 2 . . . [Article 10] is applicable not only to "information" and 'ideas' that are favourably received or regarded as inoffensive or regarded as a matter of indifference, but also to those that offend, shock or disturb the State or any section of the population."[52]

In another context, it said in *Dudgeon*:

"Although members of the public who regard homosexuality as immoral may be shocked, offended or disturbed by the commission by others of private homosexual acts, this cannot on its own warrant the application of penal sanctions when it is consenting adults alone who are involved."[53]

The qualifying remarks in each quotation—"subject to paragraph 2", "cannot on its own"—point to a significant difference between the formulation of Articles 10 and 8 (the relevant provision in *Dudgeon*) of the Convention and the freedom of speech guarantee of the First Amendment. The Convention expressly allows for legitimate interference by the authorities with the protected rights. An important part of the Court's jurisprudence is concerned with setting the limits of a State's power to interfere with a fundamental right in such a way that the rights do not appear to be completely contingent on the discretion of the State and yet, at the same time, not substituting its own (the Court's) judgement for that of the national authorities on every occasion. Accordingly, the Court allows the State a "margin of appreciation" in the exercise of its powers of limitation.[54] What is involved is not a simple balance of two factors, the individual's right and the public interest but the resolution of an equation with several factors of different weights. Recourse even to this mathematical metaphor is misleading: there is a substantial element of judgement involved with respect to every factor in the equation, let alone to resolving it. Nonetheless, the Court has elaborated certain tests or indicators which it will adopt, both to help it towards consistent solutions and to take account of what the Court calls the "subsidiary" role of the Convention to that of the national legal orders in secur-

---

[51] For a strong argument as to why this has been a good thing in the United States, see L. Bollinger, *The Tolerant Society* (New York, 1986).

[52] *Handyside* v. *United Kingdom*, ECHR A/24, para. 49 (1976).

[53] *Dudgeon* v. *United Kingdom*, ECHR A/45, para. 60 (1981). In *Laskey* v. *United Kingdom*, ECHR 109/1995/615/703–705 (1997) which involved the criminal punishment of persons engaging in sado-masochistic, homosexual acts, the Court upheld the interference with the applicants' right to respect for their private life on the ground that it was necessary for the protection of health and found no need to decide whether it was for the protection of morals (though there is little doubt that it would have done so) paras. 49–51.

[54] The literature is substantial. For a recent contribution, see H. Yourow, *The Margin of Appreciation Doctrine in the Dynamics of European Human Rights Jurisprudence* (The Hague, 1996).

ing the protection of human rights.[55] One of these is the search for a "European consensus" to see if there is a view of a particular matter, for instance on the criminalisation of adult homosexual relations, which has been widely endorsed by the Convention States. The existence of such a consensus will not, of itself, resolve the matter against a State, but it will be evidence that its solution is not necessary for or proportionate to the aim which it has identified as being the object of the interference. The Court has been criticised for not adopting a more scientific approach to the search for the European consensus[56] and, since it is a demanding exercise, much may depend upon the exertions of the parties in demonstrating that one does (or does not) exist for the particulars of their case.

An applicant will want to be able to say that the fact that other States have not found it necessary to interfere with the exercise of rights of persons in their jurisdictions means that it cannot be necessary for the defendant State to act as it has towards him. In *Handyside*, the applicant tried to reinforce his claim that his conviction and the forfeiture of his book were unjustified by reference to the fact that the book circulated freely in other European States and, indeed, in other parts of the United Kingdom. The Court's answer to the first contention was that the practice of other States did not bear on what was the exercise of a *national* margin of appreciation and, to the second, that Article 10(2) provide a power to States to act, not a duty to do so, so that the failure of the British authorities to have obtained a national proscription on the publication of the book did not show that they were without justification for obtaining one in the local areas where prosecutions had succeeded.[57] At both the national and the local level, therefore, the European Court allowed for diversity of enjoyment of the right of freedom of expression.

In *Dudgeon*, it was the government which was making the "local" argument in support of its power to interfere with the applicant's Article 8 right, here the right to respect for his private life. The Court would not accept the British government's claim that "profound differences of attitude and public opinion" as to matters of morality between Northern Ireland and Great Britain could justify a more repressive regime in the Province. Even conceding the accuracy of the government's assertion, the Court was not prepared to allow local community standards to prevail over what it regarded as a very important right.[58] The Court has made bold claims for the value of political expression, in which it includes matters of general public interest,

[55] See D. Harris, M. O'Boyle and C. Warbrick, *Law of the European Convention on Human Rights* (London, 1995), 290–301.

[56] L. Helfer, "Consensus, Coherence and the European Convention on Human Rights" (1993) 26 *Cornell International LJ* 133.

[57] *Supra* n. 52, para. 57.

[58] *Supra* n. 53, para. 56.

as well as high politics.[59] Public figures (with the exception of judges[60]) must tolerate criticism they find offensive as well as unfounded,[61] governments must accept the dissemination of information they believe they have good reasons for keeping secret.[62] The rule, like the American rule, is a strong one, despite the qualified formulation of the guarantee in the Convention. It leaves only a little space for national or regional differentiation. Interfering with political expression available elsewhere runs a serious risk of falling foul of the "necessary in a democratic society" test.[63] However, the rule is not unqualified. One State will be able to interfere with racist expression, even though another may see no need to do so, with the result that the same form of political expression may be prohibited in one Convention State on ground of its content, while being allowed to circulate in another.[64] Even then, the restrictive national law must be narrowly drawn and focused on those who use the racist expression and do so in ways which, in the local conditions, require stern action, if it is to be justified under Article 10(2).[65]

This approach to racist expression has been followed because, although there have been occasional doubting voices, the Court as a whole has consistently taken the view that Article 10 covers all forms of expression—nothing is excluded by reason of its content, whether because it is too controversial[66] or because it is too bland.[67] The result is that the emphasis in the case law is on the interpretation of Article 10(2) and, in particular, whether an interference with freedom of expression is "necessary in a democratic society". It has been said already that several factors on both sides will have to be taken into account when the Court is dealing with this matter, such as who the speaker is, whom he is speaking to, what he is speaking about, in what terms he speaks, what is the measure of the act of interference and so on, with due weight to be given to the fact that a fundamental right sits on one side of the equation and applying the standard of proportionality to the act of interference.[68] There is an obvious danger for an international tribunal that it will get sucked too deeply into the details of the particular application, with the result that its judgements will be of limited precedential value or provide uncertain guidance to national decision-makers or that it will undertake a task of evaluation which is better done by

[59] See, among others, *Lingens* v. *Austria*, ECHR A/103 (1986); *Thorgeir Thorgeirson* v. *Iceland*, ECHR A/239 (1992).

[60] *Praeger and Oberschlick* v. *Austria*, ECHR A/313 (1995).

[61] *Lingens supra* n. 59; *Oberschlick* v. *Austria (No. 2)*, ECHR 471/1996/666/852 (1997).

[62] *Verniging Weekblad "Bluf"* v. *Netherlands*, ECHR A/306–A (1995).

[63] *Observer and Guardian Newspapers* v. *United Kingdom*, ECHR A/216 (1991), para. 67.

[64] For a survey of the Convention case law on this topic, see D. McGoldrick, *The European Convention on Human Rights and Racist Speech* (forthcoming).

[65] *Jersild* v. *Denmark*, ECHR A/298 (1994). Note also *Faurison* v. *France*, UNHRC (550/1993), 2 *Butterworths Human Rights Cases* 1.

[66] *Lingens, supra* n. 59.

[67] *Groppera Radio AG* v. *Switzerland*, ECHR A/173 (1990) (pop music).

[68] See D. Harris, *supra* n. 55, 386–416.

a national authority.[69] The much-publicised criticisms of the previous British government about the competence of the European Court, though by no means confined to freedom of expression cases, did include the charge that the Court construed the margin of appreciation too narrowly and failed to allow for diversity "particularly on those moral and social issues where the view of what is right may legitimately vary".[70] It proposed a resolution of the Committee of Ministers which would set out certain principles for the Court, one of which was that:

> "account should be taken of the fact that democratic institutions and tribunals in member States are best placed to determine moral and social issues in accordance with regional and national perceptions."[71]

An investigation of the jurisprudence on freedom of expression suggests that such a warning to the Court is not necessary. While the Court has adopted a robust view of the protection of political speech, its concern for that which falls in other categories has been less resolute, the other cases invariably involving moral and social issues. It is familiar learning that the Court does not regard the "objectivity" of the various aims for which State may interfere with freedom of expression as being identical.[72] In particular, it has singled out the "protection of morals" as being a criterion with respect to which a State enjoys a wide margin of appreciation.[73] The reason for this is that the Court has been unable to detect a "European consensus" which would fill out the subjective notion of "morals" and, therefore, provide the Court with some guidance about how it should discharge its subsidiary supervisory role. That is not to say that the Court has never been prepared to declare that a State has exceeded its margin of appreciation in the protection of morals. It did so in the *Open Door* case, but there "political" speech was in issue and there were arbitrary elements to the interference which offended the proportionality requirement of Article 10(2).[74]

The position is different when the Court has had to adjudicate on "artistic speech" but, before we look at that, it is necessary to consider a significant difference in the content of the rights protected by the Convention and the Bill of Rights. It has been said already that the combined interpretation of the freedom of religion and freedom of speech clauses of the Bill of Rights has left no room for a criminal law of blasphemy in the United States.[75] The same is not true under the Convention. While it probably is not an obligation of States under Article 9, the freedom of religion provision of the

---

[69] Note the very close examination of the television programme in *Jersild, supra* n. 65.
[70] See Editorial, "Reform of the Court: the Foreign Office Position Paper" (1996) 1 *European Human Rights Law Reporter* 229.
[71] *Ibid.*, 231.
[72] *Sunday Times* v. *United Kingdom*, ECHR A/30 (1979).
[73] *Open Door and Dublin Well Woman* v. *Ireland*, ECHR A/246 (1992).
[74] *Ibid.*, paras. 67–77.
[75] *Supra* n. 6.

Convention, to enact a criminal blasphemy law, such a law does not of itself violate the State's obligations under Article 10 not to interfere with the freedom of expression of the blasphemer.[76] The explanation is that a properly crafted blasphemy law may be justified as being necessary for "the protection of the rights of others", here the *fundamental* right of religious belief of the believers. Here, it is not the lack of objectivity of the aim of the interference which accounts for the wide margin of appreciation of the interfering State. Quite the contrary: the fundamental right of the others must be ascertained according to the Convention standards. There will be a conflict of rights between the speaking blasphemer and the offended believer. The Court allows a wide margin to a State to resolve this tension and it is hard to see how it could do otherwise, in the absence of some notion of hierarchy of rights in the Convention itself. The matter is of relevance here because, of course, in many cases, the claim to interfere with expression on moral grounds, to protect people who find the expression offensive to their moral conceptions, will make reference to moral standards founded on religious belief.[77]

The issue was before the Court in *Handyside*. The interference of which the applicant complained was a conviction for obscenity and a forfeiture order of copies of a book which he had published. The book was an English translation of a work written in Danish and directed to adolescent schoolchildren. It took a generally anarchic approach to adult–child relationships and provided information on a variety of matters, including sexual relationships and use of recreational drugs. The government justified the interference on the ground that it was necessary for the protection of morals. The Court sustained the argument, noting that the wide national margin of appreciation to identify "morals", given the absence of an objective standard, extended to deciding what was necessary to protect national morality.[78] It was a significant matter for the Court that the book was directed to children,[79] a common enough consideration in such cases but one which makes the judgement of less consequence where adult consumers are involved.

When we come to examine the cases involving adults, the importance of the Court's understanding in *Handyside* of the margin of appreciation looms larger than its well-known endorsement of the values of tolerance for expression which people find disturbing, quoted above. In *Muller*,[80] the applicant was a painter who had taken part in an exhibition to celebrate the 500th anniversary of the incorporation of the canton of Fribourg into the Swiss Federation. Participating artists were invited to create works of art

[76] *Wingrove* v. *United Kingdom*, ECHR 19/1995/525/611 (1996).
[77] *Open Door*, *supra* n. 73, was such a case.
[78] *Supra* n. 52, para. 48.
[79] *Ibid.*, para. 52.
[80] *Muller* v. *Switzerland*, ECHR A/133 (1988).

specially for the exhibition rather than to display previously completed items. Muller's paintings were large and complex depictions of various forms of sexual activity among a multiplicity of actors. There was no special protection for works of art under the Swiss code from the law of obscenity.[81] The decision of the court of first instance to convict Muller and to order the forfeiture of the paintings was confirmed by two appellate courts, all of which engaged in some evaluation of the artistic merit of the paintings. Their conclusions were held by the European Court to have fallen within the margin of appreciation. "Morals", the European Court said, varied from time to time and place to place. The role of the national authorities in deciding what the contemporaneous standard in the particular district was "better" than of the international judge. That Muller had been able to exhibit similar works in other parts of Switzerland and abroad did not show that the conviction in Fribourg did not respond to a pressing social need.[82] Equally, the forfeiture order was sustained, even though he "lost, in particular, the opportunity of showing his paintings in places where the demands made by the protection of morals are considered to be less strict than in Fribourg".[83] It is hard to accept that this latter finding comports with any notion of proportionality, whatever the margin of appreciation, given the importance of factors particular to the exhibition as the justification for interfering with the paintings at all. The European Court took into account that this was an occasion to which persons were admitted free, children included, without any warning of what they might see[84]—factors which surely could have been remedied for future exhibitions. The result was that the application of the standards prevailing in a small part of Switzerland had an *erga omnes* effect of universal proportion. If local standards are to be relied upon, perhaps care should be taken to see that the consequences of the decision are local, too. The approach of the United States Supreme Court, it will be remembered, has been commended for allowing the possibility of publication elsewhere in the country, even if some States chose to condemn a particular item of speech.[85]

The approach taken by the Court in *Muller* was followed in *Otto-Preminger*,[86] though here the justification for the interference given by the State was the "protection of the rights of others", the interference being a conviction for blasphemy and an associated forfeiture order. The applicant, a non-profit-making organisation for promoting film, had been convicted of disparaging religious doctrines by proposing to show a film, *Das*

---

[81] The Swiss Constitution (but not the European Convention) does protect expressly the right of artistic freedom but the Swiss courts have held that this gives works of art no special protection against obscenity laws: *Muller, supra* n. 80, para. 18.

[82] *Ibid.*, para. 36.

[83] *Ibid.*, para. 43.

[84] *Ibid.*, para. 36.

[85] *Supra* n. 24.

[86] *Otto-Preminger-Insitut v. Austria*, ECHR A/295–A (1994).

Liebeskonzil, which dealt with the trial and conviction of a writer in 1895 following the production of his blasphemous play. The play itself was part of the film. It was to be shown in Innsbruck, in an area, Tyrol, with a very high Roman Catholic population. The Institute had taken precautions when advertising the film so that no-one could have any doubt about what it contained, and steps were to be taken to secure that no children were admitted. After viewing the film, the judge ordered that it be seized, which prevented the scheduled screenings. Later it was ordered forfeit. The decisions were confirmed on appeal. After the application was submitted to Strasbourg, the play had been performed elsewhere in Austria and later in Innsbruck, where the Prosecutor declined to act on complaints that those responsible should be charged. The Court reached the conclusion by six votes to three that both seizure and forfeiture were justified. The majority accepted that the interferences were "to protect the right of citizens not to be insulted in their religious feelings by the public expression of the views of other persons'.[87] The Court accepted that the authorities had acted to ensure religious peace in the Tyrol and to protect people from attacks on their religious beliefs in an unwarranted manner.[88] Whilst religious believers had to tolerate the denial of their beliefs by others and the propagation of opinions hostile to belief, the manner in which these views could be expressed was not unlimited. This is a rather stronger finding of what Article 9 protects than would appear from the judgment in *Kokkinakis*,[89] where the Court rejected the claim of the defendant State that the conviction of a Jehovah's Witness for proselytism was justified as being for the protection of the Article 9 right of the candidate of his attempted conversion, a member of the Greek Orthodox Church. Instead, the Court upheld the applicant's right to manifest his religion. The judgment is not terribly satisfactory in its analysis,[90] so it is perhaps not surprising that the Court in *Otto-Preminger* should not reach the same conclusion.

It could find no "European" conception of "the significance of religion in society".[91] So it was the same as for the protection of morals, the national authorities had a wide margin of appreciation to determine the necessity of interfering with freedom of expression on these grounds. The State pointed to the high proportion of Roman Catholics in Tyrol, the applicants to the precautions they had taken against inadvertent contact with the film by the advertising campaign. Far from thinking that this latter operated as a safeguard, filling the gap revealed in *Muller*, the majority said that it made the showing of the film sufficiently "public" to cause offence.[92] The Court

---

[87] *Otto-Preminger-Insitut* v. *Austria*, ECHR A/295–A (1994) para. 48.
[88] *Ibid.*, para. 56.
[89] *Kokkinakis* v. *Greece*, ECHR A/260–A (1993).
[90] See C. Warbrick, "European Convention on Human Rights: Annual Survey" (1994) 14 *Yearbook of European Law* 627–9.
[91] *Supra* n. 86, para. 50.
[92] *Ibid.*, para. 53.

emphasised the need to read the Convention as a whole and recognised that the national authorities were faced with a conflict of Convention rights. It came very close to dismissing the worth of the applicant's expression—"expressions which are gratuitously offensive to others and thus an infringement of their rights, and which therefore do not contribute to any form of public debate capable of furthering progress in human affairs".[93] There is a dilemma for those who wish to mount attacks against religious belief. If they claim their expression is "art", it will enjoy only limited protection; if they claim it is on a matter of public interest, they will be told they are not making a worthwhile contribution. The Court found sufficient evidence to support the view that the seizure and the forfeiture (which made it permanently impossible to show the film anywhere in Austria)[94] were within the margin of appreciation. Once again, the susceptibilities of people in one part of the State were given plenary effect, without the European Court regarding the outcome as disproportionate. In the more recent blasphemy case of *Wingrove*, the Court followed its judgement in *Otto-Preminger* but made no reference to the religious population whose rights were being protected by a national decision not to allow the distribution of a video-film.[95] It did not appear that the Court required any evidence that specific people would be offended by the circulation of the video or, indeed, of evidence that the video was blasphemous according to church authorities, rather than merely distasteful. The judgment makes an unfortunate collapse of the nature of expression in issue and the justification for interfering with it. The majority said:

> "Whereas there is little scope for restrictions on political speech or on debate of questions of public interest . . . a wider margin of appreciation is generally available to the Contracting States when regulation freedom of expression in relation to matters liable to offend intimate personal convictions within the field of morals or, especially, religion."[96]

The danger of this indiscriminate analysis is that matters of religion or morals which *are* political or of public interest will be susceptible to a greater degree of interference than those which are not—matters, say, of abortion or homosexuality. The Court has previously shown itself a robust defender of individual rights on these questions in the face of religiously and morally based intolerance.[97] Given the limited scrutiny to which it has subjected other forms of expression interfered with on moral or political

---

[93] *Ibid.*, para. 49.

[94] *Ibid.*, para. 57.

[95] Presumably, it was the (minority) Christian population. In *Choudhury* v. *United Kingdom*, No. 17439/90, (1991) 12 *Human Rights Law Journal* 172, the Commission declared inadmissible a complaint that the restriction to the protection of Christian belief in the English law of blasphemy was in breach of Art. 14, the non-discrimination obligation.

[96] *Supra* n. 86, para. 58.

[97] For instance, *Norris* v. *Ireland*, ECHR A/142 (1988).

grounds, particularly the widespread effects of such limitations which it has tolerated, it is important that, at the very least, these powers of interference be confined to artistic expression, so that political speech is inhibited neither in content nor in vigour.

The Mapplethorpe Exhibition in London

The Mapplethorpe exhibition which had been the subject of the case in Cincinnati was shown at the Hayward Gallery in London in the Autumn of 1996.[98] The Gallery produced an elaborate catalogue to accompany it. The Gallery was not able to display all the items in the exhibition for reasons of space, so it was inevitable that some discrimination be exercised about which photographs should be displayed. Because of the controversial nature of some of the photographs, the Gallery took legal advice about the exhibition and the catalogue and consulted the police. As a result of these consultations the Gallery took the following steps:

(a) separate entrance and ticketing of the Mapplethorpe exhibition;
(b) prominent warnings about the nature of some of the exhibits—"[a] number of works in this exhibition are sexually explicit in content, and may disturb or cause offence";
(c) restricted admission, with children under 18 admitted only if accompanied by an adult;
(d) close supervision of the display and sale of the catalogue.

In addition, the Gallery removed three photographs from the catalogue and one was excluded from the exhibition because of the sensitive nature of its content. One of the photographs was of a child. The Gallery was concerned about it, given that at the time there was great public concern about paedophilia (there was widespread coverage of contemporaneous events in Belgium). The Gallery did show the sado-masochistic portraits, even though legal advice had suggested that some of them might be a cause of concern. The decisions were taken in consultation with the Mapplethorpe Foundation. The Gallery was concerned about the risk of financial consequences if the catalogue were seized and about the chilling effect of proceedings on future exhibitions and exhibitors. Neither the Gallery nor the Foundation thought its interests would be served if a new legal confrontation were initiated, following the events in Cincinnati. There were no legal proceedings taken about either the catalogue or the exhibition.

I want to use this incident to explore further the Convention standard on freedom of expression and artistic exhibits. Some speculation is necessary to fill in gaps in the facts and to take into account that there were no proceed-

---

[98] I am very grateful to the Gallery for providing detailed information about the event and its policy and decisions. The account which follows is very largely based on its communications.

ings in England.[99] The Gallery was "chilled" by the prospects of the seizure of the catalogue, though not by the threat of proceedings about "offensive" photographs in the exhibition. It may, then, have been a "victim"[100] for the purposes of the Convention in respect of the catalogue and would likely have been excused any obligation to exhaust local remedies because of the serious obstacles to obtaining a declaratory judgment on matters of criminal law in the English courts.[101] However, would there have been any interference with its rights under Article 10? If the photographs of young children excised from the catalogue and the one excluded from the exhibition had been removed because of the Gallery's concerns about the prominence of the paedophilia debate, these look like decisions of the Gallery itself: it, rather than the State, was responsible for the decision.[102] What if there had been a successful prosecution based on including the sado-masochistic photographs? There were several possibilities of offences for which action might have been contemplated. Two of them were prosecution for publishing an obscene article and the institution of forfeiture proceedings against the Gallery, the proceedings invoked against the applicant in *Handyside*.[103] There would have been an important difference between the two proceedings. Prosecution would have allowed the Gallery to opt for jury trial rather than having the case heard by magistrates.[104] The Gallery would have been able to argue that publication had been justified on the ground that it was for the public good in the interests of art, a matter on which it could have called expert evidence.[105] If a conviction had been sustained or forfeiture ordered, there would have been interferences with the Gallery's rights under Article 10. The government would have been called upon to justify them under Article 10(2), as being necessary in a democratic society for "the protection of morals" or "the protection of the rights of others".[106] The likelihood is that the Court would have found that there was no violation. *Muller* shows that the Court takes the view that artistic expression enjoys no

---

[99] I should emphasise that nothing which follows implicates the Gallery in any of the speculation or conclusions.

[100] European Convention on Human Rights, Art. 25. See *Norris, supra* n. 97, paras. 28–34.

[101] I. Zamir, *The Declaratory Judgment* (London, 1993, 2nd ed. by Lord Woolf and J. Woolf), 174–88.

[102] There might have been a legal concern anyway because of Protection of Children Act 1978, s. 1(1) (b)—offence to show indecent photograph of a child—where there is no "artistic" defence; cf. Indecent Displays (Control) Act 1981, s. 1(4) (b)—Act does not apply to a matter displayed in an art gallery or museum.

[103] Obscene Publications Act 1959, ss. 2(1), 3(1).

[104] On the possibilities of different decisions under the different procedures and of different decisions between different benches of magistrates, see G. Robertson, *Obscenity* (London, 1979), 96–109.

[105] *Ibid.*, s. 4.

[106] In considering whether the conviction or forfeiture came within the margin of appreciation, a relevant consideration would be whether the English court had addressed the substance of the Convention point in reaching its decision.

special protection under the Convention.[107] The judgment in *Laskey*, though concerned with conduct rather than expression, shows that the Court does not attach much weight to sado-masochism as a value, so that steps taken to protect a moral climate which disapproves of it are unlikely to be regarded not serving a pressing social need.[108] On the other hand, the United Kingdom could not have argued that it was acting to protect a fundamental right of other people. There is no general Convention right not to be shocked or offended, only a right not to be so with respect to one's beliefs. The government's case would not have been as strong as it was in *Otto-Preminger* and, accordingly, the display of the warning signs and other precautions designed to protect children taken by the Gallery might have served to support an argument by it that the prosecution was disproportionate. *Handyside* shows that the Court takes no general objection to the definition of obscenity in English law, nor to the forfeiture proceedings as a means of enforcement, nor to the decision-making processes, whether by juries or magistrates.[109] There is some evidence that decisions of magistrates can vary from district to district, but neither in English law nor under the Convention[110] does it follow that a decision in favour of freedom of expression in one part of a State requires that the decision be the same in all parts of the State. In any event, the Mapplethorpe exhibition was not destined for any other British galleries, and so there was no scope for inconsistent decisions. Perhaps only if successful forfeiture proceedings had been taken with respect to any of the photographs would there have been any prospect of a claim in Strasbourg succeeding on grounds of disproportionality. Even then, the judgments in *Muller* and *Otto-Preminger* would have had to have been distinguished.

IV. CONCLUSION

The very fact that there can be such uncertainty about whether the Convention would provide for protection in cases such as this is a cause for concern and makes manifest the importance of an effective "artistic value" provision in national law if the exhibition of controversial works of art is to be protected against parochial prejudice, because there will not be much chance of redress at the international level. That this is the case is not, of itself, a demonstration of the inadequacies of the European Court. Ultimately, the most important difference between the Convention and the Bill of Rights is that the one is an international scheme for the protection of

---

[107] *Supra* n. 80.

[108] *Supra* n. 53, para. 45.

[109] *Supra* n. 52, paras. 53, 58. On the acceptability of general standards of "obscenity" as satisfying the Convention notion of "law", see *Muller, supra* n. 80, para. 29.

[110] *Supra* n. 104.

human rights, whereas the other is a national one. The European Court has
made it clear that there are limitations on what the Convention system may
do about guaranteeing human rights.[111] The subsidiary nature of its role
imposes limitations on a Court lacking even the legitimacy of a national
court to interfere with the decisions of democratic legislatures. The relationship of the Convention system and the Contracting States is not a "federal" one, even with the inverted commas, though it is, in Professor Stein's
phrase, a "divided power" system.[112] Though exaggerated, given the outcome of the cases, the British government's strictures in the Foreign Office
Position Paper were not without their theoretical foundations: there are limits to what the European Court may do of both a legal and a functional
nature. It is not into the Convention that we should be looking to import the
spirit of the First Amendment but, if it is thought desirable, into national
law. Nonetheless, in the field we have been considering, the First
Amendment jurisprudence does have a message which we should bear in
mind. However much we might make fun of Stewart J's "I know it when I
see it" dictum about obscenity, no definition has really done much better.
Yet it is clear that there is a widespread demand for the regulation of something which we call "obscenity". States will not abandon their obscenity
laws. Many of the difficulties in this area of the regulation of expression
arise because we are seeking rational solutions to non-rational impulses.[113]
The question then becomes, who should be the "*I*" to know obscenity when
he sees it? If it is thought proper that juries are given this power of decision,
then "local" decision-making is inevitable. The European Court is right
about the absence of a "European consensus" *among* the European States in
matters of morals but the same is true *within* national States. The risk of
arbitrary or inconsistent decisions will be high. The opportunities for discriminatory prosecution will be available. The controls which flow from the
application of the *Miller* test are desirable safeguards against the unwarranted expansion of vague obscenity laws to control valuable expression,
artistic as well as political. The lesson in relation to blasphemy laws is just
as clear, but there is no indication whatsoever that the European Court
would go the way of the Supreme Court and interpret the religious belief
provision of the Convention in such a way that it prohibited legislation
which sought to protect believers from the hostile expression of others. The
Choudhury decision[114] probably will bear re-examination in the light of

[111] See P. Mahoney, "Universality Versus Subsidiarity in the Strasbourg Case Law on Free
Speech: Explaining Some Recent Judgments" (1997) 2 *European Human Rights LR* 364.
Mahoney makes the distinction between "political and public concern speech" and "cultural
or artistic speech". This article became available to me only after this chapter was completed.

[112] E. Stein, "Uniformity and Diversity in a Divided-Power System: The United States
Experience" (1986) 61 *Washington LR* 1081.

[113] J. Finis, " 'Reason and Passion': The Constitutional Dialectic of Free Speech and
Obscenity' (1967–8) 116 *University of Pennsylvania LR* 222.

[114] *Supra* n. 95.

Otto-Preminger. The British government has been reported to be considering extending the blasphemy laws to cover other than Christian beliefs[115] on the same day that a French court has held the Church of Scientology to be a religion.[116] Discussion of matters of great public interest runs the risk of being "chilled" by these developments, even if not prohibited altogether. For those, and I am one, who are convinced that the widest possible freedom of expression in political matters, widely conceived, is an essential ingredient of democratic societies and of individual liberty, the message from the United States is that there is a need for caution in endorsing any exceptions to the basic principle.

There is, though, another view. It is that diversity in expression matters is a desirable thing; that the uncertainties which surround the absolutist position in the United States are well-founded. Accordingly, expression must be carefully scrutinised for its value, especially where it does damage. Professors Jensen and Arriola write:

> "Under traditional libertarian First Amendment doctrine, protecting some dangerous, harmful, offensive, or even oppressive speech is the price we pay for freedom. We ask questions about what counts as speech and who is identified as an affected party in the speech, so that we can be clear who is being asked to pay for what."[114]

This is an inquiry which is not intended to be descriptive, to show where the costs of free speech fall, but to provide an agenda for examining speech with a view to preferring, on grounds of content, some to others. In American constitutional terms, this is a radical, not to say revolutionary, project. There are less iconoclastic alternatives, which nonetheless present serious challenges to the orthodoxy. Professor Sunstein claims that the present position is defective, even in its own terms.[118] There is resistance to these trends, bolstered by a familiar argument in favour of strong protection for free speech—the "slippery slope": once some content-based exceptions are admitted there is no principled means of drawing the line to forbid others.[119] What the new approaches share is a common interest in diversity, of making sure that minorities have an effective voice or do not pay too great a price to indulge the dysfunctional freedoms of others. There is a search for effective answers to newly-identified problems: the prospect of States as laboratories searching for acceptable solutions to these newly identified problems does not seem the anathema it once did.[120] The Convention, of

---

[115] *The Times*, 30 July 1997, 2.

[116] *The Times*, 30 July 1997, 8.

[117] R. Jensen and E. Arriola, "Feminism and Free Expression: Silence and Voice", in *Freeing the First Amendment, supra* n. 30, 210.

[118] C. Sunstein, *Democracy and Free Speech* (New York, 1993).

[119] See F. Schauer, *Free Speech: A Philosophical Enquiry* (Cambridge, 1982), 83–5. See also Arthur M. Schlesinger, Jr., "Multiculturalism and the Bill of Rights" (1994) 46 *Maine LR* 191.

[120] Though the Court needs yet to be persuaded: see *American Booksellers Association v. Hudnut, supra* n. 33.

course, can tolerate this process much more easily.[121] The margin of appreciation loses its much-criticised character as a protection for venal State interests and becomes the laudable means for promoting diversity, or at least, not standing in its way.[122] The European Court cannot stem the tide in favour of diversity if that is the way it is flowing in the national States, in the manner in which the Supreme Court seems so far to have resisted the demands for changes in the understanding of the First Amendment. But the European Court can insist on the importance of the standards of necessity and proportionality to assess any innovations which come before it for judgment. This is the difference between the two Courts: the Supreme Court may act in defiance of the demands for diversity, even if they are promoted by many states and insist that they adhere to the values it has found in the national Constitution; the European Court relies on what the States are doing—the creation of a European consensus—as an indication of how the Convention should be interpreted and can apply it only to the dissenting minority. If diversity becomes a more predominant value than equality in Europe, the Court will find it even harder to detect a European consensus to underpin its judgments.

[121] For a recent, non-expression example, see *X, Y and Z* v. *United Kingdom*, ECHR 75/1995/581/667, paras. 47, 52.

[122] P. Van Dijk, *General Course on Human Rights: The Law of Human Rights in Europe: Instruments and Procedures for a Uniform Implementation*, VI–2 *Collected Courses of the Academy of European Law* 1, 68–72; D. Feldman, "Human Rights Treaties, Nation States and Conflicting Moralities" (1995) 1 *Contemporary Issues in Law* 61.

Index